# INSIDE

# THE

# OUTSIDER

# Inside the Outsider

## The search for meaning
## in an absurd world

by

## John Vincent

Freshwater Publishing Limited

Published in the United Kingdom 2016 by
Freshwater Publishing Limited

Freshwater Publishing Limited
PO Box 340
Prestatyn
LL19 0BP
United Kingdom

www.freshwaterpublishing.co.uk


First Edition

Cover Design by Freshwater Graphic Design
A CPI catalogue record of this book is available from the British Library

ISBN 978-0-9935738-0-4

Printed and bound by CPI Group(UK) Ltd, Croydon, CR0 4YY

This book is dedicated to my friend

Gareth Edwards

(1969-2001)

# CONTENTS

# Introduction

I first started writing this book 16 years ago after becoming fascinated with existentialism when I read Colin Wilson's bestseller *The Outsider*. I discovered I had a keen interest in and empathy towards the mind-set of existentialists or (as they are more commonly referred to as) outsiders and found myself being drawn to the writings of existential philosophers. The time it has taken to complete the book reflects other commitments in my life which have placed demands on my time, but has also allowed me to study and understand outsiders and their place within modern society.

The book is based upon two main assertions that existentialism is not some outdated philosophical idea which should be consigned to history, but is more relevant than ever in the world we live in today. My other assertion is that it is possible for the outsider to find a niche within life and a meaning to it. In order to allow the reader to properly understand these assertions, I have tried to give a true insight into the outsider and how he or she perceives life.

Within the book the outsider is explained through various traits he or she exhibits which sets them apart from people in general. I hope there will be many readers who will be able to gain something substantive from my conclusions in terms of their understanding of existentialism and the existentialist. Furthermore, I hope there will be many readers who will not only be able to identify with this book, but who will also benefit from it by applying its principles to generate meaning in their lives. It is important for the reader to note that when I refer to the outsider or outsiders within the book, I am specifically referring to existentialists rather than its meaning in any other context.

I have not written this book as an academic work as I believe it should be accessible to the widest possible readership. I have also tried to be as honest and fair as possible in my assertions and conclusions throughout the book. The book also gives an insight into society in general and at times the ominous direction it is moving towards, which often provides a powerful catalyst for existential thought. The absurd nature of modern life often makes people more existential in their attitude, as human endeavour is often eclipsed by its design - inhibiting their ability to find a definitive purpose within it. This book is about existentialists and how they can overcome the barriers towards discovering meaning.

# 1

# Contemplating Life

Beginning to think is beginning to be undermined. Society has but little connection with such beginnings. The worm is in a man's heart. That is where it must be sought. One must follow and understand the fatal game that leads from lucidity in the face of experience to flight from light.

Albert Camus - *Myth of Sisiphus*[1]

A man sits in his office one day. His attention is taken up trawling through a continual stream of data displayed on the screen in front of him and the intermittent buzz of various devices, alerting him to people's demands on his attention. He has been doing the same job for the last twelve years, a model employee with an exemplary attendance record. He has a normal family life with three children who would make anyone proud. He prides himself on being prudent and sensible in everything he does, and is in many ways unexceptional. As he sits at his desk thinking about his life, he realises something is different about today. His mind is unsettled and he cannot free himself from the sensation of how surreal everything is. He can accept he is presently sitting in his office, but as he tries to quantify what his life means beyond this, it all becomes a haze.

He tries to think about who he is and what his life actually represents in the grand scheme of things and finds himself unable to attribute any substantive meaning behind who he is or what he is striving for. It dawns on him, there is not really anything unique or tangible about his daily existence; his life simply unfolds, much the same as anyone else's. He tries to imagine what difference it would make if someone else was living his life and starts to wonder whether there would be any significant difference. As he looks around his office wall, gazing at his certificates and awards from his company, he thinks to himself, "is this what I amount to?" He starts to feel nauseous as it dawns on him his life is defined by an inescapable inevitability. He walks outside feeling as though he is going to be sick at any moment, hoping the fresh air will clear his head and allow him to dismiss these futile notions. Yet, unbeknown to him, his efforts are all in vain as his life and thoughts are changed forever.

The above narrative is not some figment of someone's imagination. It is a very real phenomenon, experienced by some individuals who feel drawn to seriously question themselves and why they think or do the things they do in life. For some, these thoughts and sensations can take hold quite unexpectedly, at any time in their lives, while for a few it can be virtually an everyday experience. These are people who cannot simply sit back and accept life for what it is; they must rationalise it for themselves, if it is to mean anything. They feel compelled to question their existence often asking themselves, why am I here or what does my life actually mean or represent in a broader sense? These questions often lead them to become more conscious of their actual significance as individuals who merely exist upon this planet at a certain period in time. The more they think about it, the more difficult it becomes to attribute any real degree of meaning to their existence beyond this. The enormity of these considerations naturally makes some people see life from a more detached perspective as something inevitable and unreal, making the usual things they do in life seem futile and meaningless. As these thoughts descend upon them, they instinctively try to attribute more relevance to their lives, rationalising life in the context of these powerful thoughts. Unfortunately, for many further thought simply reinforces their perception that normal or conventional life falls short of the meaning they demand from it.

Some people can relate quite closely with these feelings or may have had similar experiences at certain points in their lives. They can be very unnerving for anyone whose assurances and priorities in life are suddenly swept from beneath them. They can change a person's relationship with the world they are in, straining their ability to feel part of or satisfied with contemporary life. These thoughts can manifest themselves at any time even amongst the most confident or self-assured, who seem to have everything going for them. It does not seem to make any sense why someone who for years may have been quite content living an ordinary conventional life, suddenly find his or her perceptions have changed, making them look on life as absurd or meaningless. People are often instilled with the notion that whatever happens in their lives can be understood or worked out within the bounds of human understanding. And, while this may be true of most things, human nature sometimes defies people's reason, proving itself too unpredictable or illogical to be understood in any rational context. When people think about the characteristics and essence of human existence and its meaning, also referred to as the human condition, it can provoke certain questions which do not have any definitive answers. It can leave some people totally disorientated, unable to fathom what it is all about.

It is inevitable from the sheer diversity of human nature, that there are some people who are irresistibly drawn to question their existence and the degree of meaning they can attribute to it. In many ways, this inclination to question their lives in its wider context, is an essential part of the human condition. Successive generations have all, in their own way, strived to make sense of the world they are in, which is evident in virtually all forms of enterprise throughout history. A good example of this is through artistic endeavour where the artist often seeks to portray that unique insight or perspective which best defines or elucidates life as it is, or reflects how individuals relate to it at that particular time. The constantly evolving fashions of each new generation bears testament to this phenomenon as people continually strive to make sense of the world they are in by seeking to understand, change, or adapt themselves in accordance with it. Many people, it could be said, are in an almost perpetual state of flux, constantly readjusting themselves and their relationship with the world around them. This is often exemplified through their struggle to keep pace with today's ever changing technology and how they adapt its use to try to enhance their lives, leaving more than a few quite disenchanted with the experience. There is an indelible human need within virtually everyone to make sense of things and, from this, some individuals insist on questioning the world they are in and what their existence means or represents within it.

There is no doubt that any individual who tries to attribute a definable reason or purpose behind their existence can potentially find it a very demoralising experience. In the first place, it could be asked whether there is any distinct meaning or purpose behind their lives or is such a search bound to end in perpetual disappointment? It can leave a person in despair, frustrated with their inability to attach a tangible meaning to their lives beyond the fact they merely exist in the 'here and now'. They may start to wonder how much control they really have over what they do and how their lives pan out, or whether their lives are mere by-products of other people's expectations and society's pressures to conform to its norms or conventions. How much of their lives are real and how much is part of someone else's parody? As these people think deeper about who they are and their place in life, they naturally discard its incidental aspects trying to fathom some meaning beyond the everyday world. As they search, their insistence to rationalise life as something coherent intensifies, often escalating their demand for meaning beyond what most would regard as realistic. The more they pursue the elusive aspect of meaning in their lives, the more distant the prospect of realising this need often appears, leaving some increasingly disillusioned with life. Their perceptions can change so radically, so as to render them incapable of accepting the authenticity or reality around them. For a few, conventional life becomes perceived as senseless and absurd. These individuals are at a loss to explain why they cannot accept life in the same vein as everyone else and usually find themselves inescapably drawn deep into their own thoughts, as they attempt to remedy the enveloping feeling of insignificance and hopelessness with their predicament.

It is ironic that these individuals, who have sought to understand their lives in terms of its relevance and against a more meaningful backdrop, find their purpose and incentive for life seemingly paralysed by the depth of their insight. The gravity of thoughts which challenge the notion of human existence and its meaning are powerful enough to unravel any preconceived notion people may have had of what their lives once represented. It can leave some people wondering whether their whole lives have been some travesty of a truer reality. It is as if the more they think about their lives, the more it falls short of their expectations of it. Therefore, it is not surprising, that as this realisation takes hold, some individuals become wholly inanimate beings who appear to have had all their appetite and zest for life drained out of them. Some often become preoccupied with trying to interpret what they think and do in some sort of meaningful way and usually become dismayed at their inability to do so. Their frustration grows as they try to escape from the nothingness which opens up in their lives, whilst seeking to sharpen their understanding of it. However, their best efforts are often totally undone by its blurred and contradictory format where nothing in life makes much sense anymore. These individuals usually lose their motivation to do or achieve the things they may have once aspired to. Eventually, for some, their priorities and perceptions change so much, that day-to-day life becomes like acting out a pre-destined role in a cynically contrived soap opera.

Like Bedouin tribesmen, some people are drawn into the lonely deserts of their mind's darkest recesses; that bleak uninhabited wilderness which keeps drawing their thoughts deeper into its vast expanse. It tempts the daring individual with the prospect of a chance to glimpse life's contours with, what appears to be, an unrivalled clarity. But, the longer he or she looks further along the horizon, the more unstable the sand beneath becomes; undermining his or her assertions and creating a void where they once stood. This parched environment created by the thinking mind, compels these individuals to prioritise the more critical elements in life in a bid to sustain them within its barren habitat. They are the ones who have taken an honest hard look at themselves, only to discover that conventional life does not offer much capable of quenching their thirst for meaning. They have followed their thoughts' instincts in an attempt to make more sense of everything, only to now see their existence as an absurd series of conditioned reactions to its predictable motion. There is little solace to be found in life once a person's thoughts start penetrating its fake fringes. As a result, these people often become increasingly solitary individuals, disengaging themselves from the world around them. The sharpness of their thoughts sever the conventional umbilical, where their previous indifference and lack of impetus to question their lives' true import once bound them to some predestined role in life.

This irresistible urge to try to quantify their existence in a wider context, can lead some people to conclude that contemporary life does not contain the meaning they demand from it. This appraisal of life can reveal itself to some individuals quite unexpectedly, proving totally immune from their attempts to alleviate the resulting sensation of emptiness and despair. It is hard for anyone who has not experienced these thoughts, to understand why anyone would let themselves get embroiled in challenging notions which ultimately lead to such a hopeless juncture. But, this misses the point; these people do not set out to prove or disprove some impossible hypothesis. Their impetus to question such salient issues is simply part of their instinctive need to affirm and make sense of who they are. It is part of the human condition for a person to question the tangibility of the world around him or her, beyond its mere physical appearance. These people's willingness to confront the central issue of meaning in life often generates a need to equate greater significance to their lives. This need is not derived from a state of mind they have consciously chosen to adopt - it is a result of a their overwhelming compulsion to understand life in terms of their own perceptions and regardless of the uncomfortable revelations they often unearth in their efforts to make sense of it.

Most people may not be familiar with the thought processes of someone whose mind compels them to contemplate life's meaning or how real it is; for many people these experiences can best be described as intermittent at the best of times. However, for some people, their need to consider their lives as having more meaning than just a person who conveniently fits into a particular role within it, cannot be tamed or regulated. It emerges like part of some fatalistic flaw in human nature which appears to punish those who pursue their instinctive urge to seek out and probe life's realism for themselves. Inevitably, these individuals look on life differently to most others; they judge the reality around them according to their mind's criteria and have no inclination to use other people's benchmarks to appraise what is meaningful or significant. They usually feel unfulfilled pursuing many of life's stereotyped roles and rarely derive any satisfaction or sense of achievement from emulating others' endeavours. They simply do not see much point just automatically doing what everyone else does and fulfilling a set pattern; they require uniqueness in their lives before they can entertain any notion of authenticity. It could be said, their lives are characterised by an endless search for substance as their ability to feel satisfied is constantly thwarted by an unidentifiable parasite, which feeds itself on the fabric of everything they think and do. In some cases, the life these individuals were brought up to believe in as real, turns out to be little more than a sham revealing a huge void which cannot be filled by anything a conventional life has to offer.

Albert Camus described this urge to challenge the issue of meaning as 'beginning to think'.[2] Once people take on the mantle to explore the veracity of their realism, many begin to question how much of it is truly authentic. Can someone who strives to live a purely conventional life, religiously abiding by the norms everyone else has acquiesced to, define their lives as real? In this instance, their behaviour could be more likened to imitations of other people's protocol. Indeed, can anyone whose decisions in life revolve around other people's norms, or expectations of them, profess to be living a real life? These questions typify some individuals' unquenchable need to address more fundamental questions in their lives, beyond just going through the motions. These people often aspire to something more in life which they can consider as worth striving for and are often unwavering in their determination to find it.

People's instinct to challenge, and at times, disregard other people's precepts, is an intrinsic part of the human condition. It is commonly associated with people who reflect more on life, or who have had experiences which has lead them to look at things differently. In some cases, the powerful state of awareness which ensues is enough to destroy the seemingly unquestionable assertions which underpin what many others think and do. In their world, the fact that something is an established notion or custom, does not guarantee its legitimacy or mean it should be followed, and is no assurance of its rectitude. These people often become lost souls in society as they come to terms with their need to embrace a meaning they can authenticate for themselves - which encompasses more than just making up the numbers. These sentiments are particularly poignant to the way some people feel in the modern world; it is better known as the philosophy of existentialism, with those who think in this way aptly known as 'outsiders' or 'existentialists'.

Existentialism, unlike many other philosophies, does not comprise a set of doctrines which sets out how someone should live their life. Probably the best way to define existentialism would be to describe it as the process whereby the individual considers his or her existence in light of its meaning and in relation to the world around them. As a result, this often changes the way these individuals perceive and appraise life as it is, inhibiting their ability or willingness to feel part of the world they are in. It is a very individualistic philosophy which centres on the person's freedom to think and act by their own reason - independently of any conventional precepts or expectations, and acknowledging and respecting people's differing perspectives in life. Most people will have probably heard someone describing something as 'existential'. The word is prone to misuse by some people who run out of superlatives to describe something they do not quite understand or which appears absurd to them or 'off the wall'. Each of the key existential traits, such as individualism, despair, freedom of mind and, the inability to accept the reality others take for granted, are described in successive chapters of this book. It is important to grasp some of the background to existentialism in order to understand the key philosophers associated with it to explain how it came about.

Many of the ideas connected with existentialism have been around since ancient times. However, in terms of developing existentialism as a philosophy in its own right, most people acknowledge its two founding fathers as being Soren Kierkegaard and Fredrick Nietzsche. Kierkegaard introduced the idea that it is not society or religion which brings meaning to life, but solely the responsibility of the individual.[3] In the same vein, Nietzsche not only (amongst other things) advanced the idea of individual responsibility, but also expounded many of the absurd aspects of human existence, declaring 'God is Dead'[4] and famously proposed the idea that 'man can achieve anything'.[5] Although existential philosophy, as a term, had not even come into being by the 19th Century, both these philosophers explored key concepts which to this day, form the cornerstones of existential philosophy. As a philosophy, existentialism did not come about in a vacuum. The 19th Century was a time of great intellectual change in which people became much more open to exploring aspects of the human condition, as well as adjusting to changing times. It was a time when people were becoming bold enough to challenge and probe previously unquestionable doctrines, with the rule books being ripped up and people being prepared to acknowledge the possibility certain ideas may be flawed. Also, during this time Dostoyevsky's literature was introducing many people to the idea of the free individual at odds with the rest of society, through his portrayal of existential characters.

It was not until midway through the 20th Century, in the aftermath of the Second World War, that existentialism really came to prominence as the seminal basis for great artistic, literary, and philosophical works. Existentialism appeared to capture people's sense of disillusionment with life after the Second World War; people needed to readjust their perceptions and their relationship with a world which had been torn apart. The war had proved that nothing in life was certain, and many were faced with the daunting uncertainty of starting all over again. It made people more receptive to new perspectives, and different ways of evaluating what life was all about. Existentialism provided a catalyst for individualistic ex-pression as well as providing an avenue through which to understand people's sense of despair and hopelessness at that time. The movement, can best be summed up by a phrase used by Jean Paul Sartre in a lecture he wrote in 1946 entitled *Existentialism is a Humanism*, in which he said 'existence precedes essence'.[6] He asserted that people are not made by essence, they do not come into the world with a particular nature or destiny, they are a 'blank canvas' and, they determine what they make of their lives through their own action and volition. This is one of the central themes of existentialism, that what people become in their lives is not governed by some divine or religious destiny or who their descendants might be, but according to each individual as an equal person with a free mind capable of forging his or her own path and values in life.

Many outsiders are often acutely aware of their unique nature within society. They insist life must have some meaning to it before they can credit it with any intrinsic value. However, their ability to realise the meaning they crave for is often undone by the nature of contemporary life, where its format and the notions society promotes usually run contrary to the way they think. In some outsider's eyes, the world is underpinned by an array of absurd ideals such as, equating civilisation solely with capitalist or materialist ideologies, or technological progress through endlessly inventing new ways to dispense with the need for human enterprise. Modern society sometimes promotes, endorses and accepts doctrines which are completely at odds with what many outsiders would conceive as being conducive towards its betterment. Coupled with this notion, society seems to be becoming increasingly homogenous through people's reverence of mainstream dogma, which marginalises anyone with a tendency to think existentially or outside the norm. Society's design often rewards those who demonstrate their willingness to complement its expedient format. It could be said that, in some respects, modern society has, in many ways, become intolerant of the notion to embolden people to be themselves. It now appears to herald its ability to condition people to become receptive and obedient to a limited set of particular influences, as an achievement in itself. This flawed utopia, discounts the reality that any individual who insists on thinking for themselves could never be satisfied with a life which revolved acquiescing to collective precepts merely designed to serve or endorse the pragmatic function of the whole. As human beings people have an inherent need to preserve their freedom of thought and distinct needs as individuals in their own right and this notion is not only a central feature of existential philosophy, but is at the forefront of the way all outsiders conceive themselves.

In order for people to be accepted today as part of society there is an implied obligation they must relinquish a certain portion of their autonomy in order to ally themselves with the conduct, norms, and fashions most others have acquiesced to. Individuals who insist on being themselves or doing things in their own way will usually encounter some impediment in the way they go about their lives. And yet, it is not surprising that the more society encourages or, in some cases, deliberately limits people's ability to be or express themselves as genuine individuals, the more alienated and suffocated many people feel - especially outsiders. Most outsiders are not partial to being just part and parcel of society, especially when it appears to pursue the short-sighted benefits associated with a naïve utopian vision of rearing an increasingly uniform and, in many ways, submissive society. Outsiders cherish their freedom to think as individuals above anything else and, as a result, they often bear the brunt of some of the insular doctrines which emanate from modern society's design. They find it hard to witness the decadence which transpires when people waiver their responsibility to evaluate and decide things for themselves and simply go with what the masses think or do. The problem in today's world, is that people are easily excused from acting on their convictions or on what they truly think, when all they have to do is borrow the lame standards or excuses most others have acquiesced to. This often determines society's direction, as many now seem to measure themselves against their deviance from its norms, rather than revering their uniqueness as individuals and their ability to use their own mind as their touchstone for authenticity.

Many outsiders tend to feel alienated from society, not only by the doctrines underpinning it, but also by the way it functions. They often find it hard to warrant it with any substantive degree of meaning and are often shunned by others due to their minds' resilience to think, act, and define themselves by who they are. From their perspective, modern society is like a theatre in which the stage rules make no allowances for their instinctive expression, with parts invariably given to its thespians who have the flexibility to adopt each new role that comes along and follow its script to the letter. Unsurprisingly, some outsiders feel as though they are being somehow punished for their minds' ability to think beyond the immediacy of everyday life. Over time, a few even become so desperate of their predicament they even cling to the vain hope that the extent of their sufferance and dogged determination to stand by what they think or believe, will one day lead to some form of atonement. A few even go further than this, almost subconsciously self-punishing themselves in some way in the hope their luck in life will eventually balance itself out in the long term. This groundless hope is sometimes the only thing capable of providing a few outsiders any solace in life; the thought of having reached such a low point in their lives must surely mean that, from hereon in, things must surely improve.

Unfortunately, life never lends itself to such equanimity and usually, from an outsider's point of view, they become more and more disillusioned with a world which seems wholly incapable of accommodating their needs within it. The difficulty lies in the fact they cannot simply accept the authenticity of what is around them, which most others take for granted. They exist, but their existence means nothing to them without a meaning behind it they can rationalise for themselves. For them, there has to be more to life than simply doing what others do and existing in the same vein as everyone else. In light of this, it becomes imperative for them to preserve their minds' instincts and remain true to how and what they think, usually regardless of the drawbacks or despair which ensues. They often consider other people's realism as delusional - a reality shaped around the whims of others and propagated by a susceptibility to society's conditioning devices. They have no incentive to placate anyone by altering their outlook, especially at the expense of denying their perceptions or what they truly think. Therefore, it is almost inevitable outsiders become society's loners, trapped in an incomprehensible world unable to understand how others can accept living an existence which, to them, makes so little sense and is incapable of measuring up to their conception of a meaningful existence.

Virtually everyone can testify to having some kind of existential experience at some point in their lives. These experiences, often initiated by poignant episodes, cause people to reflect seriously on their lives and re-evaluate the things that matter to them. But, not everyone requires a catalyst to look on life existentially. For some, it is simply their indomitable need to scrutinise their lives and its meaning. Throughout this process these individuals experience the sensation of being in a world which is somehow unreal; a view which, for some, has become increasingly prevalent and it is not hard to see why. Within society today, people in general have become much more materialistic and appear to be more egocentric than they were in previous generations. In more ways than one, society today seems to be more consumer driven and it has become almost comical how some people are convinced they can happily sustain themselves through life adhering to such a baseless ideology. It could also be argued, that the emergences of a religious and, to some extent social vacuum, have also taken their toll leaving many people feeling they have nothing to fall back on or guide them through life anymore. However, regardless of the particular cause or causes of people's increasing disillusionment with modern life, or some people's tendency to think existentially, most outsiders would say that the way they think is simply derived from an intrinsic need to make sense of the world they are in. It is as if they have climbed the highest mountain to gain a unique panoramic view on life, only to find when they get there, they are unable to survive on its thin air of expectation and routine.

The anxiousness and despair which often accompanies existential thought, sometimes leads people to dismiss their perceptions as some dark passing mood. Current attitudes and dogma, even lead some individuals to believe their disaffection with life is part of some inherent flaw in their psychology. Yet, for most outsiders, much as they try to disregard their perceptions, they cannot dismiss their authenticity. They soon realise they cannot try or pretend to be anyone else but themselves. It is their unbridled thoughts which mould them into the person they are and, their motive to preserve their mind's freedom often overrides any drawbacks which ensue in their approach to life. This resilience conflicts with the notion that permeates through people's psyche today, where virtually anything which causes many to lose the satisfied perspective they have been led to expect from life, is classified as a potentially damaging state of mind; marketing proponents being the biggest disseminators of this crass attitude. In contrast, most outsiders are bold creatures who will always grapple with their existential instincts as they attempt to reconcile themselves with, what they often regard as, the senselessness of the world they are in. Some will readily admit they would love to be able to divert their thoughts from consistently expounding life's absurd format, and yet, at the same time, they also want their lives to be more substantive than the pretensions which often underlie a conventional existence. In a nutshell, life lacks the substance outsiders need to embrace a purpose within it capable of satisfying their yearning for an authentic meaning. It is therefore not surprising why so many outsiders feel unfulfilled; the modern world is often too pseudo-orientated for them to take anything substantive from it. Many are also aware they will never be totally at ease with the stale predictability of contemporary life which, in their eyes breeds an unhealthy contentment, sustaining many others through its narrow corridors.

Many outsiders stand out in life through their persistence to pursue and reconcile themselves with, what they regard as, its more critical elements. For instance, they cannot kid themselves into believing it means something by comfortably relying on others persuasive arguments or by simply trying to adopt or follow the needs or accolades everyone else aspires to. Their thoughts tend to pierce the fickle nature of what is around them, making normal everyday issues seem completely unavailing and incidental. Eventually, some outsiders reach the stage where they are prepared or, in some cases, forced to place their whole life under the scrutiny of their powerful existential instincts. Their minds will not allow them to use accommodating reasoning to convince themselves that following the same routines as everyone else actually means some-thing. And yet, this indulgence is gladly accepted by some people today as a means of furnishing them with a perception of their lives' significance.

Outsiders yearn for the profound relevance of a Shakes-pearean play, rather than the doctored and telegraphed narrative of a Hollywood blockbuster, in which originality and depth are willingly relinquished to appease the audience's taste for the banal. They develop an appetite for the genuine aspects of life and usually have an indifferent attitude towards aesthetically pleasing or materialistic aspirations. Their thoughts and actions are drawn from the way they perceive life and what it is all about, rather than being contrived from modern society's practicable mind-set. They have an inherent need to define themselves as something and want to become more than a hopeless by-product. Their worst fear is often the thought of their whole life being defined by some extraneous force or influence; of one day having to resign themselves to a middling existence in which they are destined to simply repeat a life cycle, in the same vein as countless others have done before and will inevitably do after them. In many cases, the anxiety and panic generated by the sheer gravity of such thoughts is too much for some people to bear. This explains why many people (including outsiders) feel at times they have to divert their mind from its instinctive thoughts - especially when they find themselves losing their ability to cope. The feelings of hopelessness which start to envelop them often reveal how brittle the foundations of contemporary life actually are.

Outsiders cannot help themselves questioning life, often in the hope of discovering some concrete meaning behind it. However, as they begin to do this, they lose the ability to accept it with any seriousness. They find that life never seems to contain the authenticity it once did and, some find themselves living in a dream world in which things have already lost their form and importance. Most outsiders are not prepared to go along with someone else's realism just for the sake of it. They continually challenge the validity of their relationship with the world and their existence within it, while many others simply appear to acquiesce to the way things are. Their mind provides them with a blueprint of life, with a proviso it must mean something beyond just striving to embrace the means necessary to satisfy a trite existence. This makes some outsiders particularly intolerant of the way some people proudly promote their conventional habits as forms of achievement in themselves. Existential thought can descend upon an individual with an intensity few people can imagine. Thoughts often rebound off each other without resolution, while the mind tries to construct some semblance of meaning from life - like trying to piece together a collection of smashed pottery from an unknown civilisation. The outsiders' dilemma, is often compounded by the fact that they know people usually cannot appreciate the source of their dissatisfaction with life and, it is not uncommon for them to find themselves misunderstood or even shunned, when they try to portray to others how they truly think or feel.

Most outsiders tend to disengage themselves from the general run of the mill mentality of many of those around them. They soon find themselves stepping back from life as they attempt to take in the wider picture. In their mind, people are almost perceived as part of a singular entity through their obedience to a common set of predetermined thoughts and habits. They are often bound together in their absurdity, which explains why many outsiders tend to spurn the opportunities they are offered to become a greater part of society or the community around them. Their instincts demand that their lives must measure up to their own scrutiny. They keep searching for aspects of life which might accommodate their existential instincts. The more introspective they become, the more their life appears like some perversion of nature - detached from the smoothness of any normal process as thought only seems to provoke a greater sense of discontent and despair. They feel as though they are an animal who is wholly unsuited to society's habitat, and cannot fathom why most people's incentives in life seem to be inextricably linked to their need to emulate each other, while inadvertently endorsing society's sometimes spurious design. Outsiders cannot condone the way some people continually divert their thoughts away from their minds' deeper instinctive demands, tiptoeing though life trying not to awaken what they sometimes consider to be their minds' 'demons'. They cringe at the way some people promote their own ignorance as an indispensable ingredient to a fulfilled or happy life. It is not thought, but the outsider's indomitable quest to find a meaning they can legitimise in their lives which becomes their millstone.

As outsiders think about the machinations of the world they are in, the prospects of them playing some meaningful role within it seem ever more remote, or even for few, simply ridiculous. For some, there is a nauseating inevitability about life and the roles people adopt with it. Modern society often designs itself to accommodate those who willingly apply cynical or pragmatic means to achieve their egocentric aims; those who adhere to their minds' instincts, or an idea beyond themselves, can often find themselves disadvantaged or marginalised in some way. Thus, society as it is, ceases to have any real value to outsiders and far from complimenting the merits of the way they think, often encroaches on their resolve to maintain their intrinsic self. In essence, there is much more to outsiders than their struggle to reconcile their perceptions with the world they are in. They have an array of characteristics and qualities that emerge from the way they are, which are often unacknowledged by most others. Over time, they develop unique traits in conjunction with their existential tendencies as they search for aspects of life they can connect with and consider meaningful, in a world which to them is often alien and irrational. Before delving into these, it is important to understand who the outsider is and what actually makes him or her tick.

# 2

# The Outsider

What is meant here by saying that existence precedes
essence? It means first of all, man exists, turns up, appears
on the scene, and, only afterwards, defines himself. If man,
as the existentialist conceives him, is indefinable, it is
because at first he is nothing. Only afterward will he be
something, and he himself will have made what he will be.

Jean-Paul Sartre - 'Existentialism Is a Humanism' [1]

There are innumerable misconceptions surrounding what existentialism is, and how people define 'the outsider'? For instance, some people naturally think existentialism is solely associated with individuals who are more introspective or who think profoundly about life. However, existentialism is prevalent amongst a wide cross-section of people regardless of intelligence, age or even experience of life; many of whom do not acknowledge their existential tendencies due to the way they interpret their thoughts and the intermittent way they manifest themselves. Some people also try to mask their existential inclinations by ascribing their cause to something their mind can rationalise more easily. A few, mistakenly attribute existential despair to depression or even stress. There are even some who believe existentialism is caused by some extraneous condition without realising that it is a thing in itself - the human mind following its instinct to contemplate life according to its own experience and reason. Modern life is itself a powerful existential catalyst, as people find their need to acquire meaning continually undermined by the dogma society promotes, usually narrowing the scope of their function as distinct individuals. Society forges ahead seemingly oblivious to the fact that as human beings, most people simply do not feel fulfilled playing out many of the neatly anticipated roles either imposed or expected of them in today's world.

Nearly all outsiders insist that there must be some sort of meaning to life beyond the mere fact they exist. The big problem, as far as most outsiders are concerned, is that the more they try to picture their lives against a more relevant backdrop, the less significance they are often able to attribute to it. Existential philosophers have often acknowledged that existentialism is not a formula for life, it is simply the way some individuals think and perceive what is around them; aspects of which, many people seem to identify with. The large volume of literature, containing existential themes and characterisations, testifies to its appeal amongst a wide cross-section of people. There is almost something endearing about the lone misunderstood individual trying to grapple with their realism in a world, which to them, makes little sense. It is evident that many people have a natural curiosity towards the thoughts, tribulations and characterisation of existentialists and, there is a long list of writers who have conveyed existential themes and characters in their novels. Some of the more prominent include: Sartre, Hemingway, Kafka, Joyce, Camus, Heller, Salinger, Dostoyevsky, Kundera, Thomas Mann and Iris Murdoch.[2] The sheer volume of existential literature surely undermines some people's simplistically contrived assumption that existentialism was some type of passing fad - which specifically developed from people's disillusionment with life after of the Second World War. Some academics, have even tried to pigeonhole existentialism as precisely this, a fashion-like phase which deserves to be consigned to history.

Existentialism is often difficult to define in the way it relates to the individual. It is far too fluid to be contained under any blanket definition or, by trying to identify it through one particular trait.

Existential thoughts are often unpredictable in the way they manifest themselves, usually descending on an individual without warning or reason, varying in their intensity, whilst sometimes shattering the order and assertions in their lives which underpin their realism. These experiences can range from the hopelessness of not being able to find any purpose or meaning in anything, to an intense despair with the way life is and its unreal appearance. Everyone has their own particular way of dealing with these thoughts. Some people instinctively try to divert their mind's attention onto something else, by occupying themselves with work or particular tasks to try and stop themselves from focusing on the absurd aspects of life. Others sometimes try to ally themselves more closely with other people in the hope of alleviating their despair by trying to calibrate their perceptions with those they regard as more conventionally orientated. The majority believe that forcing themselves into a routine is the best remedy, but none of these options are particularly effective in diverting the deep-rooted thoughts and perceptions of the serious existentialist. Those who experience these thoughts for the first time are often confronted by an impending fear, as they start to question the way they conceive themselves and their place in the world; sometimes drawing the conclusion that much of what they have done or striven for in their lives simply amounts to an array of hapless exertions.

The powerful nature of existential thought changes people's perceptions. The reality of the world they were once so assured of begins to break down, and their immediate reaction is to frantically try and bring some sort of order and normality back into their lives. Many use increasingly desperate and diverse measures to try to get back into their familiar routines again, as they attempt to escape and free themselves from these thoughts. The apprehension accompanying them leads some to crave the safety they associate with an uncomplicated conventional lifestyle, where they can, at times, immerse themselves in the same tripe as everyone else. A few will even go to extraordinary lengths to avoid broaching the issue of meaning in their lives, or to try to remain ignorant of it. Many people know where this could lead them, and would rather not experience the blank uncertainty and despair which accompanies confronting existential questions. They are aware of the perplexing attributes of the human condition, and also the fickle nature of life where a simple shift in their perceptions can sometimes turn their whole world upside down.

Existential thoughts have no pattern in the way they manifest themselves and, at times, leave many individuals feeling totally disorientated. A few feel like a child separated from its parent, as they find themselves out of their depth in the adult world of existentialism. These people sometimes feel completely helpless without their mother of conventionality and their comfort world of ordered predictability, and they usually turn to the playground of established customs when the blinding light of existentialism becomes too unbearable. Nowadays, more and more people are advised to steer clear of any thoughts which threaten to impinge on their carefully balanced state of mind. Their success in maintaining this sometimes depends on their mind's resistance towards adopting contrived behavioural roles or rationales, as they attempt to quell their mind's inclination to place their lives in a more understandable or meaningful framework. Their ability to feel content, often hinges on the extent to which their life lacks the meaning they now crave for. For some, it is simply a question of busying their minds enough with other things to override their mind's existential tendencies; sometimes with the constancy of menial tasks in order to give their thoughts a different orientation. However, for others their thoughts have taken them too far - their perception of life being unreal has now become their reality. They cannot return to that naïve childlike world where ignorance, or relying on the veracity of other people's precepts, once provided them with the feeble notion their lives were somehow fulfilled. These people are the true outsiders of this world. They stand out as distinct individuals within society, destined to follow their mind's natural tendency to consider their lives in the context of its meaning as their mind develops an appetite for something much more substantive.

There are some people who are undoubtedly inclined or have an affinity towards the concepts of existentialism in the way they consider their lives. However, notwithstanding this, there is generally a considerable difference between the outsider and the average person within society. One of the key differences, is that outsiders refuse to be swayed from what they think and how they perceive things, often with little regard for whatever impact this may have on their own disposition. They stand by the things they can rationalise for themselves, which often prove more durable than anything the rest of society has to offer. What they think cannot be likened to a political or intellectual point of view - it is more than this. Their thoughts define who they are, and this provides them with a powerful motive to maintain what they think or believe in. As individuals, they cherish their freedom of mind above anything else, and will defy any attempt (from whatever quarter) to unduly influence or impose any sanction upon the way they are or what they think. Some people presume that outsiders would be inclined to form themselves into groups, but most cringe at the idea of forming cliques of any kind. They are fiercely individual, and usually would not tolerate having to adulterate their opinions to accommodate any consensus, in return for the privilege of being part of any group.

The outsider's powerful sense of autonomy, coupled with their acceptance of their individual responsibility for what they do or think in life, makes them distinct entities within society. There is also no atypical profile which fits all outsiders, merely a collection of existential traits which are present, to varying degrees, within each outsider. The difficulties involved in trying to identify the outsider are exacerbated by the fact that their nature inadvertently frustrates people's attempts to categorise or define them. They do not usually fit into any set profile and cannot be singled out as a particular type of person within society. Some people's inability to classify them as a particular person or part of a definable group within society, leads them to assume the worst in outsiders, often to compensate for their own lack of understanding. The driving force which underlies the outsider's psychology is completely alien to people's general conception of human wants and needs. All that can be said, is outsiders are often distinguishable from most others by the fact they exhibit certain traits, often loosely defined, which are more or less common to all.

Camus explained the origins of existentialism as 'beginning to think'.[3] Existentialism is born from thought, generated by the mind unflinchingly contemplating life and its meaning. Most outsiders are quite happy to let the conventional world pass them by. To some, it is like watching a river, knowing it will dissipate its inane currents into the sea allowing the water cycle and the next generation to repeat the same process all over again. The inevitability of the way people's lives unfold makes outsiders crave the freedom to maintain their uniqueness as individuals. They often grasp every opportunity they can to be or define the person they are as something authentic, even if it is just to provide them with a chance to distinguish themselves from the rest of society. This yearning for freedom and, to do something inimitable or different, is common to virtually all outsiders; it is intertwined with their need to generate meaning. They would hate to feel they were just reproducing what someone else had done, or acquiescing to someone else's perception of what they should do in life. They are not prepared to accept the world like everyone else by subsisting on its unreal fringes; they need to feel they are entities who can define themselves as something tangible, formed by the authenticity of their own thoughts and instincts. The possibilities which existential thought presents to an individual are limitless and some outsiders often see mankind's greatest limitation in the way it perceives itself.

Outsiders often remain unmoved by the elements which shape or determine other people's perceptions in life. Their minds are free from the collective constraints others sometimes willingly impose on themselves. Their determined sense of autonomy gives them the freedom to confront the fundamental questions which underpin their existence. Their immunity from society's usual leverage, together with their independence, gives them a boldness to challenge or disregard existing traditionalist dogma. Many do not accept anything is beyond them when they put their mind to it; some will even go out of their way to disprove other people's established notion of what they can or cannot do. However, their inability to find a meaningful purpose in their lives often means their potential is left dormant. In some people's eyes, the outsiders' attitude to life often makes it appear they have resigned themselves to a latent existence, and therefore, their abilities and resolve are usually underestimated. It is difficult to quantify to what lengths an outsider would be prepared to go to prove a principle he or she truly believed in - a psychometric test would probably be a totally useless tool in trying to estimate this. Once initiated, the extent of the their determination to pursue something capable of bringing meaning into their lives can rarely be anticipated within the context of what most people would consider as reasonable human behaviour.

People often make the mistake of trying to appraise outsiders according to their own partialities. They rely on the assumption that outsiders are governed by the motives, rules, and enticements of people in general, and are usually left perplexed when their presumptions are way off the mark. In some people's eyes, the outsider will always be an unknown entity. Many people do not appreciate their powerful incentive to simply be themselves in life. Some people try to pick up on every little quirk in the outsider's behaviour in an attempt to build up a profile they can rationalise for themselves. And yet, even when they have drawn their conclusions, many people still do not have a clue as to what really makes the outsider tick.

Some outsiders can be very audacious in life. They believe that they, and indeed any individual whose resolve is strong enough, can surmount virtually any obstacle. Unfortunately, their willingness to properly challenge themselves in life, is often undone by its absurd nature and the way they appraise what is meaningful. Having said this, when outsiders do get the bit between their teeth, they can, at times, excel beyond most others; refusing society's half measures and setting the bar by what they value or define as worthwhile. As such, they are often averse to endeavours in which they are obliged to temper these instincts by amalgamating their consciousness amongst everyone else. They thrive on challenges where they are left to their own devices – where they have the freedom to apply themselves in their own way. They do not see any achievement in developing a flair for the frivolous or trivial skills of life. The real challenge for them lies in the standards they set for themselves, the mind challenging its will to project itself to generate a meaning it can qualify as real. The challenge facing most outsiders is often in trying to bridge the massive gulf between what they define as important in life and what most others prioritise or aspire to.

It is important to bear in mind that the driving force behind the way many outsiders think is to simply see life for what it is, in its plainest format. It is also important to make the distinction between existentialism and mental illness, such as schizophrenia, paranoia or extreme delusions. It can sometimes be quite easy for someone suffering from one or other of these ailments, to mistakenly believe they are seeing things objectively and claim their despair or perspective of things is attributable to some existential disposition. Therefore, it is important to bear this distinction in mind as it could lead some people to rely on existentialism as a reason why they think the way they do, which may disguise an underlying mental or emotional condition. There are clear differences between someone who thinks existentially and someone who has a mental illness. Outsiders are usually distinguishable through their knack of seeing things for what they are, without people's usual motives or bias. Their detached demeanour often disguises a willingness and need to embrace anything which might bring some meaning into their lives. Their exposure to life may be the same as everyone else's, but their mind filters out the dim light of absurdity, making them wholly receptive to the brightness of substance and meaning. It is their ability to remain totally unmoved by the mundane aspects of life which forms their detachment and provides them with a perspective that, in many respects, enables them to recognise the often inevitable patterns of human behaviour. Many outsiders also exhibit a talent for being able to place people, changes or events within a wider context; a faculty which often adds to their quandary. As the German philosopher Schopenhauer explains:-

> In the first place, no man is happy but strives his whole life long after a supposed happiness which he seldom attains, and even if he does it is only to be disappointed with it; as a rule, however, he finally enters harbour shipwrecked and dismasted. In the second place, however, it is all one whether he has been happy or not in a life which has consisted merely of a succession of transient present moments and is now at an end. [4]

Outsiders sometimes feel as though they are trapped in a life made for someone else. Their candid perceptions enable them, at times, to anticipate certain eventualities, but it is precisely this ability to see through life which inhibits their ability to bind to it. They often see themselves as entities suspended in some past life, watching society move forward like a giant clock constantly revolving around a fixed point. To the outsider, society's only real claim to progress is in time and its form, like the clock's continual revolutions, seldom changes from one generation to the next. In this respect, some outsiders look upon society almost like a stagnant pool, geared towards supporting anything which remains on the surface feeding on life's simple organisms, while there is little sustenance for any creature wishing to thrive on the complex organisms which reside beneath. Many outsiders feel as though they have been left to suffer this habitat, starved of the freshwater environment they require to nourish them on a diet of transition and change, and trapped by the slow nature of evolution, always one step behind their will to attach meaning to their lives.

Some outsiders cannot escape their penetrating analysis of life. The more they look at what people generally do or aspire to, the more they cannot help thinking that people's needs are merely dependent upon what they have been conditioned to or led to accept as authentic. As some outsiders see it, people simply spend their whole lives striving for the enticements and accolades offered up by each successive generation, a situation which only reinforces most people's established mind-set. Unfortunately, within society, people are becoming increasingly conditioned. It is fast reaching the stage where those who do something out of the ordinary or wholly unconventional are often castigated, often for making a deliberate attempt to defy others collective standards. The upshot of this insular attitude is reflected in modern society by the way it takes a dim view of and, at times, stifles individualism within its conditioned sphere.

Some people within society today now even selectively choose which thoughts or articulations to give credence to, and increasingly ignore opinions or attitudes which do not complement their contrived perceptions. These people appear to be oblivious to the reality, that without independent minds to question society's rational basis, it has nothing to buffer itself from becoming more and more absurd in the way it evolves. It is inevitable that everything becomes much easier to excuse, in a society which is fast losing its ability to scrutinise itself. More and more people today are being governed by the devices and propaganda which streamline the masses down a single road, often kept in check by being taught to fear the consequences and upheaval which would ensue if society were to suddenly alter its course. It seems most people have discounted the fact that with the absence of autonomous thought, ideas and opinion, society's development becomes like an uncontrollable disease, rapidly evolving its form to disguise its expedient nature and immune from the ineffectual remedies of acquiescent opinions and eulogistic attitudes.

Some outsiders have no respite from their mind's existential predisposition, which becomes pivotal to the way their lives unfold. These outsiders sometimes feel as though their willingness to become or do something meaningful with their lives is undermined at every turn. They could never consider just going through the motions in life as a worthwhile aspiration and their stark appraisal of it, often gets dismissed out of hand by others as being negative or derived from some pessimistic view of life. People often deride outsiders for their apparent loss of faith in life and sometimes even classify their need to preserve their individualistic nature as conceited. However, in most cases, the simple fact is outsiders have not found anything substantive enough in life which they feel they can seriously latch onto or strive for. Many outsiders just do not accept the way society fashions itself; they believe it is stuck in a perpetual cycle, often continuously re-inventing its doctrines to accommodate its irrational nature. Some outsiders even reach the stage where they lose all purpose in living itself, which most people take for granted. They find themselves unable to live on hollow aspirations and the world most other people accept as authentic ceases to have any value to them. Sometimes, the only thing they can really console themselves with is the thought that their mind has furnished them with a lucidity - enabling them to consider something more meaningful than is contained in many people's everyday dream world of modern life.

Outsiders often feel like a fly caught in a spiders web, knowing if they do not struggle to at least do something, they will feel increasingly trapped; whilst also aware that if they struggle too much to break free, they are only hastening the inevitable confrontation between themselves and the world they are in. There does not seem to be any easy way out for the outsider. If they try to express their sentiments to others, they are always given the 'good advice' of how it is too impractical to think the way they do, and how they should just acquiesce to the way things are and go with the flow. The trouble is, they do not have any occasion to adopt this innocuous formula to life. They feel suffocated in a world where they believe many people prefer to live in their conventional bubble, rather than experience life riding on their mind's instincts. People in general confound outsiders by incessantly following their predictable and safe routines throughout life, sometimes perceiving any small unanticipated interruption in its pattern as some great tragedy. In today's world, people seem increasingly willing to accept an existence which comprises little or no real authenticity. Many feel safer residing in their contrived realism, and allowing themselves to be cajoled into today's mass market world, where nearly every aspect of life, including people, have cynically become commodities. Indeed, how can anyone take themselves seriously by adopting such a flimsy philosophy to life? Maybe the Algerian born French writer Albert Camus had the answer when he attempted to explain why some people are so content to embrace a conditioned existence:

> It is essential to consider as a constant point of reference in this essay the regular hiatus between what we fancy we know and what we really know, practical assent and simulated ignorance which allows us to live with ideas which, if we truly put them to the test, ought to upset our whole life. [5]

The most vexing aspect of existentialism is the way thought undermines the authenticity of a reality which virtually everyone else has acquiesced to. Outsiders cannot just go through life like everyone else; they would not feel as though they were living a real life without exercising their need to question its basis and test its substance. They can also be impulsive, having an aspiration one minute which may seem to be the most important thing in the world, whilst the next finding themselves helplessly transfixed as their mind unravels its potentiality. Life for outsiders often feels like trying to piece together a complicated jigsaw, with pieces which do not quite fit together, often leaving them in a state of despair. But this is not true of all outsiders, as many live their lives on the existential cusp, managing to tame their deep existential urges so they do not impact too much on their day-to-day lives. These individuals have learnt to be vigilant of their minds wanderings, knowing when it is time to turn away from analysing life's stark realities, when the nausea gets too much. These people know how much they have to rehearse life's routines in order to divert their thoughts direction and, unlike the more serious outsider, they feel a bit more secure in the knowledge they can, to some extent, check their thoughts' intensity when the need arises.

Existentialism and conventional thought could be considered as the most polarised aspects of human thinking. Those who go through life abiding by other people's protocol can often feel safe, knowing they are less likely to put a foot wrong by imitating what everyone else says or does. Whilst, on the other hand, existentialism advocates a total freedom of mind by championing the individual's need to think instinctively and define themselves according to their own values and conclusions. Too many people now prefer to follow the established advice of their contemporaries, who coin proverbial phrases such as: 'It's not good to think too much' or 'ignorance is bliss'. In order to embrace such an attitude, people are obliged to shy away from their minds' impulses. Nowadays, many people build their perceptions of life like ivory towers, where many things, no matter how innocuous, are avoided at all costs, just in case it undermines their mind's fragile foundations. As a result, many people deliberately limit their freedom of thought, often because they have been taught to fear the ramifications of trusting the mind to its own devices. Unfortunately, more and more people can now be found recanting corny maxims straight from the ever increasing number of puerile self-help books, as they attempt to carefully steer themselves through life, dodging anything which threatens to infringe on their ability to maintain a happy pretence.

The bold individual, who disregards or veers from people's established behavioural norms, is often considered to be some type of threat to society. Whenever a sensational murder trial is underway, the media often strives to serialise every snippet of the accused's past in order to pinpoint what turned the seemingly normal person into a ruthless or remorseless killer. Every little quirk is often magnified to fit the facts around a hypothesis which inevitably reaffirms the dangers associated with the anomalous individual. Nothing escapes the resourceful journalist seeking to place the wayward individual into a context which compliments people's faith in their own perceptions. Consequently, the loner or person who does not mix well in society often gets branded in much the same way as the criminal or social deviant. Not surprisingly, the outsiders' insistence to follow their instincts in the way they conduct themselves is often derided, with a few eager to draw comparisons between them and the twisted individual. Thus, it seems that anything will do to satisfy people's ignorant understanding and, outsiders often prove themselves as easy scapegoats for a society which is becoming increasingly illiberal in its attitude towards anyone different or who, by their very nature, do not make themselves amenable to its circumscribed comprehension.

Throughout history, the people who made the greatest impact on society invariably gained their insights from a wide range of ideas and experiences. If we had not had these bold individuals, prepared to go against the grain and do something different, we would never have had the scientists, inventors, writers and artists who have shaped society so profoundly through the ages. It could be said that the greatest danger facing society today is not from some extraneous source, but is more from people's susceptibility to the forces which condition them. Large swathes of the population now embrace society's doctrines at will, like the initiates of a close-knit religious cult. It seems many people do not appear to appreciate the precarious state of modern society, as they unfortunately become increasingly susceptible to the devices which condition them. What is more worrying, is how easily people can be swayed by the propaganda of hypothetical scenarios, even being led to believe their 'way of life' is somehow imminently under threat if their nation does not initiate military action and/or invade another country.[6] And at the same time, many people paradoxically harbour an exaggerated apprehension towards the lone disaffected individual, who might one day happen to go off the rails. The reality is that the greatest threat to any civilised society today, is not from the individual, but from the conditioned masses themselves. Most people find it difficult to envisage how irrational they can become, when they allow their scruples to be dissipated into some kind of collective consciousness. They often do not realise how dangerous this mind-set can be, sometimes resulting in the most sane people doing the most inconceivable and even cruel things. Furthermore, if we discount the notion that certain sections of society, groups of people or particular nations are simply 'evil', then it could be said that it is precisely people's vulnerability to being conditioned or manipulated that has precipitated humanity's worst crime against itself – genocide.

Society is more assured of itself when it feels it can confidently categorise people by reducing the causes of human behaviour into simplistic precepts. It has almost ceased to matter whether such classifications are entirely accurate. Some people nowadays seem increasingly content to believe they know something, than to actually know it. This is evident in the way some people learn things today, which often amounts to visiting Google and reading a few brief words on a subject, rather than gaining a comprehensive grasp of what that subject is about. In conjunction with this, some people are showing an increasing lack of willingness to accept, or even explore opinions which are not in accord with mainstream dogma. But, what could be more absurd than heralding mediocrity and adopting the borrowed values of others as the benchmark for appraising another point of view. It seems that far fewer people nowadays have the time, or indeed inclination, to test the validity of an opinion or an idea for themselves. This state of affairs exasperates outsiders as they strive to distinguish themselves from the prevailing mentality around them. It is a complete anathema to outsiders how some people are often too apathetic, or even too fearful, to project what they truly think and be who they are in life. In contrast,  most outsiders would never willingly submit themselves to the dictates or expectations of others; they are shaped by their own thoughts and must exist on their terms.

> So long as the mind keeps silent in the motionless world of its hopes, everything is reflected and arranged in the unity of its nostalgia. But with the first move this world cracks and tumbles : an infinite number of shimmering fragments is offered to the understanding. We must despair of even reconstructing the familiar, calm surface which would give us peace of heart. [7]

The problem many outsiders face is their thoughts have taken them beyond the pale. They have reached the end of the line, and found they cannot withdraw into that comfort zone of just accepting life again, without despairing with it in some way. These outsiders have lost their innocence. They have become incapable of recreating that carefree attitude to life, in which they may have once accepted things without question. Consequently, they develop an incredible resilience by evolving to withstand the increased pressures of deeper waters;

they learn to accept the dim light of life and do not offer any excuses for the way they think or the way they see things. They know they cannot manufacture or immerse themselves in someone else's realism to give themselves some peace of mind; they cannot delude themselves by trying to emulate someone else. These outsiders live on the fringes of society, usually with no other option than to accept their despair with life which, for some, grips them every day. The river cannot be diverted; thought has carved out the gorges of conviction which now run too deep to be altered by the climate these outsiders find themselves in. They cannot be enticed to become part of society again on the premise that it offers a naïve type of equality to all those willing to be carried blindly along with it. Their thoughts are inescapable and all that seems left is to live in a virtual void, where glimmers of hope are usually quickly extinguished by their mind's longing for something more.

Existentialists, by their nature, can neither deny nor alter their perceptions. They do not deliberately set out to prove that the world around them lacks the meaning they demand from it. This is simply their minds' conclusion, as it starts piercing life's many guises. Some people, it seems, give themselves an implied privilege to proudly uphold what they do, justify what they have done, and excuse themselves for the things they have omitted or failed to do. To a few, it does not matter what they do in life or how they conduct themselves, as long as they can convince others of their supposed respectability. Some people are adept at shrouding themselves in accommodating moral, ethical or academic justifications, to protect themselves from any blemishes on their character. Outsiders sometimes feel as though they are alone in witnessing some people's duplicity. By their nature, they often become proficient at discerning people's lowest common denominator and the true vested and pragmatic needs they serve. From a wider perspective, they often cannot bestow much credibility on many of those around them, or society as a whole for that matter which often reconciles its principles according to its form, rather than using its principles as a source for its design and as a platform for improving itself. From an outsider's point of view, any society that convinces its masses of the veracity of its doctrines through conveniently deceptive rationales or spurious precepts, to disguise its true nature, is not really worth being part of.

This explains why most are continually drawn towards the gravity of their own perceptions. They become increasingly immune from other people's feeble persuasions, and tired of watching those around them accept weak or dogmatic excuses for society's obvious, and in many outsiders' eyes, predictable oversights.

It is unfortunate existentialism is often considered by some as a form of mental illness. Thinking existentially is sometimes misdiagnosed as a clinical mental illness (or vice versa) as in some instances the symptoms, at first glance, can appear very similar. Mental illness is essentially a defect of the mind, whilst (it could be argued) existentialism is simply the mind becoming more conscious of itself in its attempt to come to terms with its perceptions and define its own parameters of meaning. Having said this, existentialism is generally regarded by the medical profession as a damaging state of mind. The attitude which seems to permeate through the psychiatric world is that any thoughts which are not part of the norm, or which have the potential to cause people despair in any way, should be supressed or avoided at all costs. Unfortunately, existentialism often gets branded in much the same way. The massive array of drugs available to people who show the slightest signs of mental unease, and the unnerving frequency with which these are prescribed, especially anti-depressants and beta-blockers, typifies this attitude. Many of the drugs on offer today are specifically designed to subdue aspects of people's mental faculties and, while they may be essential in treating genuine mental illnesses, it is worrying that some of these drugs are at times prescribed with alarming ease and frequency.

Regrettably, too many people today are all too willing to castigate existentialism as either a sign of some mental failing or, even as some believe, an immature attitude to life. The problem with this, is that the outsider's dilemma is not solved by trying to suppress their thoughts, alter their state of mind, or by giving them a course of drugs to inhibit their mind's ability to function effectively in the short term. What is actually wrong with the individual (who it is presumed does not suffer from any mental illness) judging life according to their perceptions and then drawing the conclusion it is absurd? Are these individuals supposed to hypnotise themselves with the demeaning jargon of self-help audio books to bring them back into line with the way everyone else thinks? Are they meant to condition themselves or force themselves to accept a fake form of contentment with life? An extension of this methodology would also imply that any individual, with a radically different outlook on life, should be considered as exhibiting some type of mental disorder.

It is sad, that so many people today are often treated as social outcasts purely on the basis that they perceive things differently from the majority of others. People's respect for the uniqueness of individual thought and opinion seem to be increasingly cast aside, as modern society seems to strive towards a utopian model - inducing increasing numbers of people to think and act in a more uniform way. The idea that technological advancements, in terms of the information we have at our disposal and the effectiveness with which people now communicate, has created a new generation of individuals with an increased spectrum of views and opinions is a misconception. Apart from the crackpots, fanatics and conspiracy theorists, people in general have become more mainstream in the way they nowadays think and behave. It is interesting to imagine what concoction of drugs van Gogh would have been prescribed had he lived today. Furthermore, it would be highly optimistic of anyone to expect that he could have generated the deep insights portrayed in his paintings whilst being prescribed some of the typical mind-suppressant medicines handed out to so many people in the western world today.

Most outsiders do not believe they have a niche in society or an avenue through which to instinctively express themselves. Their relationship with the world can only be described as tenuous to say the least and this is probably where Camus derived the now famous title of his book *The Outsider*. Existentialists generally prefer to keep themselves to themselves, as their reality clashes more than contrasts with the world around them. Some existentialists can also be very intolerant of people who dare not veer off their conventional path in life, believing they base their lives on precepts which have little or no real authenticity. It does not make any sense to the outsider, why so many people often squander the means necessary to define themselves by what they think. On the other hand, outsiders often get accused of being deliberately obstinate, but this completely misses the point. Most outsiders, ultimately aspire to be able to one day embrace life like everyone else and feel part of a society which is capable of realising its pretensions and, concerning itself with (what they regard as) its more substantive aspects, as a platform for improving itself. It may appear paradoxical, but many outsiders often aspire to the prospect of playing a greater role in society; however, in most instances, contemporary life proves itself wholly inept at satisfying their need to feel fulfilled in any meaningful way.

Modern society seldom contains the means to entice outsiders to become a greater part of it, yet in spite of this some outsiders are still prepared to tolerate its social fringes. It may appear contradictory, but some outsiders even go to extremes, sometimes prostituting themselves by acting out their part on the social scene. These outsiders disguise their despair in order to feel part of something, even if it is for a brief moment, which goes some way to making them feel less alienated. It has ceased to matter that they realise the futility of their attempts to relate to the people around them; what is important to them, is that they satisfy their inherent need to feel part of something, and close to others, for a time, to alleviate their sense of isolation. Most are aware, they will usually only feel a sense of emptiness by congenially trying to connect with others, but some outsiders are desperate and will always try to fit in somewhere hoping one day to derive something worthwhile from the world around them, while aware of the probable outcome. Outsiders can be creatures of extremes and, the extent of these extremes should not surprise anyone, when seemingly contradictory measures are used as a tool to bridge the solitary wilderness between their realism and, from their perspective, other people's holographic world. Therefore, even though it may appear at times that some outsiders are as much a part of society as anyone else, this inference can be misleading. Life has taught them how to play their part in society, so at times it is difficult to distinguish them from just another face in the crowd.

Camus' novel *The Outsider*, describes the sensations all outsiders feel from time to time of living life while lacking any real passion for it. The book's protagonist Meursault, is virtually in-different to what goes on around him. He lacks any of the normal zest for life that others appear to possess and resigns himself to routinely drifting through it from one day to the next. People are incomprehensible to him, and yet he does not despair with this even though he considers living amongst them as something strange. Meursault accepts life the way it is, believing there is nothing he can do to reconcile his need to understand it against its senselessness format. He accepts his situation, so much so that he does not see any point in despairing with it. The book centres upon an event in which Meursault becomes embroiled in someone else's dispute and inadvertently shoots a man dead. During his trial Meursault is given every opportunity and virtually pleaded with to repent for what he has done, but to no avail. He is even advised to show some sign of remorse which would allow the court to be lenient with his sentence, but shows a total lack of appreciation for the principles of mitigation. The story demonstrates the injustice of Meursault's case, as the magistrate yearns for him to show them some indication of regret for what has happened. Camus makes it clear in the story that the magistrate would accept his regret as a mitigating factor, even if it is only in response to concern for his own welfare (which could be understood in the context of a normal human response), but Meursault does not show any sign of penitence.

> Then the magistrate stood up as if to indicate that the examination was over. Only he asked me in the same manner whether I'd regretted what I'd done. I thought it over and said that rather than true regret, I felt a kind of annoyance. I had the impression that he didn't understand me. [8]

> I didn't much regret what I'd done. But, I was surprised that he[the magistrate] was so furious about it. I'd have liked to have explained to him in a friendly way I'd never been able to regret anything. [9]

Camus' Outsider does not feel remorse or regret for what has happened, his mind rejects these sentiments. Meursault's actions were unintentional, but from an existential perspective he thinks – why regret it when there is nothing anyone can do about it now, it has already happened? It is quite evident Camus' character finds difficulty expressing or feeling any kind of emotion; he probably considers emotion as too self-indulgent for his existential nature. Meursault is different from the majority of outsiders, as even though he is portrayed as emotionally detached from society (to which he feels absolutely

nothing for), he quietly submits to his place within it. Notwithstanding this, Meursault does exhibit a prevalent trait common to
all existentialists - they are invariably honest in the way they present
themselves to others. Meursault does not see any reason to mask
what he thinks and, therefore, has no motive to lie to anyone. He
makes sense of his life by being completely honest with himself and
others. He understands nothing of most other people's appeasing
habits, and the thought of etching a more endearing portrait of
himself in someone else's imagination to obtain a more lenient
sentence, does not even cross his mind. He decides who he is,
governed by the substance of his own unbridled thoughts, and cannot
be anything other than true to himself.

In day-to-day life, Meursault seems to take everything in his
stride, while feeling totally unconnected with what goes on around him.
He just plods through it, trying to make the best of his circumstances in
the only way he knows how. He has no hankering for self-preservation
and, of course, no motive to mitigate his circumstances by hiding his true
thoughts to the magistrate - which eventually becomes his undoing. His
frankness during his trial cannot be understood in the context of a
normal person's response under the circumstances. The court inevitably
infers that, if his actions were accidental, he would be remorsefully
pleading with them to understand his unfortunate state of affairs.
However, he does not show any reaction during the court proceedings
and the court duly interprets his indifference and blunt responses to
their questions as confirmation of his callous nature, allowing the
prosecution to paint a disturbing picture of him as a person. The court,
in turn, has an unshakeable faith in its ability to understand Meursault;
in much the same way society believes it can pigeonhole the outsider.
The court's unerring attitude only adds to its complacency, making
the magistrate incapable of appraising Meursault fairly. *The Outsider*
highlights the gulf between the existentialist and society, demonstrating
how easily they can find themselves unjustly or inaccurately classified
within the limits of other people's understanding. Society as a whole,
often thrives on its ability to neatly compartmentalise each individual
within it, and often will not relinquish this faith by entertaining any
suggestion that it might sometimes be mistaken in its conclusions.
Meursault finds himself against the full force of this unerring prejudice:

He [the magistrate] announced that I had no place in society whose most fundamental rules I ignored, nor could I make an appeal to the heart when I knew nothing of the most basic human reactions. [10]

The story concludes with him being sentenced to death.

Even though *The Outsider* is widely read and frequently quoted, Camus' characterisation of Meursault is not wholly typical of most outsiders. Even though life does not make much sense to him, he does not despair with it. He has given up all hope of finding anything in it capable of meaning something to him. In this respect, he sees despair as a futile response and just takes what comes without trying to qualify the things going on in his life. In contrast, most outsiders do despair with life. In many ways, existential despair can be considered as a positive reaction to life's absurd format, as it does not just demonstrate an individual's disillusionment with it, but also their expectation of possibly reconciling the difference. It does not serve any purpose for an individual to abandon their hope of ever being able to change the circumstances they are in, if they believe things, from their point of view, do not make sense or could be improved. Sometimes outsiders wish others could actually empathise with their plight, but all too often no-one, it seems, really wants to see their lives in the context of its meaning or against such a blatantly honest backdrop. In many ways, outsiders find themselves like artists amongst a bunch of novice painters gazing on their abstract view of life. The outsider, like the artist, is able to see through the picture and understand its meaning and symbolic significance, while the novice is unable to penetrate its façade, unable to see it other than as a scene from a picture postcard. The artist is usually frustrated by his or her inability to translate what they see; the novice must experience it for him or herself in order to discern its meaning. The outsider often feels like an artist before his time, despairing with the way people's conditioned nature renders them incapable of seeing into the dimensions of life, or grasping its meaning for themselves.

It is hardly surprising outsiders often struggle to function in life like other people. Their lives are characterised by a continual search for some aspect of it which will generate a drive within them to want to achieve something, but often the more they search the more disillusioned they become. Their imperative, to attach meaning behind their existence, sometimes leads them further away from the things they may have once valued or aspired to. The romantic outsider (the opposite to Meursault), is usually never settled in anything he or she does. These individuals stand out by their untiring willingness to try new and different challenges. On the face of it they appear like eternal optimists, chasing an ideal which in the end always proves illusive; finding something in life to strive for and apply themselves to wholeheartedly and without reservation. These outsiders frequently jump from one thing to another with an enthusiasm which soon tapers off almost as soon as it manifests itself. It is as if, once they have lived the experience, or succeeded in what they have challenged themselves to do, they instantly feel the need to move on to something else. Some people would say this shows a lack of dedication or resolve, whilst others might put it down to the fact that such individuals have a great appetite for life. However, in the case of the outsider it invariably represents someone desperately searching to find an unequivocal purpose in life; something sufficiently meaningful to put their heart and soul into. This explains why the romantic outsider is often willing to embrace any challenge; there is more to be gained than merely overcoming the challenge - they would never pass up any opportunity to potentially discover something which they could define as being worthwhile. The stakes could not be higher for the outsider; to subsist in life resigned to a dormant existence by a conception of their own impotence, or to try every means at their disposal to find a pursuit capable of igniting all their imagination and energy to achieve it.

All outsiders aspire to live a fulfilled life, but most of the time it does not seem to offer much within it that is worth pursuing with any real degree of conviction. From the outsider's standpoint, many people live virtually the same kind of life, striving for similar goals while feeling equally proud of their accomplishments. People often cheer themselves into a frenzy, each convincing the other that every small endeavour equates to some momentous achievement. It seems that every piffling deed deserves a feather in the cap, magnifying the relevance of what people do, until in some cases, their inflated conceit makes them oblivious to the inconsequentiality of what they have actually accomplished. Outsiders are not prepared to follow convention and simply go through life trying to perfect whatever endeavours society tends to hold in high regard at a particular time. As such, their options are often narrowed. Despite this, their relentless search for meaning continues in the face of all adversity, as the alternative is often too wretched to contemplate. Many often channel their despair into pursuing increasingly extreme undertakings in life and, this explains why some are so unpredictable in what they do. They are usually fiercely independent and refuse to relinquish what they think; everything must first pass their mind's rigorous scrutiny before being given any credence. They are well aware of the gulf between the way they appraise life and others deference towards it. They realise that people generally have little understanding of what actually drives them and this usually strengthens their determination to disregard protocol and other people's 'good advice', through their insistence to make their own way through life by learning from their own mistakes.

Most outsiders refuse to be counselled or dictated to by anyone. It may seem at times, they deliberately go out of their way to frustrate others' expectations of them, but this explanation is often only advanced to fill a gap in some people's comprehension. It would probably not even cross their mind to be deliberately obstinate just for the sake of it. The reason some outsiders tend to be so shockingly unconventional, is that at times they feel they need to counterbalance and even shake up people's more orthodox mind-set. These people sometimes presume legitimacy behind what they think and do merely because it is accepted as some established norm. For instance, some outsiders often use seemingly contradictory means, not just to prove a point, but also to highlight the paradoxical nature of a particular set of circumstances. They sometimes go to great lengths to accentuate the importance they place upon their freedom and autonomy, instinctively resisting any force or framework which they feel indiscriminately classified by. They detest all forms of unnecessary bureaucracy, especially when they believe its purpose is contrived from curtailing people's freedom of expression. It is often difficult for outsiders to feel any real empathy for people within modern society, especially when they witness so many squandering their freedom to think and act as individuals, often without a qualm for the type of society it engenders.

Outsiders find it difficult to grasp why some people willingly relinquish such a large portion of their autonomy to society's trifling incentives. Society appears to commend anyone with a proven track record of appeasing populist or authoritative dictates. People often feel pressurised into discarding or suppressing what they truly think, allowing themselves to be marshalled into increasingly narrow clusters. The whistle-blower exposing unfairness or corruption, who would have probably been praised in the past for his or her courage in doing the right thing, nowadays faces losing his or her job or even going to prison. These days, people are encouraged to look up to those who fall in line, while the person who seeks to project themselves beyond this naïve dogma, is often seen as an impediment to people's ability to get things done. This often explains why the way outsiders think is at such odds with society, especially in today's world. They are not a piece of clay which willingly submits to whichever mould it is assigned, but the hardest of all stones which resists being bound to anything or shaped by the conditions around it. They have an unremitting determination to exist according to what they think. It is this, which holds them steadfast against any temptation to deny themselves and abandon their mind's principles, for the privilege of floating anonymously along with society on a tide of other people's paradigms.

The outsider's powerful determination to adhere to what he or she thinks is drawn from their need to exist as something tangible in life. This is why they are unwilling to relinquish any part of themselves or their perceptions, to effect some favourable short-term change in their circumstances. They are renowned for their candid nature and, lack any incentive to use unscrupulous levers to drag themselves through life, when all this does is make them part and parcel of an increasingly Machiavellian world. Society will often use whatever means it can to compel outsiders to reaffirm the veracity of its design in order to authenticate its doctrines. It is usually the most impressionable who gain first prize in implicitly embracing these doctrines, while the weak-minded are not far behind, requiring a little more persuasion. The irresolute are usually the next to fall in line, requiring a bit more time to decide what they get out of it, while those who have already declared their opposition, wait for someone to come up with a conveniently spurious rationale to disguise their blatant submission. These days society's doctrines gain their legitimacy in the same shabby way ill-conceived Commons bills become law.

Inevitably, the outsider's unwillingness to be swayed from what they truly think frustrates others. Many people simply cannot fathom what outsiders gain or what their motives might be for following their intractable instincts, when the upshot is that they often become at odds with those around them - like someone who wears the wrong style clothing at a golf club function. Their determination to maintain their principles and the things they believe in leads some to define them as moralists, however, this label is wholly misleading. The fact that they stand by what they think, is not due to any moral indoctrination, but simply because that is the way they have chosen to conduct themselves. Outsiders take responsibility for what they think; they decide for themselves what values or principles, if any, to adhere to. Furthermore, they cannot tolerate, nor see any reason to involve themselves with anything which interferes with their mind's certainty. They just cannot find a credible rationale for compromising themselves when pitched against their freedom to choose who they are and their mind's will to be itself; in their eyes the alternative simply leads to a meaningless existence. In a world which is now filled with so many irresolute people, the outsider's truth and certainty of mind become paramount to who they are, which they will never renounce to any person or group unable to offer them anything capable of overriding their need to define themselves by what they think.

At times, outsiders can come across as insensitive or cold individuals. They are not generally moved by (as they see it) many people's inconsistent sentimental displays and usually perceive things from a more detached perspective. Having said this, they can be as upset as the next person over a tragic set of circumstances, but generally speaking they take a much more philosophical view. Some outsiders do not even show much emotion; many consider sentiment to be based upon selfish presumptions, which are self-imposed by people who seek to rely on their expectations of a particular person or set of circumstances. In most cases, people's immediate natural reaction to an unfavourable or unexpected change is to be surprised or sometimes upset, and yet, many outsiders often seem to have an almost nonchalant attitude to changes or upheavals in their lives. Many outsiders believe expectation it too much of a liberty to take from life as the only real expectations outsiders they have are the ones they demand from themselves. This would appear to give them the ultimate freedom to do anything they want. However, the freedom outsiders realise from exploring their mind's unreserved potential is often rendered redundant by their inability to find the unequivocal purpose they often seek. The dilemma becomes the paradox - thought negates life. Therefore, the totality of freedom which accompanies existentialism is curtailed by its very nature, which in many cases, renders their freedom academic.

Outsiders are often left to digest the irony that just as their mind strives to explore the possibilities open to it, things seem to lose their meaning. From their perspective, conventional life often does not contain enough gravity to galvanise their will and fix their mind on achieving anything. Many quietly hope one day an opportunity will present itself, enabling them to do something exceptional or something which has the potential to have a meaningful impact on their lives. Many outsiders can also be quite altruistic, ready to stand up against any repressive system or for that matter any form of injustice. However, it is sometimes difficult for outsiders to find a motive to uphold others freedoms, when so many nowadays simply acquiesce to the way things are. There is no doubt, over the years, people have become increasingly impressionable to the array of subtle influences which condition them, especially in the way they think and behave. For instance, in the commercial world, many people's respect for raw originality has already been superseded by their veneration of the hollow principles of mass-market success. There appears to be less and less people, who actually want to liberate themselves from the existing mind-set around them, and define themselves according to their mind's criterion. This explains why modern society is like a concrete jungle to outsiders who long for the rural diversity, where they can only quench their mind's demands by existing as naturally free individuals.

The strong features of individuality, freedom, truth and the endless search for meaning are attributes virtually all outsiders possess to varying degrees. It is these hallmarks, often subtly disguised, which sets them apart from most others. At the same time, nearly everyone can profess to having experienced existential thoughts or been confronted with existential dilemmas at some point in their lives. They may have woken up one morning feeling helplessly adrift, wondering what they are doing with their lives, or whether their life has any real degree of meaning to it. Obviously, this happens to some more frequently and intensely than to others, and this book is principally concerned with those whose existential instincts dominate their lives, making it impossible to reside comfortably in the cushioned world of other people's realism. These outsiders are the exceptions in society, who cannot accept life seriously and exist without any real connection to the world around them. In many ways, they live an isolated existence, in a world hopelessly inept at nourishing the calling of their thinking minds. A world which shepherds the masses in a singular direction and frowns on anyone who harbours an aspiration to acquire a more substantive meaning to their lives. These outsiders despair with a society they perceive as increasingly concerned with revering its ability to organise and guide its population down an increasingly narrow pathway, rather than cherishing people's versatility to embrace and promote their qualities as individuals within it. The world for these outsiders is unreal and, as such, they are compelled to turn to themselves for answers; they cannot live on the diet others blindly swallow by deluding their true instincts and doing themselves the injustice of simply subsisting within it.

# 3

# The Unreal World

**The criteria which have been bestowed on the "true being" of things are the criteria of non-being, of naught, the "true world" has been constructed out of contradiction to the actual world: indeed an apparent world, insofar as it is merely a moral optical illusion.**

Friedrich Nietzsche - *Twilight of the Idols* [1]

In the outsider's world, life must hold some meaning to it in order to be granted any significance or taken seriously. The problem they have is that their thoughts continually strip away life's veneer exposing its contradictory nature and lack of meaning. As a result, they fail to find anything substantive to latch onto, and life as they perceive it becomes almost fictional. They cannot simply accept the realism everyone else takes for granted and things seem to carry on around them wholly unconnected with the things they believe actually matter. To many there is a nauseating inevitability about daily life and subsequently they find it hard to attribute any authenticity to the way it unfolds. To them, it is like watching the endeavours of some celebrity on a television show, even though it may amount to something in some people's imagination, it has no relevance in real terms. There is a stark contrast between the things which preoccupy most people's attentions in life and what outsider's value. Much of the time normal life does not strike them as real or authentic and this generates an inertia which undermines their willingness to do or dedicate themselves to anything with any serious conviction.

The clash of perspectives in the way outsiders and others appraise things, touches virtually all aspects of their lives. They can walk down a busy street with a number of other people and have a completely different interpretation of what they have witnessed. This concept was acknowledged by Eduard Husserl, a nineteenth century philosopher, who founded the theory of phenomenology.[2] In it, he proposed that there is no objective reality and what people perceive is dependent on their experience of things and how their senses interpret what is around them. Consequently, there is no definitive right or wrong way of looking at things; everyone is a product of their experiences and the way their mind defines the world they are in. This is especially poignant in the case of the outsider who often takes a long hard look at other people's underlying reasons for what they do in life, trying to identify with something they can regard as tangible or which resonates with them. However, the deeper they delve, the more it becomes plain that many people's lives are dominated by a succession of needs instilled in them by society which are often pursued without question.

From many outsiders' point of view, people appear predictable in the things they do, from the continually revolving fashions they follow and even down to the opinions they adopt. They see people so immersed in the rigmarole of day-to-day life, that any incentive they may once have had to address more substantive aspects of their lives, seem to have drained out of them long ago. It is true, that many people's pace of life now runs at a million miles an hour, leaving them with little time or inclination to consider their lives or its meaning in a wider context. It is as if modern life conspires against the individual's penchant to consider their lives from a more meaningful perspective. Communication is now instant with people struggling to keep up with the constant demands on their attention. Some people are literally 'driven to distraction' and inevitably lose their inclination and willingness to consider their lives against a more profound backdrop. In addition to this, society subtly reinforces the idea that it is foolish for people to try to attribute a meaning behind what they do in life, as it usually just leads to unhappiness or some psychological impasse. This ideology permeates through society, convincing people to divert their thoughts away from confronting anything outside its safe conventional remit or anything else which may upset the applecart.

In life, some people find themselves having to check their thoughts when they feel themselves looking into the meaning and relevance of things too much; a few have done it for so long the habit is almost subconscious. However, by doing so these people are deliberately obscuring their minds' natural impulse to see things for what they are. Many of these people try to ensure their attentions remain focused on marginal or incidental aspects of their lives. Like a child who adheres to the pronouncements of overprotective parents, these people keep their thoughts firmly on the surface, only to one day find themselves totally out of their depth when they inevitably experience the real world outside. In these people's lives, minor disruptions are often considered as major events as their reality becomes a world where the immaterial is prioritised over and above its more salient aspects. Unfortunately for some, this forms the basis of their realism in the modern world and as someone worries about how they will be able to afford the next must-have fashion accessory, they may not have a pang of conscience for the poverty or depravation on their doorstep, or that thousands may be needlessly starving to death in some Third World country.

Within some people's narrowed perceptive sphere they have no occasion to concern themselves with a large scale human catastrophe unfolding thousands of miles away. For a few, their closeted outlook on life robs them of the imagination to empathise with the plight of people less fortunate than themselves, while their self-absorbed attitude leads them to discard anything which they think has no direct bearing on their lives. People's realism in the modern world is often further obscured by their increasing hedonism, flagrantly promoted by the commercialisation of people's needs. It appears, no-one really frowns anymore on anyone who shamelessly pursues a purely selfish aspiration, even sometimes when they display a total disregard for the wider repercussions their actions may engender. It has also become much easier for people today to rely on others collective indifference as an excuse for not embracing any responsibility beyond themselves. This self-induced nonchalance is the real cancer of our time - it spreads quickly amongst those who are more conditioned within society, gradually eclipsing their empathy and moral conscience until eventually, their obligation to do something is whittled down to the egocentric self and, the immediacy of their fickle or self-serving aims in life.

In society today, it seems people can go through life resting on their pretensions and still hold their heads up high. From the outsider's standpoint, it is as if some people selectively choose what they want to see and hear as they bodge their way through life. Some outsiders often feel like grabbing some people by the scruff of the neck just to try to make them aware of the realities they seem so blatantly oblivious to. Outsiders are poles apart from most other people in terms of their outlook. In some ways, they can be likened to someone who has suffered a near death experience who now sees life in a completely different vein from before. The more they look into life trying to discern what it is all about, the more they become aware of people's fruitless idiosyncrasies, with some feeling as though they are mere spectators in a Greek tragedy. They cannot condone the way some people resort to their well-rehearsed habit of justifying the relevance of their lives by peddling their spurious assertions, often like unscrupulous car salesmen. They cannot identify themselves with a world which designs itself to revolve around satisfying people's increasing hedonism, while propagating an in-difference to the truer realities of life; hardly a credible doctrine on which to base any prospective society.

Outsiders generally feel trapped in this world like Hamlet's father's ghost, condemned to wander in a place where they no longer belong. Their candid outlook offers them a perspective which is far too authentic to be dislodged with people's usual psychological trickery. Their heightened sense of awareness and stark analysis of life does not wane over time, and strikes some with a blinding brightness rendering them incapable of naïvely looking on life like others do. Everything they see is refined through their existential perspective often turning what they see into a meaningless haze and the people into indistinguishable shadows, where there is no perceptible difference between one person and the next. Most outsiders find it impossible to unconsciously accept life without challenging the relevance of their role within it. The more they think and consider it in this context the more they see though it, undermining their prospects of discovering anything capable of stimulating their senses or rousing their imagination. In many cases, their disaffection towards contemporary life is made complete by their weariness towards society's self-perpetuating motion and people's indifference towards even acknowledging their realism. Few people open their minds and attempt to understand the person inside the outsider, who is often just simply searching for something capable of generating a meaning within his or her life, which they can qualify as real.

The outsider's detachment from the usual humdrum of everyday life, often allows him or her to see further along the horizon. They remain outside the immediacy and concerns of the everyday world which appears to dominate some people's conventional habits, subsequently bringing an objectiveness in the way they see things. Their perspective is not easily distorted by any emotional or self-indulgent needs they may harbour towards others or society as a whole. Their mind's conviction to appraise things in its own way is enhanced by their ability to affirm their perceptions against the predictable way life around them seems to unfold. They also refuse to condone anyone who squanders their ability to appraise things for themselves by placing their blind trust in those who, they believe, are more qualified to sweet-talk them through life. It could be said that nowadays, fewer people actually think for themselves; many preferring to ally themselves with mainstream dogma or to whatever the prevailing attitude or consensus might be. This in turn, manifests itself through a lack of opinion and scrutiny within society, offering little protection from those in authoritative positions wishing to run roughshod over the rights of individuals, or make decisions absent of any notion of fairness, common sense or legitimacy. Some would argue that society has already reached this stage.

Many of the things in life which usually motivate people in general, or which people believe define them as individuals, often do not have any real meaning to the outsider. Most people's conception of what it means to be successful or what leads to contentment in life often revolves around things like having a good job, maintaining a good standard of living, or raising a family they can be proud of. The remarks of the advertising millionaire, Jacques Seguela, who said anyone who does not own a Rolex by the time they are fifty is a failure,[3] typifies the shallow and naïve way some people are conditioned to define achievement. These aspirations usually do not offer anything worthwhile to the outsider in terms of how they define success or achieving anything in life. People's usual notions of attaining a good career, a good salary or becoming affluent, are usually completely incidental to the things outsiders conceive as being meaningful or leading to any real sense of contentment.

The question of whether or not someone is respected by their peers or considered successful, has no bearing whatsoever on the way outsiders appraise other people. They often have a completely different set of criteria in the way they define achievement and its role as a prerequisite for feeling satisfied with their lives. Unfortunately, the way most people generally define success is often dependent upon established notions, behaviours, and others prevailing attitudes they are taught to identify with achievement. Virtually every day some well-respected and/or successful member of society becomes undone by their sometimes ruthless or dissolute nature, with some conveniently ignoring the fact that these character traits are often indispensable ingredients to those intent on reaching the top in society's pecking order. It is even more worrying that as time goes by, more and more people seem to accept this behaviour as part of the format of modern life. It is beginning to reach the stage where it does not matter how someone reaches his or her goals in life or how fickle their achievements may be. Some people have already acquiesced to what is fast becoming the new norm, where expediency now qualifies as an acceptable motive to deem an action justifiable. Many people now pride themselves on their versatility in being able to contrive a situation to their advantage or persuasively convince others of something which, even a child would sometimes recognise, as plainly short-sighted or erroneous. And yet, this ability is sometimes held in high regard and, in some cases, promoted as a valuable skill within society; presentation often accepted as a suitable substitute for substance in the modern world.

There is little doubt some people's unwillingness to question the tangibility of life around them distorts their perspective of it.

Outsiders find it hard to appreciate the twisted realism of people who choose not to confront any wider or more profound issues or think for themselves. For some, it is much easier to follow the well-trodden path of abiding by the things most others esteem or are conditioned to. It is as if there are many people who do not want to go down that precarious road of finding out what really lies behind their cosmetic realism. It seems as though outsiders are condemned to bear witness to this parody, people's continual highs and lows, and their consternation when the predictable order of their society is affected by the undulating machinations of modern life. From an outsider's point of view, many people exist in a cartoon world where they give themselves the liberty of altering the scenario often through redefining the plot or the ending when they feel the need to shirk the reality of what happens next.

Many outsiders often wish they could just wake up one morning without having that fateful feeling of having to muddle through another hapless day. And yet, the real irony is, it is the outsider who finds him or herself being counselled on the meanings of life - much like solving a problem by conveniently reattributing its cause. It seems they are the ones who need to be constantly advised 'just live life and enjoy it, there are no reasons or deeper meaning beyond this'. Indeed, how can such a solution provide any answers, when it discourages people from addressing the questions their minds generate? But, maybe we should not be too dismayed by this modus operandi, as avoiding the issue is a practice which is now commonplace. It has been transformed into an art form by today's politicians and corporate spin doctors, rendering some people oblivious to the unscrupulous nature of decisions made on their behalf. Outsiders find out early on they cannot draw their sustenance in life from other people's axioms; they are struck by the revelation that life, by its lack of tangibility, has in their eyes lost much of its meaning. Their frustrations are often amplified as no-one else appears to appreciate their perspective or even entertains the idea that life could lack the meaning some people demand from it. It is shameful to think that today's society, which presumes it is more socially advanced than any before it, often promotes naivety and indifference, as essential ingredients to maintaining people's notion of a happy life.

Outsiders face an uphill struggle, often grappling with their own sanity as they try to come to terms with the fact they cannot seem to find a horse to back in the merry-go-round of modern life. Some try to force themselves to accept life in the same vein as everyone else, but soon find they are only deceiving their true instincts. They cannot deny the way they perceive things and often feel frustrated by the fact they feel they have to resign themselves to such an ineffectual existence through their inability to find a meaningful aspiration within the absurd world they are in. Their thoughts give them little respite and like the tidal pressures of the sea constantly pound the shoreline, unravelling society's prefabricated doctrines which distort its natural appearance. Many people's general aspirations in life are not usually considered by outsiders as avenues which actually lead to anything. All some appear to want from life is to subsist within it, choosing the path of least resistance at every turn while often trying to grab as many cheap benefits as they can along the way. There appears to be less people today who are prepared to persevere and work towards creating or doing something which is not considered practicable or capable of producing an immediate material benefit in some way. The transient nature of modern life makes it appear increasingly unreal to the outsider as they vainly attempt to project their instincts on the fabric of a world which is unable to properly measure up to their objectivity, truth and need for meaning.

Some outsiders often reach the point where the void created by their realism and other peoples' world cannot be bridged. The two continents finally break away, evolving independently. These outsiders soon realise how lonely their world can be as their alienation only seems to lessen the possibility of reconciling the two. At times, there does not appear to be anything capable of bridging the gulf and all that seems to lie ahead is a life of quiet despair. To them, it is as if many others prefer living in a pseudo-reality and society's design appears to facilitate this penchant. With increasingly mainstream dogma now permeating through most things society does, the myth that individuality and diversity play a much more prominent role within it today is still maintained by some people. A prime example is the advanced technological gadgetry people now have at their disposal, which has opened up a new world of opportunity for them to access more information and to communicate at an instant. This in turn, has led to the misconception that through embracing each new technological innovation and the increasing time people spend on social media and trawling the net, they are somehow broadening their perspective and augmenting the grasp of life and their environment. However, the net effect has actually been the opposite, with people increasingly feeding themselves on and regurgitating the same sort of tripe, while usually missing out on the rich experience of real life.

The explosion in social networking has had a major impact on people and the immediate world around them. Many people's lives are now defined by constant communication, either through following each other's alter-ego or amongst an ever expanding army of 'supposed' Facebook friends. Whilst on the face of it (excuse the pun), many people believe this constant communication enhances their lives through empowering them as individuals to project their views to others, communicate more and know what others are doing every minute of the day. However, the irony for those who choose to envelop themselves within this social networking bubble, is that it often detracts from their ability to feel unique as individuals and less fulfilled as a real person. As each new experience is immediately shared with others, it often has the effect of eroding its authenticity and meaning on their lives. For some, the end ceases to be the experience of doing something, but how it is portrayed and received by others. Everything some people do is relayed to others without holding anything back, leading some to feel quite inadequate as genuine people in their own right.

Many people who frequently post content about themselves on networking sites are sometimes more concerned with portraying their alter ego; with a few having missed the whole point behind why they communicate in the first place. It would be difficult for anyone to update their status every ten minutes of the day without eventually writing drivel. Some simply do not acknowledge how their uniqueness and integrity as an individual is undermined by its overexposure, with a few experiencing an unnerving empty feeling when they lay bare their lives to others. If someone were to pick a networking site and trawl through a person's communication, the chances are they would probably not find much which they could consider as substantive or unique. The fact that people are interacting with increasingly advanced technology, disguises the reality that communication has become a frenzied exchange of information where they now devour increasing hogwash, while exposing themselves to predominantly mainstream material. Regardless of this, there is an inherent need within everyone, to varying degrees, to envisage themselves as autonomous individuals. Society's design facilitates this illusion by giving people the opportunity to embracing each new fashion as it comes along, the illusion of differentiation provided by product advertising and, the number of society's tailor-made accolades they can potentially acquire before they are all washed up. It seems that some people are quite content to portray themselves as being distinct individuals within society, whilst disguising the fact they often have no real inclination to become the actual person behind their pretence.

Life is usually a nebulous experience as far as most outsiders are concerned. Sartre described this sensation as 'nausea',[4] while Camus described it as perceiving life as 'absurd'.[5] Yet, these words rarely reflect how terrifying these perceptions can be to someone experiencing these thoughts and sensations for the first time. Their whole life can suddenly be turned upside down in an instant, leaving them totally disorientated with who they are, or whether their life has any real meaning to it. Nearly everyone could probably say they have experienced moments when they were not certain of themselves, but few can say they have experienced watching their certitudes in life collapse into a haze of meaninglessness. For some, these experiences come and go in an apparition like way as if it were some supernatural phenomenon, however, when they strike, they can undermine the assertions which may have underpinned a person's whole life. Most people feel mightily relieved when these sensations pass with time and count themselves fortunate not to be amongst the few who feel as though they are constantly living an unreal life in a make-believe world. In most cases, the impulse to consider life's meaning and see it in its most transparent form is beyond any human control. Once the mind sees something for what it is, it often cannot be coaxed or manipulated into perceiving it in a more genial way. Some people are unwilling to entertain any notion that their life may be part of some pseudo-reality, many have a well-rehearsed knack of dismissing such predications. It could be said, people's unimpeachable faith in modern society has resulted in a farcical situation, in which each successive generation not only creates its own expedient ideals, but more absurdly corroborates them for itself.

Herman Hesse's *Steppenwolf*, provides one of the most powerful fictional accounts of an outsider's view of life. Hesse's novels are all concerned with people's tribulations in life, and their struggle to come to terms with the gravity of their perceptions. In Hesse's *Steppenwolf*, the main character Harry Haller believes himself to be half man, half wolf. The book is prone to misinterpretation; however, the symbolism used by Hesse is a clear reflection of Harry's strife, his mind's existential inclinations straining against his shallow carnal instincts. The greatest challenge in Harry's life is his struggle to reconcile living with his deeper perceptions, and the book provides a good example of the conflict of realities which ensues when the existential mind grapples with the irrational world it finds itself trapped in:

> I cannot understand nor share these joys, though they are within my reach, for which thousands of others strive. On the other hand, what happens to me in my rare hours of joy, what for me is bliss and life and ecstasy and exaltation, the world in general seeks at most in works of fiction; in life it finds it absurd. And in fact, if the world is right, if this music of the cafes, these mass enjoyments and these Americanised men who are pleased with so little are right, then I am wrong, I am crazy. I am in truth the Steppenwolf that I often call myself; that beast astray who finds neither home nor joy nor nourishment in a world that is strange and incomprehensible to him. [6]

The things which furnish people with their enthusiasm for life have no meaning to Hesse's character. Harry's existential instincts are too entrenched to be swayed by other people's perceptions or realism. This typifies the outsider's experience as their attempts to adopt people's usual mode of thought or behaviour invariably leave them feeling empty and longing for something more tangible in their lives. Some people today cannot even fathom why someone would choose to be completely honest with themselves and those around them when it may not serve their immediate disposition. A few people even end up perplexed when they try to second-guess the motives of an individual who adamantly stands by a chivalrous principle he or she honestly believes in, especially when the obvious choice for many would be to just to go with the flow. Why complicate life or make it more difficult by stubbornly trying to defend an impractical ideal or truth? Why not just accept things as they are and do what everyone else does? Why make life difficult when everyone else sanctions people's behaviour even at times when it is based purely on their own selfish concern for themselves? It could also be asked, why should anyone adhere to what they believe in when society is able to seduce the most so-called 'respected' within it, to become servile components within its ranks?

Some people today have become so utilitarian in the way they think, they have little conception of what actually induces someone to go against the grain and vehemently stand up for something they believe in. This lack of understanding fuels people's insular attitude towards the outsider. Instead of respecting their strength of conviction, outsiders sometimes find themselves derided as naïve idealists for upholding perceptions or opinions which are at variance with most others, or which do not quite fit in with people's notions of feasibility or practicality in modern life. People generally today have little patience with those they find difficult to understand, who do not endorse society's predetermined norms or, who do not make themselves amenable to what most others think or do. The outsider's defiance in adhering to what he or she thinks insults others by implication. In addition, some people hate to admit their inadequacy to discern others motives in life. To compensate, they often ensure that every thought or action must fit into a framework they can rationalise for themselves. It is sometimes essential that some people fill their void of understanding and, this over-zealous need for a convenient and explanatory rationale is at times exacted at the expense of an entirely accurate appraisal. Those who map out life assured of their unerring outlook, usually come unstuck by their inability to anticipate its pitfalls. Elements of the unknown do not exist for long in a society so willing to attach a reference to anything which serves to preserve its faith in its understanding and its ordered perception of itself.

Regardless of the immense difference between the outsider's realism and most other peoples, it is the realism of the majority which predominates. It is always the rules and, at times, limits of their understanding that outsiders find themselves measured against. As a result, many outsiders keep their thoughts firmly to themselves as others usually find their perceptions far too disparaging for some people's obliging outlook on life. This is aptly demonstrated by Harry Haller's observations in *Steppenwolf*:

> Their (people in general) life consists of a perpetual tide, unhappy and torn with pain, terrible and meaningless, unless one is ready to see its' meaning in just those rare experiences, acts, thoughts and works that shine out above the chaos of such a life. To such men the desperate and horrible thought has come that perhaps the whole of human life is a bad joke, a violent and ill-fated abortion of the primal mother, a savage and dismal catastrophe of nature. [7]

Outsiders, by their nature, tend to express themselves bluntly. Their language clashes with the accommodating dialogue others sometimes use to excuse their flippant propensities. As far as most outsiders are concerned, it seems no-one wants to witness or accept the stark realities of life. To them, it seems people appear to be much happier maintaining the notion that society, as a whole, is somehow continually bettering itself, regardless of what it does or how it does it.

It is a sad fact of life that some people nowadays do not tend to look at the merits of their unique thoughts, but at their deviance from whatever seems to be the consensus. It has almost become accepted practice now, to rely on others lack of resolve when people's anchors of principle prove too flimsy against society's opportune tides. Some are accustomed to tasting the falseness of their realism, only to creep back into their shells of conformity, unable to inhabit the deeper waters of life. Society commends anyone who demonstrates a willingness to revere its precepts, and these days increasingly takes a dim view of those who insist on acting according to their own thoughts or reason.

Throughout history, mankind's progress was made possible through individuals who not only had ideas and thought things through for themselves, but who also had the confidence to disregard other people's protocol and carry through what they believed in. These individuals refused to accept those who tried to counsel them on what could or could not be done. They projected their own vision and sought to change things by advancing a different alternative, regardless of the hurdles they faced. These days, it is becoming more difficult to find many people with uniquely defined values or opinions, especially on more substantive issues. It could be said that nowadays people in general are thinking less for themselves and, from an outsider's perspective, society is becoming increasingly decadent as a result; a few may even go so far as to say it is already showing signs of imploding on itself. In fact, it is hard for some outsiders to feel optimistic about modern society when people are often flagrantly encouraged to live mindless lives, made possible through nurturing an indifference to the unpalatable realities around them and sustained by a willingness to accept a spoon-fed perception of 'real life'.

Existential thought could, in some ways, be considered as a natural human reaction to society's encroaching standardisation and its effect of stifling people's abilities to think and act autonomously. Modern society seems obsessed with trying to systematise more and more aspects of people's behaviour, often employing the most cynical means to bring this about. In many ways, people have already been reduced into formulas for the sake of increasingly convenient accounting. There is less scope for individuals who attempt to pursue or do something which is often not sanctioned by some form of authoritative body or consensus. Many people have been brainwashed into obsessively pursuing materialistic aspirations throughout their lives. They have developed an overreliance on never-ending technological advancements which now dominate how they interact with their environment, and are slow to grasp its adverse effects. However, who can complain when people's apparent or instilled needs are being satisfied?

It is a paradoxical human condition which often makes people more dissatisfied with life once their apparent needs have been fulfilled. However, contrary to modern dogma, most people will never be satisfied aspiring to the fickle ends modern society promotes. Some people are oblivious to the reality that their needs are constantly being replaced by new ones. They tirelessly strive to better themselves through these instilled wants, with the emphasis on enhancing their affluence, standing within society, or gaining career success. For this model to function effectively, enough people must be conditioned to embrace this constant succession of needs. This often involves commending those who think less for themselves, whilst bestowing accolades on those who prove themselves tractable enough to buttress this naïvely presumed notion of progress. As early as the nineteenth century, Friedrich Nietzsche realised the precariousness of the doctrines underpinning people's conception of human progress. Nietzsche, probably more than any other philosopher, sliced through people's pretence within society, exposing their irrational nature:

> Whoever has seen deeply into the world has doubtless divined what wisdom there is in the fact that men are superficial. It is their preservative instinct which teaches them to be flighty, lightsome and false. [8]

Even though Nietzsche died in 1900, his insights are still relevant and, it could be argued, especially poignant with regard to the way the world is today. His trademark was his strikingly blunt conclusions on life. His works expounded many absurd aspects of people's lives, usually through advancing controversial ideas which many agreed with, but were too afraid to admit to themselves. Nietzsche was renowned for his ability to turn previously unquestionable doctrines on their head, demonstrating the ease with which life becomes absurd once thought changes a person's perspective on it. He considered most people's perception of the world around them like a photographer's camera angle, demonstrating there are no certainties in a world whose appearance is merely determined by its interpretation, which in turn is simply dependent upon their existing preconceptions. Nietzsche realised how people's realism was often distorted to suit whatever system of taboos they were encouraged to follow at a particular point in time.

> Nowadays there is a profoundly erroneous moral doctrine that is celebrated especially in England: this holds that judgments of "good" and "evil" sum up experiences of what is "expedient" and "inexpedient". One holds that what is called good preserves the species, while what is called evil harms the species. In truth, however, the evil instincts are expedient, species-preserving, and indispensable to as high a degree as the good ones; their function is merely different. [9]

Over the years Nietzsche's candid insights have led many people to question their assertions in life. This is also the outsider's dilemma; no matter how hard they try, they find it extremely difficult to embrace any thought or action without scrutinising it enough to bring it into question. The reality which many people believe in as authentic often collapses when challenged by the existential mind, which ravages and devours virtually everything for its lack of substance and meaning.

From an outsider's perspective many people's lives appear to revolve around a continuous, but at the same time futile process of striving to fulfil an established set of conditioned needs. Modern society tends to pride itself on its versatility to cater for the tastes of everyone, but conveniently ignores the fact that it increasingly goes about achieving this end by creating an increasingly homogenous society. Once people's minds are tuned to respond to a narrow set of stimuli, people's wants become much easier to satisfy; in effect, a mass-produced parody for a mass-produced people. In some instances, those with influential or authoritative roles within society, often appear to congratulate themselves on promoting people's homogenisation and increasing their subjugation. It is fast becoming a world which classifies being at variance with the predominant view as inflexibility, having an opinion as being obstinate, and thinking too much, as a sure sign of some mental illness; some would argue this is already the case.

It is tragic, that so many people are either discouraged from or do not show much inclination to explore their instinctive thoughts in life. Many people have been taught to steer themselves away from any thoughts which might disturb their ability to maintain their conditioned equilibrium. Society has already reached the stage where it can manufacture virtually anything it wants in increasingly easier and more efficient ways and, there appears to be an implied prerogative that people's needs can be catered for in much the same way. It is already evident nowadays, that people do not appear to show the same imagination, willingness or patience to work diligently towards achieving a goal which may not produce some immediate gratification. People's expectations often revolve around the speed or efficiency with which they can achieve their ends - in many ways regardless of how synthetic, unoriginal, or short-lived these achievements prove to be.

We now live in an age where everything must be reduced into simplistically labelled frameworks or naïve terminology so everyone can feel assured they can rationalise their lives in an understandable context. Even leisure, expressing an inherent human instinct to feel free and pursue pleasurable experiences, has now been re-defined as a separate and exclusive aspect of people's behaviour. We are constantly witnessing the emergence of new vocabulary such as 'quality time', being used to denote periods when people do something natural, like spending some time with their spouse or family. The implication that every human thought, action and reaction can be divided up and measured by contrived formulas, infers that the human mind itself can be made to function as a mere product of its surrounding influences. This ideology has infiltrated into many different aspects of people's lives and, the strategies underpinning it are often employed with a cynical disregard towards the dignity of individuals who merely wish to think, do things for themselves, or simply make their mark in their own way. From their own experience, outsiders cherish people's freedom to be individuals in their own right and do not believe there is any justification for treating people other than as autonomous and distinct human beings.

The notion of dehumanising people into functional commodities is not something which is particularly frowned upon any more. It is easy to be duped by the new fashion of abiding by procedural and political correctness within society today, which implies that fail-safe systems are in place to ensure people are treated with fairness, dignity and respect. And yet, in the workplace, some companies continue to treat their employees as little more than dispensable commodities - often considered a necessary prerequisite in order to attain the target-driven success many organisations demand. In some sectors of society, people are not even treated as human beings anymore, but merely as functional entities which exist to serve a specific purpose, usually promoted as essential to serve people's needs as a whole. In some respects, many people within society appear oblivious to the consequences of this one-dimensional notion of progress, as society becomes more prepared to disregard anything which impedes the effectiveness of achieving its specific ends. In its eagerness to fulfil the often greed-driven or short-sighted goals it sets for itself, society often nurtures individuals who think less for themselves and become increasingly acquiescent to the controlling influences around them. The outcome of this narrow-minded ideal is the eventual creation of a zombie like society which devours anything placed in front of it; while those who think for themselves become more and more disenchanted with an increasingly debased society - which appears to contradict the principles of Darwinian theory.[10]

It is unfortunate that some people have become so molly-coddled within society today; they have lost much of their ability to deal with things outside its conditioned sphere. As people are reduced to mere conditioned components within it, they lose their impetus to probe anything beyond its cushioned interior. Once this occurs, people often relinquish their responsibility for what they think, amalgamating their conscience with everyone else so that eventually everyone's responsibilities become no-one's. Within such a society, no-one feels any compulsion to strive for anything much beyond what the person next to them may have done or accomplished. This absolving attitude exacerbates most outsiders. They could never condone hiding behind society's paradigms. To do so would be tantamount to admitting that their mind (which seeks to understand things for itself) is a defective component of nature, which needs to be prevented from exploring its urge to define things for itself. This explains why true existentialists cannot be bargained with. They refuse or renege on what they think - some would even declare that death is preferable to an anonymous existence, subsisting on the tasteless fruits of a choreographed world.

Probably the most graphic of all fictional portrayals of an outsider, is contained in JP Sartre's *Nausea*. The story centres upon a disillusioned writer, Antoine Roquentin, and his constant struggle to attach some credence to a world which, to him, appears totally meaningless. Roquentin finds himself unable to bind to a topsy-turvy world whose logic, form, and nebulous nature are totally incomprehensible:

Now I don't think about anybody anymore; I don't even bother to look for words. It flows through me more or less quickly and I don't fix anything, I just let it go. Most of the time, because of their failure to fasten on to words, my thoughts remain misty and nebulous. They assume vague amusing shapes and are then swallowed up: I promptly forget them. [11]

Sartre's character typifies the frustrations felt by all outsiders from time to time, through their inability to connect with those around them. As this frustration grows, some outsiders start to lose all sense of direction in their lives. As their perceptions begin to take hold, they soon discover they can no longer see anything clearly through the confusion it generates. Life appears contradictory and meaningless, with the chances of finding an unequivocal purpose within it appearing increasingly unrealistic. Yet, regardless of this, most outsiders' faith in their thoughts' authenticity remains unquenchable. They consider their perceptions as pure, held steadfast by the truth of their minds' unbridled thoughts and incapable of being tarnished by society's usual vices or bias. Sartre's Roquentin provides a powerful insight into the outsider's frustration with society and people's conception of its infallibility:

And meanwhile, a vast vague Nature has slipped into their town, it has infiltrated everywhere, into their houses, in their offices, into themselves. It doesn't move, it lies low, and they are right inside it and they don't see it, they imagine that it is outside, fifty miles away. I see it that Nature, I see it... I know that it's submissiveness is laziness, I know that it has no laws, that what they consider it's constancy doesn't exist. It has nothing but habits and it may change those tomorrow. [12]

Miguel de Cervantes' most famous work *Don Quixote,* expounds this theme through the comic events which result from the protagonist's twisted realism. Don Quixote and his servant Sancho Pansa set out across Spain in a quest to carry out the deeds of a noble knight. Unfortunately, Don Quixote's attempts to perform his virtuous and philanthropic deeds are thwarted by his adoption of an antiquated custom of chivalry, which nobody takes seriously anymore. He shows a total lack of appreciation for the realities he encounters, and his mind's inclination to perceive things in a particular way, tends to override what he actually sees. The book describes the inevitable comic failures of Don Quixote's endeavours, resulting from the complete contrast between his realism and the circumstances he finds himself in. In some ways, Don Quixote's plight parallels many existentialists. Their realism is often completely different from most other peoples and, when they do attempt to apply their instincts or values within life, these sometimes prove wholly incompatible. However, there is one glaring difference in this comparison; whilst Cervantes' character has little grasp of what is real, outsiders by their nature, often have an appreciation of life in its starkest form.

This theme of contrasting realities between the individual and the circumstances he or she find themselves in, was the hallmark of Franz Kafka's works. He often placed his characters in unreal situations to expound their blatantly absurd circumstances. For instance, in *The Castle*, a land surveyor called K finds himself excluded from admittance to a castle and also alienated by the people of a nearby village. Since circumstances also prevent him from going home, he is left destitute with nowhere to go. The book typifies Kafka's talent for creating absurd scenarios, but the meaning of *The Castle* is allegorical, the man like the existentialist finds him or herself alienated from a society which he or she could never join, nor be part of. Kafka's works took the concept of the absurd to its extreme, demonstrating his talent for creating unreal narratives. His most renowned work, *Metamorphosis*, is the story of a man who wakes up one morning to suddenly find himself transformed into a giant insect.

In Kafka's *The Trial*, a man is arrested, but throughout the book, no-one actually tells him what he has been arrested for. As absurd as this story sounds, this scenario has been created in modern times by a democratic country which regards itself as civilised - through the treatment of detainees in Guantanamo Bay.[13] Many people find it surprising that Kafka's apparently ridiculous stories were ever published at all, but his appeal should not be under-estimated. The popularity of his works at the time reflected the way people are able to empathise with his absurd tales and appreciate their underlying allegorical themes. In fact, Kafka used his narratives to highlight people's plight, through their loss of individual freedom and subsequent sense of alienation within society. It is evident that Kafka's seemingly innocuous tales were used to convey his vision of what lay ahead for the Czechoslovakian people, under the heavy bureaucracy of Soviet totalitarianism. His works stand out as poignant warnings of the way people's rights were soon to be overridden and, in many respects, completely ignored by the Soviet's need to assert its political ideology.

Many will have experienced times in their lives when their perceptions have changed in the face of extreme or unusual situations. Kafka's works demonstrate how a person naturally perceives his or her circumstances as unreal when confronted with extreme bureaucracy or, for instance, when their freedoms are curtailed by a particularly repressive political system. However, some people often associate unreal circumstances through their experiences of conflict or war. One of the most explicit and controversial wartime novels ever written was Erich Maria Remarque's *All Quiet on the Western Front*. The book recounts the author's experiences of life in the trenches, as a German soldier during the First World War. Remarque's work, illustrates the utter sense of disillusionment and inconceivability felt by the individual, plucked from the placidity of a youthful peacetime adolescence, to experience the contradiction, horror, and senselessness of war.

> Now we would wander around like strangers in those landscapes of our youth. We have been consumed in the fires of reality, we perceive differences only in the way tradesmen do, and we see necessities like butchers. We are free of care no longer - we are terrifyingly indifferent. We might be present in that world, but would we be alive in it. [14]

One of the most familiar pieces of literature, characterising the individual's struggle to come to terms with the realities of war, was Joseph Heller's *Catch 22*. First published in 1961, Heller based his book on his own experiences as a bomber pilot during the Second World War. *Catch 22*, describes the tribulations of Captain Yossarian, assigned to an American bomber squadron, and his attempts to extricate himself from his obligations as a bomber pilot, due to their short-life expectancy. Each time he tries to get himself relieved from duty, in order not have to carry out the mounting number of missions, he finds that the rules change making it virtually impossible to complete his tour of duty:

Yossarian: 'Can't you ground someone who's crazy?'
Doc Daneeka: 'Oh, sure. I have to. There's a rule saying I have to ground anyone whose crazy.'
'Then why don't you ground me? I'm crazy. Ask Clevinger.'
'Clevinger? Where is Clevinger? You find Clevinger and ask him.'
'Then ask  any of the others. They'll tell you how crazy I am.'
'They're crazy.'
'Then why don't you ground them?'
'Why don't they ask me to ground them?'
'Because they're crazy, that's why.'
'Of course they're crazy,' Doc Daneeka replied. 'I just told you they're crazy,  didn't I? And you can't let crazy people decide whether you're crazy or not, can you?' [15]

Even after Yossarian completes his allotted number of missions his efforts to extricate himself from flying are still thwarted, often by the most absurd rationales:-

'But the Twenty–seventh Air Force says I can go home with forty missions.'
'But they don't say you have to go home. And regulations do say you have to obey an order. That's the catch. Even if the colonel were disobeying  a Twenty-seventh Air Force order by making you fly more missions, you'd still have to fly them, or you'd be guilty of disobeying an order of his. And then Twenty-seventh Air Force Headquarters would really jump on you.' [16]

Catch 22 is undoubtedly an anti-war novel, Heller's satirical show-piece to highlight its irrational nature. Yossarian's hopeless situation compels him to take a very sardonic view of life. The book brings to the fore the unreal and hopeless feeling which envelops the individual, placed in a life-threatening situation at the hands of incompetent pen-pushing bureaucrats. Heller's book expounds the extent to which war, and the contradiction and bureaucracy that go with it, naturally create absurd circumstances for those who find themselves as a pawn within it - a situation with which some who have served in the military, in recent times, may be able to identify with.

        There are innumerable parallels between Yossarian and the outsider, such as the way his day-to-day life becomes unreal. The book descends into what can only be described as a cynical comedy; the resultant human reaction to closeness with death, where there seems little chance of any reprieve. The book shows how an individual's attitude inevitably becomes existential in nature when continuously placed in dangerous situations. It describes how Yossarian becomes incapable of carrying on his life in the same vein. He finds it difficult to take life seriously anymore and as such, everything around him becomes more and more unreal. And yet, Yossarian has one major difference from the majority of existentialists - his sense of the unreal is induced by circumstances. He is like those countless thousands of people who have seen or experienced great adversity, major events in their lives, or who have found themselves trapped in completely absurd or paradoxical circumstances.

Unsurprisingly, some of the most prominent existential writers faced extreme circumstances in their lives. Some might even argue their experiences were a necessary prerequisite, enabling them to generate their unique insights into existential thought and characterisation. Both JP Sartre and Camus actively fought for the French Resistance during the Second World War. Dostoyevsky too, faced extremely poignant challenges in his life. He was arrested for being a member of a free-thinking literary circle and subsequently sentenced to death. After being lined up in front of a firing squad, he was given a reprieve at the last moment by the Tsar, and spent the next four years in a prison camp and six more in enforced military service, enduring conditions of extreme hardship. Under these circumstances, it is not surprising Dostoyevsky's subsequent works contained a deep understanding and empathy with existentialism and how the outsider perceives life. In Dostoyevsky's case, it was probably the extraordinary events and the circumstances he endured, which gave him his level of insight into the existential psyche.

The popularity of authors such as Dostoyevsky, Heller, Sartre, Kafka and Camus, to name a few, demonstrate existentialism's wide appeal. All these authors have portrayed outsiders in their works, often placing them in wholly unreal situations as the springboard to illustrate their existential characterisation. Many people seem curiously attracted to situations where the clever paradox of reason, transfers normal people from their everyday world into one where nothing is really certain. Some authors also create unreal situations within their narratives in order to use their symbolism as a satirical tool. This can range from the tangled webs of inescapable bureaucracy woven by Kafka, to the absurd wartime drama created in Heller's *Catch 22*. Maybe some people have an inexplicable need to test the extent of their realism and escape from the usual day-to-day world they are in to feel part of that existential world, which differentiates them if only for a moment, from the unchanging motions of normal life.

Even though most people's personal experience of existentialism is usually intermittent, these experiences keep tapping on the outsider's door as if some unsatisfied part of their mind yearns for sustenance which a conventional life makes no provision for. At some point in their lives, most outsiders will be forced into making a stark choice. They know they cannot dismiss their minds' conclusions and the way they perceive life; their thoughts are too authentic and too much part of them to be dismissed out of hand. Like Roquentin in Sartre's *Nausea*, the tingling unreal sensation they experience tends to envelope their lives, often giving them little respite. This is how it is for many outsiders who cannot just set aside their perceptions. The outcome of this conflict of realities is that some outsiders increasingly disengage themselves from the world in general. They become at odds with an environment in which they cannot seem to find a niche to satisfy their minds' yearnings. They often get frustrated with the people around them who to them, appear to wallow in a contentment derived from a faith founded on an increasingly closeted outlook of life. As a result, many outsiders live an isolated existence, forced to reside on the fringes of a world which seems too irrational and absurd for their participation in it. They exist, but their inability to bind to the unreal world around them or to make sense of it in any meaningful way, leads them to despair.

# 4

# Despair

I can no longer distinguish the present from the future and yet it is lasting, it is gradually fulfilling itself; the old woman advances along the empty street; she moves her heavy mannish shoes. This is time, naked time, it comes slowly into existence, it keeps you waiting and when it comes you are disgusted because you realise that it's been there already for a long time.

Jean-Paul Sartre - *Nausea* [1]

There is an immense contrast between the outsider's appreciation of life and how others interpret it. The void created by these differing outlooks means that for many outsiders, their perceptions are never properly reconciled with the world as it is, which leads many to despair. Existential despair should not be confused with the normal frustrations people experience day to day. It can encompass a complete sense of hopelessness with life and even living itself, with the individual unable to see any way out or solution to his or her predicament. It can lead to a complete impasse in some people's lives in which there is nothing left to do as most things just seem futile. Despair is also generated by these people's alienation from the rest of society and their inability to connect to the world, in a way they can consider as worthwhile or constructive. For the outsider, the irreconcilable clash of realities often culminates in a complete loss of faith in life, the paralysis of not being able to feel, connect with, do, or aspire to anything meaningful within it.

Most outsiders tend to experience existential despair periodically, but for a few it can be unrelenting, defying any mental control they try to place upon it. When it strikes, it naturally makes them start searching for something positive in their lives, anything which might bring light at the end of the tunnel to generate more of an incentive towards life. Some outsiders try to block out or divert their mind from its irrational and contradictory aspects. A few even try to convince themselves they have mastered their despair by relinquishing all hope of ever gaining anything substantive from the world as it is. These outsiders completely disengage themselves from life, resigning to the notion they could never gain or feel anything for it. In which case, even despair becomes futile and they simply take what life throws at them regardless, like Camus' character in *The Outsider*. However, it is hard to see whether there could ever be any positive outcome for these outsiders in the long term, if conquering their despair requires them to concede all hope or expectation of reconciling their need for meaning with the world they are in. In effect, this is the same as nulling their senses to make life around them a bit easier to cope with. Yet, what distinguishes humans from virtually all other animal species is precisely their ability to create and exercise some control over their environment. It is important to bear in mind every outsider has their own way of dealing with the despair they experience. It is also important to understand where this despair stems from if they are to have any prospect of understanding its nature and potentially having some control over it.

Existential despair often emerges from a deep frustration with life and the predicament many outsiders find themselves in. It manifests itself as a complete sense of futility towards what a person does and even living itself. Its source usually stems from the issue of meaning and the perceptions which emerge from many outsiders' failure to attach any meaning to what is around them. Their attempt to apply their own bench mark to normal life invariably falls short of their expectations of it; to them, it seems ridiculous no-one else appears to appreciate life in the same vein. This unrealised need for meaning changes their perceptions, usually making everything frustratingly unreal and driving a wedge between themselves and the world around them. Their priorities and values in life change accordingly closely linked to their need to preserve their freedom of mind, individuality and, their responsibility for who they are. They despair with many others who seem perfectly content to go through life enclosed within their own tailor-made dreamworld. Their frustrations are magnified by their inability to feel any connection with contemporary life. Their inability to find a meaningful purpose behind their own existence makes everything else seem hopeless. In some respects, despair can be considered as the outsider's natural reaction to society's absurd format and the helplessness they feel when they find themselves powerless to shape, change or make sense of the irrational world they are in.

Contrary to what some people may think, virtually all outsiders aspire to be able to reconcile their perceptions with the world they are in. They want to be able to make sense of life and ideally bring it in line with the way they think. Unfortunately for them, these hopes are continually dashed often through their minds' confirmation of its absurd format and the sheer gulf that exists between their conception of how they think it should be, and how it actually is. They sometimes look around at other people's self-satisfied expressions, wondering how on earth some of them can regard themselves as having done or achieved anything, when all they appear to do is aspire to the usual mediocre aspects of everyday life. They do not believe an existence which revolves around the puerile notion of satisfying each new hedonistic or populist fad that comes along, is capable of encompassing anything substantive. They cannot take seriously, or respect anyone, whose life comprises doing what everyone else does, without ever having considered whether it amounts to anything remotely meaningful. Furthermore, they have little regard for anyone who relinquishes their natural instinct to appraise life in their own way, in order to placate others expectations of how they should be or think. The problem is that this is how many people tend to go about their lives, while outsiders are often left to sit back in despair watching them just carry on, basking in the illusion of their lives' verity. As Camus explains:

It is a matter of living in that state of the absurd. I know on what it is founded, this mind and this world straining against each other without being able to embrace each other. [2]

Most outsiders try desperately to keep alive some prospect of being able to engage with life and draw something from it. They try to believe that at some stage in their lives they will find some solace or niche for themselves in its contrived design, even though for most this hope seldom materialises. The notion they can set aside their thoughts, in order to play a more inclusive role within society, is usually not an option. They cannot kid themselves into thinking they can escape from their despair by trying to inhibit their minds' instincts or maintain some satisfied pretence. This is in stark contrast to the mentality which underlies some in today's world, where maintaining a façade or some alter ego has become a preoccupation, for a few, eclipsing who they are in real life. Outsiders have no inclination to be anyone but themselves. However, maintaining their thoughts and perceptions within life often renders them without any anchor to the world they are in, leaving them drifting aimlessly though it, not knowing whether the waves of its irrational sea will one day consume them or simply toss them onto the rocks.

The constant despair some outsiders experience leads them to believe they are afflicted by some strange type of chronic mental illness, which no amount of thought or rationalisation can ever cure. On the face of it, it appears that the only way to alleviate their symptoms is to try to stop themselves from thinking, but for most, this alternative is out of the question. They would never entertain the notion of submitting themselves to some sort of primitive existence by repressing their instinctive urge to probe the essence of things, or to become indifferent to the lack of tangible meaning in their lives. In this instance, they would in effect be demeaning themselves, conceding they are incapable of defining who they are according to what they really think and feel. Most outsiders are bound by their need to exist as entities in their own right, even if this means accepting a lonely existence, isolated from the rest of humanity. Their thoughts cannot be watered down or made to just disappear; they are usually, too entrenched in reason to be displaced by the coercive pressures society brings to bear. Even though their despair and utter sense of hopelessness may be painful to live with at times, it is usually subordinate to their need to be true to themselves by preserving their minds' integrity.

The difference between the way outsiders and other people see life, leads some outsiders to question their own understanding and the possibility that they may be the ones whose outlook on life is wide of the mark. Some often wonder whether they have missed some essential hiatus in life, or whether they have become too preoccupied with the notion of attaching meaning to their lives, rendering them incapable of ever being satisfied with life as it is. Some even question if what they are searching for in life actually exists? Whether there is any meaning to be found within it? These considerations tend to haunt some outsiders who sometimes consider their inability to release themselves from their thoughts' intensity as a failing on their part. They get increasingly frustrated by their powerlessness to remedy their condition as their prevailing sense of hopelessness leaves some quite despondent towards life in general. Yet, further thought often just reinforces the authenticity of their perceptions, strengthening their need to fix meaning to their lives. As a result, they become increasingly immune from, and averse to, society's mind-numbing mentality. This in turn compounds their predicament as those around them appear increasingly trite in the way they think and behave. Some outsiders soon find themselves anticipating society's echoing trends, like a scientist predicting the behaviour of rats in a simple experiment. Their judgement is untainted by any motive or expectation other than to look upon things plainly and for what, if anything, they mean. This often give them an aptitude for seeing life much more clearly, but also exacerbates their despair towards it. It is therefore no surprise that some existentialists over the years have been dubbed as visionaries.

The outsider faces a real predicament. Life's lack of meaning drains their incentive to latch onto a definitive purpose - a realisation which they cannot ignore, and which has profound implications on their lives and how they perceive it. A conventional existence rarely provides the means necessary to ameliorate their perceptions, or make their outlook more appealing. Coupled with this, many outsiders find themselves constantly having to overcome a succession of obstacles as their will to preserve their incompatible single-minded nature is tested time and again. Their willingness to thwart society's attempts to define them can provide a few outsiders with a contrived sense of purpose in their lives, but for most the routine merely becomes a tiresome, and in some cases, tedious exercise. Having said this, the pressures society exerts upon them is often unrelenting and is usually never properly allayed until they have conceded some portion of themselves to its collectivist ideology. Unfortunately, the outsider's dogged resistance to these pressures usually results in them being branded as unnecessarily stubborn or just bloody-minded. They often have to accept their alienation from society, even though it often adds to their quandary. Paradoxically, their isolation can strengthen their resolve by forcing them to rationalise things for themselves. In addition, the more others try to compel them to submit to society's mandate, the more resolute they often become in terms of sticking to what they think. Their mind's reaffirmation of life's lack of meaning and its irrational make-up inevitably leads many to look at the causation of their despair beyond themselves - to cease believing their difference from others is caused by some flaw on their part.

> I could not bear this tame lying, well-mannered life any longer. And since it appeared that I could not bear my loneliness any longer either, since my own company had become so unspeakably hateful and nauseous, since I struggled for breath in a vacuum and suffocated in hell, what way out was left for me? [3]

It seems as though the outsider, and the rest of society, are set on a collision course. The clash or perspectives seems too great for each to exist simultaneously. Each trying to eclipse the other and unfortunately, it is outsiders who usually end up feeling left in the shadows. Naturally, they believe their realism is the most authentic and cannot embrace the reality so many others unquestionably accept. Most existentialist's psychological histories are littered with failed attempts to bind to contemporary life, usually by trying to force themselves into a niche in which they already know they could never belong. These attempts to connect with life emerge from a built-in human need to relate to their environment; as Aristotle concluded, humans are to all intents and purposes 'social animals'.

It may seem paradoxical, that while many outsiders are drawn towards a need to relate to society in some way, some deliberately disrupt this relationship when they get the unnerving sensation their lives are just panning out like anyone else's. It is as if once their lives start becoming too predictable, or start resembling the usual pattern of others general behaviour, the more they feel like breaking free and casting it all aside. Trying to live this kind of life can make some outsiders feel like they are falling down an abyss where they have nothing substantive to latch onto anymore. All outsiders, to varying degrees, have an inherent need to escape from the choreographed world and prosaic mentality they are often exposed to. And yet, the odds always seem to be stacked against them as their realism seldom has any standing or place within society. It is easy to see why some outsiders attribute their disaffection with life as a failing on their part, rather than its cause being their minds' frustration with life stemming from its overly placid milieu - making no allowances for the freedom, spontaneity and complexity of the existential psyche. Sartre's *Nausea* provides a good insight into the way some outsiders perceive society and its indisputable routines:

> How far away from them I feel, you on this hill. It seems to me that I belong to another species. They come out of their offices after the day's work, they look at the houses and the squares with a satisfied expression, they think that it is their town. A good solid town, they aren't afraid, they feel at home. They have never seen anything but the tamed water which runs out of the taps, the light which pours from the bulbs when they turn the switch, the half breed, bastard knees which are held up with crutches. They are given proof, a hundred times a day, that everything is done mechanically, that the world obeys fixed, unchangeable laws....... The idiot's. It horrifies me to think that I am going to see their thick, self-satisfied faces again. They make laws, they write populist novels, they get married, they commit the supreme folly of having children. [4]

Outsiders sometimes envisage society as an entity trapped in a perpetual cycle, with people responding like clockwork to each new circumstance as it transpires, regardless of its inevitability. Many outsiders see society continually making the same kind of mistakes without seemingly learning anything from them. They are often frustrated with the way some people need to be affected by some catastrophic event before considering addressing an issue with any real foresight. Many outsiders think that most of the time society generally reacts in a kneejerk way to events which befall it. They despair with the way some people go about resolving their predicaments, usually by doing too little too late and, often never really doing enough to change anything. As the outsider sees it, some people seem to be oblivious to society's oversights as their predetermined behavioural norms simply reinforce the authenticity of its status quo. As the outsider shifts the onus of his or her despair onto the absurd world they are in, they begin to find it more difficult to step back into the blind spot of other people's realism. When they begin to focus their despair on the irrational aspects of what is around them, they soon lose patience quietly conceding to others cannons, and this explains why some outsiders feel an impending need to make their mark on life in their own way. However, much of the time, they feel powerless to effect any change on people's mentality as all around them most are just content to live virtually oblivious to, what outsiders regard as, the wider implications of their existence or what meaning lies behind it.

> Men, too, secrete the inhuman. At certain moments of lucidity, the mechanical aspect of their gestures their meaningless pantomime make silly everything that surrounds them. A man is talking on the telephone behind a glass partition; you cannot hear him but you see his incomprehensible dumb-show you wonder why he is alive. [5]

To some outsiders life around them appears wholly transparent, compounding their despair. They watch many others seeking to derive their contentment in life by immersing themselves in an increasingly synthetic realism; an idea which to them is a total anathema. In fact, anyone who is prepared to break down the usual motives which belie people in general would probably find quite a few lacking any significant aspiration to do anything really out of the ordinary or different from the norm. It seems as if there are increasingly fewer people within society today who show any real inclination to distinguish themselves in life on their terms; too many now seem to fashion themselves on emulating what has been done before or what everyone else does. In many respects, the format of modern life saps people's ambition to create something original in its own right; it seems to accommodate the opportunist or person who develops a knack for hitting some fashionable market at the right time. As a result, many are easily dissuaded from doing anything truly unique or exceptional in their lives, usually opting for the safe bet of striving to become an atypical person within society through abiding by its standards of mediocrity. The consequence for anyone who refuses to condone or legitimise this heedless philosophy, often leads to them being excluded from society's ever diminishing standard deviation.

Modern society usually prides itself on its ability to accommodate people's diverse needs and opinions within it. Yet unfortunately, people generally have little empathy or understanding towards the outsider's disaffection with life. Some will invariably maintain the notion that society is always improving itself through continually enhancing its understanding and flexibility to accommodate people's distinct needs. The disproportionate status afforded to any minority group which shouts loud enough, and society's drive towards absolute political correctness (often peddled by those who do not think for themselves) is, to some extent, ample evidence of this. The technology and communication revolution of recent times, has led to a presumption that everyone is being brought closer together creating a new era of tolerance and understanding. It is true that people are now exposed to much more information through the media, internet and some people's relentless need to constantly communicate. However, for many, instead of broadening their perspective it has narrowed it, as people have simply chosen to ally themselves more closely with mainstream dogma and the skewed perspective they inevitably become conditioned to.

It is not information as such which broadens people's minds, but the quality of that information in terms of its scope, objectivity and the arguments which emerge from it. In addition, people need to be encouraged to think for themselves and draw their own conclusions. Unfortunately, the biased and distorted way in which information is now presented to the public at large, has made people more partisan to established precepts. In many respects, this has made them less willing to acknowledge or accommodate people's more diverse or idiosyncratic needs and opinions within society. There is seldom any platform within the mainstream media for anyone with a vastly different or radical point of view. The media itself has virtually become a closed shop with respect to its shameless agenda driven bias, whether this be political, corporate, or otherwise. Original and independent thought have become casualties of an underlying trend within society to feed people on populist or carefully contrived ideas. It is as if people are being marshalled down increasingly narrow corridors, being encouraged to embrace whatever the prevailing view may be and adopt an almost standardised outlook on life. This worrying trend has dire consequences for society's future, but probably more worrying is the number of people who seem to be unaware they are being led down the garden path.

It is widely acknowledged that most people underestimate the extent to which they are influenced by or conditioned within society. Over the past few decades the media has enveloped people's lifestyle and culture, through their progressive exposure to it. In many ways, some have become increasingly gullible with respect to what they see, hear and subsequently believe - especially with regard to some of the drivel spurted out by the mass media. It is now easier to sway public opinion on a wave of emotional innuendo than ever before. This has reached pandemic proportions where the creation of perceived, or even unfounded threats, are enough to galvanise public opinion behind the most absurd decisions, such as endorsing a completely erroneous and unnecessary war upon another nation. These decisions sometimes being made without a qualm for the consequences which transpire or the human misery it creates. It seems that all that is required for such threats to be taken seriously, is to ensure they are wrapped up in persuasive arguments and terminology for most people to swallow, such as the unsubstantiated claims which led to the invasion of Iraq, asserting it had 'weapons of mass destruction' and the threat being posed as 'serious and current'.[6]

As society becomes more mainstream in its outlook, the net result is often that people in general become less discerning. Some have already adopted the philosophy where they draw comfort from embracing the most widely held opinions or conventional attitudes within society. This in turn undermines society's strength, curtailing people's ability to appreciate diverse opinions and to value others perspectives within it. Unfortunately, more and more people are showing an increasing intolerance towards anyone, such as the outsider, who refuses to embrace society's doctrines. Inevitably, the outsider becomes marginalised within society, left to witness its ominous evolution where people today are often rewarded for becoming increasingly tractable. Many often have little conception of the depth of the outsider's despair, the extent of which is vividly reflected by Harry Haller (Herman Hesse's portrayal of an existential character in *Steppenwolf*):-

> A wild longing for strong emotions and sensations seethes in me, a rage against this toneless, flat, normal and sterile life. I have a mad impulse to smash something, a warehouse perhaps, or a cathedral, or myself, to commit outrages, to pull off the wigs of a few revered idols, to provide a few rebellious schoolboys with the longed-for ticket to Hamburg............or to stand one or two representatives of the established order on their heads. For what I hated and detested above all things was this contentment, this healthiness and comfort, this carefully preserved optimism of the middle classes, this fat and prosperous brood of mediocrity. [7]

Harry's despair in *Steppenwolf* is in stark contrast to the quiet despair most outsiders experience. It seems his despair has reached breaking point, turning him into an anarchist or some kind of seditious radical intent on harming society. However, it is unwise to draw hasty conclusions when appraising the outsider. Harry's despair stems from his urge to break up the monotony of what, he regards, as people's absurd routines in life. He wants to draw attention to how meaningless their lives have become, by surrendering their true instincts to such ineffectual predictability. Like many existentialists, he believes it has become all too easy for people to disregard what is real in life, and immerse themselves in mindless conformity. At the same token, it is also very easy for someone to dismiss Harry as a madman, but the simple fact is, he wants to make people realise how fickle their existence has become. Many might contest Harry's, or any outsider's right, to question or judge how others go about their lives, but it could also be said that at least someone is prepared to stand up and question the substance which underpins people's unassailable mind-set.

The attitude which now tends to permeate through modern society is that people should shy away from trying to equate any real meaning to what they do in their lives, because such aspirations can seldom be realised in the grown-up world of necessity and compromise. These days, the individual who harbours a vision to

change something in any significant or dramatic way can sometimes find themselves disparaged or frowned upon. People's general
inclination to project their opinions, question society, or the basis
upon which it advances itself, seems to have diminished over the
years. Fortunately, there will always be people who are prepared to
voice their opinions within society and, sometimes, it is outsiders
who feel the strongest compulsion to do so. They usually despair
more than most, and it could be argued, are best placed to scrutinise
society through their detached perspective of it and their willingness
to quantify and even challenge the essence of others behaviour. They
refuse to take anything for granted and often have a knack of
undressing people's pretence, exposing the true needs they serve.
Unfortunately, their candid perceptions are seldom held in any
regard by others who often find their stark perspective incompatible
for their accommodating outlook on life. As a result, the outsider's
role invariably becomes the spectator; left to witness (as they see it) an
unfolding tragedy where ignorance reins as the essential ingredient to
anyone choosing to immerse themselves in modern society's deluded
ideal of a happy life. The fantasy world of contemporary life is ideally
suited for the timid mind of the non-thinking person. Some people
even accuse outsiders of being conceited or elitist in their outlook,
but this conveniently obscures the real reasons behind their despair.
The fact is; many outsiders become increasingly fatigued by some
people's endless parodies, relentless hypocrisy and inability to step
back and see things for what they really are.

While some people seem perfectly content to embrace conventional run-of-the-mill lifestyles they are often averse to any attempt
to portray their lives in this way. Many place a great emphasis on
trying to convince themselves and others, of their uniqueness as
defined individuals within society; many like to envisage themselves
as being extraordinary in some way. Modern marketing techniques
are designed to accommodate this pretence, convincing people they
can become exceptional by buying their way out of the norm, whilst
in effect, creating the new norm. Some people are quite content
being bridled to society's herd instinct, but human nature dictates
they are averse to conceiving themselves as part of some uniform
multitude. Marketing strategies often revolve around creating a need
within people's imagination and connecting this to a means by

which people can dress themselves in the illusion of differentiation. This usually has the result of cajoling them en masse to want a particular brand, product, or even to be swayed towards a specific point of view by media protagonists. The outsider despairs with such duplicity, unable to understand why some people cannot seem to see through it. As far as they are concerned, people are very much like compulsive gamblers, who with a small amount of success become convinced of their own infallibility. The outsider's despair lies in not only knowing they will probably lose their money, but knowing that no amount of argument or persuasion is going to stop their inevitable behaviour. They feel helpless to affect any sense of realisation within people when confronted with an apathy, whose source stems from conventional routines on the one hand, and indifference on the other, the two great dividends of our modern advanced society.

There is no doubt, despair and the hopeless sensation it generates, are difficult for outsiders to deal with at times. Those who try to release their despair by expressing how they feel or how absurd they think life is sometimes get branded as being obtuse or even twisted in some way. As a result, outsiders seldom have a voice in a society whose language they find easily discernible, but whose irrational nature renders it deaf to their vivid discourse. Their hope of finding others who may be able to empathise with their predicament is made more difficult by society's conventional mould, where people have become increasingly selective in what they choose to acknowledge. The Americanised phrase 'Don't go there', did not take long before it was snapped up into people's vocabulary. More and more people now become uneasy when philosophical quandaries manifest themselves. Many are afraid of confronting issues head on, often fearful to unearth too many contradictions, making the pretence that their lives may amount to something in the grand scheme of things less easy to maintain.

Notwithstanding this, there are some people who are fascinated by what goes through the mind of the truly despairing outsider. This was borne out by the success of the screenplay *Taxi Driver*, written in 1976 by Paul Schrader. The play revolves around a disillusioned cabby, Travis Bickle, who despairs with the seedy underworld he witnesses, while picking up customers in the early hours on New York's streets. It depicts Travis, as a character craving for a way to alleviate the despair he feels towards society's moral decadence. The screenplay, influenced by JP Sartre's *Nausea*, was soon made into a film and became an instant success. It provides an insight into the loneliness which accompanies outsiders as they come to terms with their thoughts and the varying intensity of their despair:-

> Loneliness has followed me all my life. The life of loneliness pursues me wherever I go: in bars, cars, coffee shops, theatres, stores, sidewalks. There is no escape I am God's lonely man......I am not a fool. I will no longer fool myself. I will no longer let myself fall apart, become a joke and an object of ridicule. I know there is no longer any hope. I cannot continue this empty flight. I must sleep. What hope is there for me? [8]

Throughout the play Travis becomes more and more disillusioned with the people he encounters. He does not feel any enthusiasm for their trite dialogue and feels trapped by his impotence to affect any change on what is around him or to do something of any significance. He also struggles to distinguish himself through trying to apply his principles in everyday life, and refuses to accept that he should just become part and parcel of society like everyone else and senselessly subsist within it. His is a classic case of a man whose instincts are struggling against the tide of mankind's modern day mind-set; the current which draws others along as they obediently float with it. Travis becomes increasingly desperate as he carries out his insipid role as a New York cabby. He feels an impending need just to do something, before he gets swallowed up into society's characterless void. Travis searches for ways to separate himself and escape from the ominous predictable way his life unfolds. He starts thinking of desperate schemes to express his altruistic sentiments to generate some meaning in his life. The final scene ends in a bloodbath, in which Travis rescues an underage prostitute from the exploitation of a criminal gang. However, Travis' real challenge lay in his own mind; his heroic actions were only a circumstance of his need to do something to add some tangibility to his existence. Travis' true conflict was his struggle to acknowledge and prove to himself that he could exist as someone within society, capable of applying himself in a meaningful way. In the end, Travis felt compelled to exercise his own veracity to alleviate his despair. He could not tolerate becoming just another nondescript character which society often cultivates to fit into its carefully cultivated bed of roses.

Despair, nausea and alienation are experiences which affect all outsiders in one way or another. And yet, despair usually has the greatest impact on the individual, creeping up on them unexpectedly and being completely unforgiving. Like a tornado, it sweeps away everything that is not held steadfast with some meaning to it. For some outsiders, the sense of loneliness which accompanies this despair makes their alienation feel all the more real, as Harry Haller expresses in Hesse's *Steppenwolf:-*

> The passing years had stripped me of my calling, my family, my hope, I stood outside all social circles, alone, beloved by none, mistrusted by many, in unceasing and bitter conflict with public opinion and morality; and though I lived in a bourgeois setting, I was all the same an utter stranger to this world in all I thought and felt. [9]

The world can become a strange and incomprehensible place for some outsiders. It seems that whichever way they turn, they are destined to carry the burden of this despair with them throughout their lives. The way they think compels them to see themselves as separate and distinct from the rest of humanity, while the way in which others inaccurately define their nature usually completes their alienation. In the end, some gradually become more and more cut off from contemporary society. Their predicament often causes them to resign themselves to a lonely individualistic way of life and society's failure to understand their existential plight, compels them to keep their despair carefully hidden away, like some incurable disease.

There will always be a number of existentialists who cannot sit quietly by, trying to quell or manage their despair. These outsiders refuse to lie down and just let things blow over. The anguish they feel often cannot be contained and, like a swelling abscess, something has to give in the end. These outsiders become like Hesse's character Harry Haller or even Travis Bickle, where their despair has reached a defining stage, compelling them to project their perceptions in increasingly desperate attempts to breathe freely in the smog of other people's realism. Despair, in itself, does not provide any answers to the outsider, and sporadic outbursts of frustration or even provocation towards others, generated by deep despair, do nothing to alleviate their frustration in the long run. Many outsiders just feel they need to do something, even if it is just to rock the boat a little, but this rarely serves a constructive purpose. More often than not, this only drives the wedge still further between the possibility of reconciling their realism with the world they are in. Despair is simply the outsider's natural reaction to their continual exposure to the 'déjà vu' reality of modern life. It offers no solution in itself, but presents an indication to them of what they must be prepared to endure in life by pursuing their minds' instincts.

Every outsider will have experienced the sensation of living in an unreal world and the despair which accompanies it. Most consider themselves lucky that their despair comes and goes and it does not become a permanent facet of their lives. These outsiders are usually able to manage their despair, so that its intensity does not overwhelm their ability to function in life like everyone else. Some even devise elaborate strategies to suppress their minds' yearnings, tempering their instinctive urges in accordance with its incompatibility. These people have already chosen how far they are going to let the existential pendulum swing, as each new day brings with it a carefully stage-managed performance. However, for others, the existential burden which descends upon them cannot be suppressed. In a senseless world, these outsiders are compelled to preserve their thoughts' certainty and adhere to their own perceptions come what may. As Descartes said "I think, therefore I am".[10] Society rarely understands the resilience of a mind which will cling to its precipice whatever circumstances are thrown its way and, these outsiders have little choice other than to define themselves in life by their minds' conclusions.

# 5

# The Existential Dilemma

From the moment absurdity is recognised, it becomes a
passion, the most harrowing of all. But whether or not one
can live with ones passions, whether or not one can accept
their law, which is to burn in the heart they simultaneously
exalt, that is the whole question.

Albert Camus - *Myth of Sisiphus* [1]

Existentialism is not a blueprint for the way someone should live their life; it is merely a human compulsion to understand and place existence in some meaningful context. Having said this, it often poses a real dilemma for many outsiders who are unsure where these existential tendencies might lead them or what, if anything, lies at the end of it. Some fear if they give into these powerful existential instincts, they will lose their ability to function or cope with life. They know at times their despair can rage like a wildfire as their thoughts ignite life's sapless core, leaving nothing in its wake but a scorched landscape where only the deep rooted elements of life have a chance of being propagated again. Life's transience proves highly combustible matter in the outsiders' world, as these flames transform the façade around them into an uninhabitable wilderness, where many start to doubt whether they can nurture any meaning in their lives from its infertile conventional soils. A number of crucial questions emerge in every outsider's mind, such as, what philosophy should they embrace to find some solace in their lives or what do they need to do to accept life and be content with it like everyone else? Should they stick to a set of well-rehearsed routines like others, and try to stop themselves from becoming too pre-occupied with how little sense things appear to make? Or, should they pursue their mind's natural impulse as it strives to understand itself and the world around it regardless of the consequences which might ensue?

The question of what many outsiders do next is never a simple one and, for most, often presents a massive dilemma. Is it really wise to follow the mind's instincts as it strives to break free from the synthetic reality it is exposed to, should people discipline themselves to suppress their existential urges, concealing their disaffection with life by convincing themselves they are just being foolish? Should they strive to liberate themselves from the chains which bind them to society's realism or, immerse themselves in the pedantic details of everyday life, hoping their mind will not ascend to address the wider implications of their existence and its meaning? Indeed, the real question to consider is to what extent people can live with themselves once they have made their choice? Some outsiders cannot ignore their minds' conclusions and yet, at the same token, find it difficult to cope with the heavy burden existential thoughts impose on their lives. Most people do not want to have to deal with the despair, alienation and nothingness that accompanies thinking existentially. For some, it is often just a question of how much bull they are prepared to put up with, and how far they are prepared to go to convivially embrace a life which they cannot properly accept as real.

Sooner or later all outsiders have to take an honest hard look at themselves and decide where they 'lay their hat'. Existentialism is not for the faint-hearted and the sheer sense of hopelessness it generates explains why many people try to steer clear of their minds' existential inclinations, which often provoke questions which have no definitive answers. It also does not make any sense for anyone to live their life in limbo and yet, many outsiders seem to end up in this exact quagmire. They cannot accept life seriously and, therefore, do not have any incentive or reason to consciously want to become anything or move their lives in any particular direction; for many, it is predominantly circumstances which determine how their lives unfold. They feel as though they are in an inescapable quandary and for some, it ceases to matter what they do as they already regard many endeavours in life as being pointless. Virtually all outsiders are aware they need to maintain some sort of link to the world and the people around them, often regardless of how absurd they think it is. Most outsiders will often do whatever they need to in order to preserve their ability to engage with life, regardless of how little sense it makes or whatever contradictions ensue. Unfortunately, society always exacts its own price for granting this privilege in order to be accepted within it. As such, many outsiders feel pressured to curb their instincts and forego their demand for meaning or aspiration to define themselves according to who they are. As Roquentin (Sartre's character in *Nausea*) admits:-

> But I remained close to people, on the surface of solitude, quite
> determined in case of emergency, to take refuge in their midst's in so
> far as I was an amateur at heart. [2]

For most outsiders the variables in the equation are always fluid. Their existential propensities tend to come and go and this explains why most choose to maintain some sort of bond with the world they are in, even though this relationship is quite loose at the best of times. Many need the comfort of knowing they can re-engage with life if their thoughts start infringing on their ability to sustain themselves within it like others do. These outsiders live in both worlds, extreme and incompatible, where the experience of one usually cancels out the other. At times, their mind rejects the idea of adopting this vacillating approach, but deep down they know they cannot totally escape from it. Their existential leanings are not strong enough to warrant relinquishing everything by allowing their minds' instincts to run riot; they still crave the safe normality a conventional life has to offer. Some even develop elaborate subconscious strategies, slipping from one to the other, in order to pacify their minds' demand. They crave the freedom of mind which existentialism gives them, but they also fear its potential ramifications should their thoughts encroach upon their ability to passively accept enough of contemporary life to get by within it. These outsiders know the role they need to play to maintain their place within society, where they can at least rely on its routines from time to time as an antidote against their thoughts' intensity.

The friction generated by the contrast between the outsiders' realism and other peoples is never fully allayed, even at the best of times. In a way, it is as if two vastly different worlds are trying to exist simultaneously; with some outsiders quite content to flip from one to the other providing them with an obscure type of balance in their lives. A few can even subjugate their existential instincts to give themselves some respite, even though deep down they may be aware they cannot really tolerate anything but the genuineness of their true thoughts. Some outsiders do not need to choose between one world or the other; they can step in and out of each almost as if they were shifting between realities. Once they feel they have had enough of society's stifling sauna, they can step into existentialism's cold shower. The most important decision for most is not *whether*, but *how much* freedom to entrust to their mind as it strives to lay claim to a reality it can authenticate for itself? Getting this balance right becomes a crucial issue in many outsiders' lives. They know themselves well enough to realise their mind behaves like some semi-domesticated animal. If they do not give it enough freedom, it is likely to become frustrated and there is more chance they will end up doing something rash as it strives to break free; while they are also fearful of giving it too much freedom, running the risk of losing that link with the everyday conventional world, where they may never find a way back.

There are some outsiders who can be so consumed by the nothingness and despair they experience; the only solution they see is to cut themselves off from the world altogether. These individuals are the ones whose existential tendencies are more acute, whose lives have reached a defining stage, where they can no longer tolerate the false or make-believe world they may have once been part of. They have no other option than to turn to themselves for sustenance as the nausea of having to stomach the pseudo-reality of contemporary life is just too much. This view is illustrated by Sartre's Roquentin, as he discovers he cannot sustain his congeniality with those around him against the backdrop of his mind's conclusions:

And I know very well that all the bachelors around me can't help me in
any way: it is too late, I can no longer take refuge among them. [3]

Roquentin realises he is unable to renege on what he thinks. He
cannot dither about who he is anymore and must be true to his
instincts if, crucially, he is going to feel anything for himself. He is
typical of the more resolute existentialist, unwilling to accept the
trade-off of a compromised equilibrium. These outsiders refuse to
shy away from, or hide from what they think; to do so, would be
tantamount to admitting to themselves they merely exist at someone
else's whim. In this instance, they may as well declare to themselves
they just exist as a by-product of someone else's world. To accept this
would mean admitting they are incapable of making any truly free
choices from the shackles of society's pressures to conform or their
need for acceptance within its ranks. Most outsiders would never
entertain the notion of living by such precepts. However, it is the
lesser of two evils which faces most outsiders; to cope with the
despair resulting from an insistence life must amount to something,
or shirk from these thoughts, hoping to preserve an ability to maintain
some sort of place within society.

The Nausea hasn't left me and I don't believe it will leave me for quite
a while; but I am no longer putting up with it, it is no longer an illness or
a passing fit it is me. [4]

I exist by what I think.......and I can't prevent myself from thinking. [5]

Roquentin acknowledges he can neither control his thoughts n act
contrary to them; he is in effect declaring that his mind above all else
determines the person he is. He can no longer see himself as part of
any community and has chosen to become totally free by his resolve
to act on his mind's reason. He has tasted this freedom and, like many
existentialists, knows he cannot transgress and betray himself by
denying any element of his natural thoughts.

In *Notes from the Underground*, Dostoyevsky refers to the
outsider as 'the real man of the Russian majority'. The book has

been hailed as a revelation of Dostoyevsky's deepest reflections and centres on a single character coming to terms with life and his mind's existential orientation, referring to the outsider's 'will to be itself' as 'consciousness':

> Though I did lay it down at the beginning that consciousness is the greatest misfortune for man, yet I know man prizes it and would not give it up for any satisfaction. Consciousness, for instance, is infinitely superior to twice two makes four. Once you have mathematical certainty there is nothing left to do or to understand. There will be nothing left but to bottle up your five senses and plunge into contemplation. [6]

Many of Dostoyevsky's works are characterised by a protagonist's struggle to come to terms with his or her freedom of mind against the prejudice of orthodox attitudes; their lives often being undone by the incompatibility of their nature to the world they are in. His narratives often reflect the outsider's dilemma, facing a world in which they are rarely appreciated or even visible, unable to envisage how or where they might play a constructive or meaningful role within it.

Unfortunately, the outsider is already at a disadvantage in respect of trying to find a niche for him or herself within contemporary life. The ethos which tends to actuate much of what society does often implies it is better off when, people as a whole, abide by an established set of norms and doctrines. Changes within society often reflect this constant frenzy to maximise its social and functional efficiency, which in many instances are simply orientated towards creating a more uniform society. The gullible usually prove to be the greatest proponents of this model, often classifying anything which brings it about, regardless of the means, as 'progress'. It is a very naïve hypothesis which presumes that the more mainstream and conventional people become within society, the more their needs are somehow being satisfied. Yet, society seems to be ominously moving towards this impasse, with some people even envisioning it as some sort of epitome of mankind's achievement. Indeed, where is the progress when to bring such an ideal about, people are required to discard their willingness to think for themselves? What is really to be gained by any society which seeks to attain the short-term goal of submitting to the needs the majority have been conditioned to entertain? Outsiders themselves will always be distinct individuals within any society and, the existential mind actually becomes something through its refusal to accept many of the crass notions which underlie people's general behaviour.

Most outsiders go through their lives feeling a deep sense of frustration. Everything is measured against other people's realism, which is sometimes based upon presumptions they cannot give any credence to. If something does not fit into some people's conception of how things are or should be, then it sometimes just gets dismissed out of hand. This attitude is evident in the way some individuals, especially outsiders, are often reproached by others, especially when they try to express things which are deemed radical or at variance with the rest of society. Some often find themselves chasten by society, even before due consideration has been given towards the merits, or otherwise, of what they think or have to say. This is reflected in a wider context in the way certain laws are contrived and sanctions imposed on people, preventing them from expressing particular opinions or disclosing particular information. This practice has at times been cynically facilitated through an obscure application of laws which were never conceived for this purpose in the first place.[7] The most high profile of these being related to whistle-blowers, who nowadays find themselves on the wrong end of the law regardless of how well intentioned their actions may be. Indeed, what behaviour does this promote with regard to people's individual integrity? This also has disturbing implications for society's future, when those in positions of power or authority can use an array of legal means to decide what people can or cannot express, even to the extent where it overrides the interests of the public at large.

The power to limit people's freedom of speech is a big step beyond the small-minded doctrine of political correctness. If someone expresses an opinion which is either irrational or wide of the mark, then surely reasoned argument and discussion are sufficient tools to ameliorate such opinions or render their merits as unfounded. Surely, in any progressive society, the emphasis should be on enhancing people's understanding of things to acquire their support or acceptance, instead of trying to 'shut them up'. Nowadays, there seems to be more of an emphasis on gagging people. The initiators of such measures are, in many instances, merely advertising their ineptitude in being able to win the rational argument. Moreover, those who resort to such means, obviously do not put that much faith in people's ability to judge the import of certain information or opinion for themselves. By their nature, outsiders generally believe in the principle of a more open society where information should be exposed to public scrutiny. This principle strikes at the core of their existential beliefs. It also explains why most outsiders detest all forms of attempts to suppress self-expression or conceal information where the arguments to support such actions are, in all but the most extreme cases, lacking any proper reasoning or justification.

The thing which marks outsiders out from most others is their insistence to maintain their freedom of mind to think or appraise things in terms of its meaning. Their detached perspective can, at times, make their judgement and opinions highly objective. Yet, this objectivity, when taken to its extreme, can also become their undoing, leaving their perspective or judgement absent of people's usual emotional penchant or partialities. Outsiders have an uncanny ability to step back from things, enough to feel totally impassioned about the circumstances around them. This ability, to be emotionally disengaged from life, can also have its positive side; they can often be the best placed to, for instance, make decisions in times of a crisis. However, sometimes their lack of sentiment in the way they appraise things can lead people to judge them as callous individuals who lack any empathy for others circumstances. These presumptions do nothing to aid the outsider's predicament. However, neither does the fact that a few outsiders mistakenly believe their objectiveness gives them some sort of prerogative to bring about whatever outcome they believe to be justified. Some outsiders presume, because they are inclined to weigh up things from a more meaningful perspective, they have some sort of right to impose their beliefs on others. Such an attitude not only sets a dangerous precedent, but is often difficult to reconcile against their regard for people's freedom to think and act for themselves. People invariably learn from their own mistakes; they do not generally learn anything when someone decides for them what they should do or think - this is true of any society or nation as a whole. The chaos which has ensued in the Middle East and North Africa, from toppling dictatorships where people's freedoms were previously heavily or brutally repressed, bears testament to this.[8]

Many outsiders' ability to perceive things from a detached perspective makes them more dispassionate towards life. It is often easy for someone to say what they would do in a hypothetical situation, and naturally much harder to make those decisions in real life. For instance, is it ever justified to cause some sort of harm in the short term, in order to bring about a better outcome in the longer term? Dilemmas like these are played out in many outsiders' minds and some find themselves in a real quandary when their emotionally detached foresight challenges their natural human sentiment. Some outsiders often make the mistake of believing they can formulate emotionally detached decisions, on purely objective grounds, regardless of their repercussions on others or their own state of mind. This theme is aptly portrayed in Dostoyevsky's *Crime and Punishment*, in which the protagonist Raskolnikoff is a man tormented by his mind's existential inclinations and the hopeless situation he is in. Being aware of his intellectual abilities, he is also desperate to change his family's circumstances, but is forced to discontinue his university studies due to his lack of finance and begins pawning what few possessions he has left just to survive. His friend Razoumikhin describes him thus:

> One might almost say that there exists in him two natures, which alternatively get the upper hand. Sometimes he is extremely taciturn; everything and everybody seem against him, and he will lie in bed and do nothing! He never indulges in raillery, not because he is a sarcastic turn, but rather because he disdains to waste his words. He never cares to hear what anyone has to say, and takes no interest whatever in what is occupying the attention of everyone else at the time. He has a high opinion of his own ability, not altogether without justification, I will own. [9]

Raskalnikoff's existential nature is evident from the above passage, but as an outsider he does not stop at simply despairing with life or his situation. He is desperate to get out of the rut he is in and the burden it is placing on his family, but finds himself at an impasse due to his inability to support himself financially. Raskalnikoff gradually changes from someone who merely despairs with his situation to a person who develops a strong resolve to change his circumstances, no matter what. This concept of the outsider who resolves to take action, regardless of the consequences which ensue, was expounded by Nietzsche and has become known as the 'Superman theory'.[10] This theory proposes that existentialists, due to their freedom of mind, can become or achieve virtually anything they want as they alone determine what they do in life.

Raskalnikoff's ability to see through life without the usual human sentiment, leads him to conclude that his life and the contributions he will eventually make are more important than most others around him. In his mind, he believes he can disregard the effects his conscience may have on his state of mind. His lack of finance has forced him to discontinue his education, and has led his sister to consider marrying an unsuitable older man simply to use his wealth to help him continue his studies. With these considerations playing heavily on his mind, Raskalnikoff formulates a plan to solve his predicament. As he sees it, it comes down to a basic equation. He concludes his life is more important to humanity than the old lady with whom he is pawning his meagre possessions, and, therefore, in his mind he is able to justify the idea of killing her and using her wealth to alleviate his family from the burden of trying to finance his education.

> Her oddness interests me. But I tell you what I would do. I would kill that demonstrable old hag, and take all she is possessed of without any qualm of conscience. [11]

His rationale, that his life is ahead of him and immeasurably more important than the old woman who preys upon others misfortune in order to enrich herself, is sound to him in principle. In fact, Raskalnikoff deliberates more on the manner of the pawnbroker's death than on the death itself. His undoing is the belief his detached existential perspective will enable him to put into practice his objective without adversely affecting on his state of mind. His utilitarian approach takes no account of his conscience, and this is where his actions begin to unravel themselves and he immediately finds himself tormented by what he has done. In his mind, he has already disco unted the possibility that his own human instincts might be affected by such a cold-blooded murder and, as a result he agonises over the fact he has just murdered another human being:

Let us grant that she has been a mistake all along! She has always been an incident. I wished to complete the thing as quickly as possible. It was not a human being, it was a principle I destroyed! The principle I have destroyed, but I could not step over it, I am no farther than before. All I could do was to kill. [12]

Raskalnikoff's step was putting into practice a theory which his existential instincts could rationalise, but his conscience could not. Similarly, no outsider should presume their existential detachment gives them an implied freedom to disregard their natural human sentiment towards others in the choices or decisions they make. This attitude is not dissimilar to someone who becomes convinced of their own omnipotence, and in turn imply they have a right to dictate to others or force them to do something because they may believe 'it's the right thing to do.' A phrase ominously used with increasing frequency in political dialogue these days.

It is inevitable that on occasion a few individuals interpret their existential nature as giving them an implied right to decide things for others, believing their existential disposition makes them better placed to do so. Outsiders have to bear in mind that, like Raskalnikoff, they cannot always apply what they think in life in its strictest sense regardless of their scruples, and without risking awakening their conscience and bearing the repercussions. Moreover, most outsiders would probably agree that any action designed to bring about a particular outcome exacted through deliberate or foreseeable harm to others is, in all but the most highly extreme circumstances, unjustifiable. Unfortunately, there has been an irresponsible and reprehensible precedent being set in recent years, that 'being at war' provides the extenuating circumstances necessary to discard ethical dimensions and the basic principles of morality – at times on the basis of a political whim. This is typified by the causation of civilian casualties during military campaigns in recent years, or as it has become known these days through that casual and emotionally disconnected term 'collateral damage'. If people accept, or more to the point, believe in the political rationale and necessity for the succession of wars which have occurred in recent times, in particular Iraq and Afghanistan, then can they really argue that this need has justified the deaths of countless thousands of civilians?

Outsiders often have to accept that life will always be an uphill struggle as they try to preserve what they think and what they believe in. Their blatantly honest and stark views unnerve some people who, at times, think they are deliberately trying to provoke them into some kind of reaction. The trouble is; outsiders cannot claim to be living any kind of life unless they define themselves by who they are, shaped by the uniqueness of their own thoughts. This concept is powerfully demonstrated in the play *Taxi Driver*, whose hero Travis Bickle like Raskalnikoff, is not prepared to just live in the realism everyone else accepts, by becoming one of life's expendable accessories:

> Wizard: 'Travis, look, I dig it, let me explain. You choose a certain way of life. You live it. It becomes what you are. I've been a hack twenty seven years, the last ten at night. Still don't own my own cab. I guess that's the way I want it. You see, that must be what I am. Look, a person does a certain thing and that's all there is to it. It becomes what he is. Why fight it? What do you know? How long have you been a hack, a couple of months? You're like a peg and you get dropped into a slot and you got to squirm and wriggle around a while until you fit in.'
> Travis: 'That's just about the dumbest thing I ever heard, Wizard'. [13]

Throughout the screenplay, Travis is tormented by the un-scrupulousness and crookedness of people around him. He feels as though he is the only one who witnesses society's moral decadence, believing he must do something to redress the inequities within it, rather than just conceding to its format in the same vein as everyone else. Life for him cannot accommodate his need for honesty, or his will to distinguish himself from the lacklustre society he is exposed to. Eventually, he reaches the stage where he cannot contain his overwhelming instinctive urge to break free and do something. He despairs with those who willingly acquiesce to people's immoral demeanour and cannot understand why no-one else seems to feel any compulsion to do anything about it. Travis does not want to become just another nobody in a meaningless unprincipled society, and the play typifies the despair many outsiders experience in the modern world. Society's lack of responsibility for itself and its lack of real meaning, gradually push Travis to the end of his tether, compelling him to act.

Some outsiders can easily identify themselves with Travis' or Raskalnikoff's characterisation and usually, these are the ones who see their chance of fitting into society as the most remote. However, in contrast, there are some outsiders who long for the simplicity of calibrating their thoughts and routines with the rest of society. For a few it can even provide them with a brief respite from the despair they experience. Some can even numb their consciousness, drifting into a contrived comfort zone, allowing themselves to be carried along by someone else's impetus. This capacity for escapism varies with each individual, but for the more serious outsider it is something they know they could never develop a talent for. In fact, many outsiders would never even consider trying to dull their mind's sharpness; there is no stepping back from what they perceive as real life. They do not believe they could find any sustenance within it by immersing themselves in someone else's realism or by entertaining themselves with its fickle gimmickry - often only made possible at the expense of the self. It would be like declaring to themselves that their identity, as a person, is superfluous in this life; that they may as well just exist as a number whose sole purpose is just to add another insignificant number to the overall sum. These outsiders believe their destiny is unwritten, it is of their own making and above all, they will always cherish and defend their right to exist according to their own mandate. This view is recanted by Schopenhauer:

> He will understand, rather, that although when he dies the objective world, with the medium through which it presents itself, the intellect, will be lost to him, his existence will not be affected by it; for there has been much reality within him as without.
> Whoever does not acknowledge all this will be obliged to assert the opposite and say. 'Time is something completely objective and real which exists quite independently of me. I was only thrown into it by chance, have taken possession of a little of it and thereby attained an ephemeral reality, as thousands of others who are now nothing have done before me, and I too shall very soon be nothing.........' I think the fundamental perversity, indeed absurdity, of this view has only to be clearly stated to become obvious. [14]

Schopenhauer's extract gives a blunt insight into how some outsiders weigh up life. He describes those who do not take stock of themselves and the reality of their situation, as people who become 'nothing'.

Once someone starts to renege on what they genuinely think or believe in to pander to someone else's whim, they lose that portion of themselves which makes them who they are. They simply join the countless millions of others, who with all their pretensions may never even consider how meaningless or absurd their lives may actually be. In the outsider's mind they become Schopenhauer's 'nothing' and, therefore, in hindsight it could be argued it is of little consequence whether they have existed or not. If they had not existed, someone else would simply be in their place carrying on in probably the exact same way. To some extent, people have created their own expendable niche within modern society, each making their uniform pint-sized contribution with some not even bothering to question what it is all actually for. And yet, it is surprising how many people are curiously drawn to the existential mind-set as the human antidote to modern life. Of these, there are a few who eventually conclude they can only reside in the more authentic existential world. This was the decision that Don Juan arrived at in George Bernard Shaw's *Man and Superman*:

> Don Juan: 'But even as you enjoy the contemplation of such romantic mirages as beauty and pleasure; so would I enjoy the contemplation of that which interests me above all things: namely, Life: the force that ever strives to attain greater power of contemplating itself. What made this brain of mine, do you think? Not the need to move my limbs; for a rat with half my brains moves as well as I. Not merely the need to do, but the need to know what I do, lest in my blind efforts to live I should be slaying myself.' [15]

There is no inducement which would tempt the true outsider to suppress their existential thoughts, which although cause them such despair, enable them to conceive themselves as distinct and their existence as unique within life. Once outsiders make the choice or feel compelled enough to follow their existential urges, the challenge begins to find a tangible purpose in life through which they can apply their incompatible instincts.

# 6

# Seeking Purpose

I am free: I haven't a single reason for living left, all the one's
I have tried have given way and I can't imagine any more. I
am still quite young, I still have enough strength to start
again. But what must I start again?

Jean-Paul Sartre - *Nausea* [1]

Outsiders often cannot escape the predicament they find themselves
in. The more they analyse life, searching for something more
substantive within it, the more its meaning simply drains away.
Eventually, some outsiders feel disinclined to do anything. They try
to imagine what they must do to escape from the dormant quagmire
they find themselves in. Some have already dismissed the idea of ever
being able to live a normal sort of life like other people. Many simply
cannot free themselves from their stark existential perspective which
keeps scrutinising and mocking the absurd nature of what is around
them. At times, their mind behaves like some wild unstoppable beast,
smashing the fabric of the world around it, making it impossible to
evoke that content demeanour others appear to exude in their daily
lives. Most outsiders feel they need to challenge themselves, not only
to authenticate their realism, but to satisfy their need for some kind of
purpose and direction in their lives. At this stage, few can conceive

their journey has only just begun as they desperately search for something to latch onto or do, which they can consider as being worthwhile. They cannot dismiss the prospect that in all life's vicissitudes, they will eventually come across something capable of providing them with a purpose they can believe in, capable of furnishing their lives with a meaning they can claim as authentic.

Unsurprisingly, a few outsiders tend to reproach themselves for the way they are. Some even obsessively analyse each past experience, trying to discover what brought them to this existential impasse. It is as if fate has dealt them a bad hand, making them destined to wander through life like Frankenstein's monster, with their despair akin to the monster's features, thwarting their attempts to be, or feel part of, the world they are in. Many outsiders fail to find any answers to explain why they just cannot accept life and be satisfied with it, apart from the realisation that certain experiences, or the way they think, may have prompted them to consider their life in a different context. Some find it difficult to come to terms with the fact that they have been singled out, like some diabolical mischance, to endure the despair they feel towards life and its lack of tangibility. Many feel as though they are trapped in a hopeless world like the characters in Beckett's *Waiting for Godot*. Their thoughts carry the only substance they understand and this pierces through the reality of a world they often find themselves an utter stranger to. The more they dwell on their perceptions, the more they feel convinced they could never find a clear and worthwhile purpose through life's conventional avenues or merely through emulating others endeavours. Undaunted by this revelation of the self, most outsiders continue their search for something they can at least aspire to - even though they often consider life around them as absurd, senseless and often devoid of anything capable of justifying their serious participation within it.

Many outsiders' lives are typified by this endless quest to discover something capable of providing them with an enthusiasm for life. This sounds a simple undertaking to anyone naïve enough to believe it is possible to conjure up an incentive for it by adopting other people's conventions or readjusting a few lifestyle routines. The outsider could never be satisfied with an existence which revolved around trying to fulfil someone else's trite conception of 'la dolce vita'.

They insist on more from life than perfecting some self-indulgent habit, or even (as some people do), bypassing the concept of meaning altogether, as a necessary requisite for feeling satisfied with it. Their nature precludes them from adopting Machiavellian type doctrines to prise out some purpose in their lives, trying to convince themselves the end justifies the means. Their principles are usually far too resilient to be subordinated to any paltry motives designed to affect a desired result regardless of the means they employ. For the outsider, there is no getting away from the fact that what they do in life, reflects on the way they conceive themselves. It makes them reliant on being true to their minds' instincts, whilst the tragedy is that they are rarely given the scope to properly apply these instincts, in a way which to them resembles anything meaningful.

Unfortunately, for most outsiders life often becomes a daily process of trying to make the best of it, and tolerating the irrational circumstances they are confronted with. And yet, it does not seem right that they, above anyone else, should go through life resigned to making the best of a bad lot. Living in a state of suspended animation, is as absurd to most outsiders as adopting someone else's philosophical perspective, just for the sake of it. They are well aware, if they based their existence on trying to imitate what others do, they would soon end up despising themselves. At the very least, they must maintain some prospect of enhancing their lives through projecting their instincts and being true to themselves. This explains why some are often prepared to embrace any opportunity, no matter how slight, to further an aspiration which might be capable of fixing some meaning to their lives. As Colin Wilson, author of the bestseller *The Outsider* explains, finding a purpose can be a formidable undertaking for outsiders, whose despair often inhibits their ability to generate a motive to do anything in the first place:

> Freedom posits free-will; that is self-evident. But will can only operate when there is first a motive. No motive, no willing. But motive is a matter of belief; you would not want to do anything unless you believed it possible and meaningful............. And belief must be belief in the existence of something; that is to say, it concerns what is real. [2]

The biggest hurdle facing the outsider, trying to seriously accept the world around them and find a purpose within it, is often life itself.

Modern society tends to design its principles to fit its expedient format. The flexibility with which some people devise endless rationales, to support whatever point of view they choose to embrace at a particular point in time, is sometimes championed as a valuable skill - especially by those who embrace it as their philosophy to 'get on' in life. More often than not, the spurious yet convincing advocate, is preferred to someone genuinely trying to do the right thing. The individual, who sees through society's pretence, is usually side-lined in favour of the unscrupulous opportunist, who has an aptitude for making him or herself amenable to whatever partiality serves their current disposition. People's regard for truth seems to have been supplanted by society's increasing veneration of those who demonstrate a proficiency in being able to reinvent themselves every five minutes or manipulate others perceptions, usually creating a blatantly misleading or even false impression of the way things actually are. This practice is commonplace within society today, where the emphasis often centres on portraying a particular perception to others, rather than conveying life's realities.

It is hard for many outsiders to see how they could earnestly apply themselves to the intangibility of the world. Wherever they look, they cannot escape from the sensation that life is something unreal which almost exists in parallel to their reality. It could be said the media is probably the biggest culprit for widening the blurred line between the real and make-believe; infiltrating into virtually every aspect of people's lives. Its effects, especially in recent years, have been to imbue the masses with its dogma where information is sometimes delivered with or according to some skewed agenda. The careful choreography behind the reporting of politically sensitive issues, such as military interventions, bears testament to this; the public seldom provided with the means to appreciate the realities of frontline combat or understand the true causes of people's strife in the world. Instead, people are shielded from any uncomfortable revelations or anything which does not fit the narrative, with the media sometimes focusing on marginal issues which lead people to presume that circumstances cannot really be as bad as all that. Sometimes the public are even bombarded with too much information in an attempt to distort or detract from the significance of a particular piece of news. Many crucial and important aspects of news are sometimes not even given the airtime they warrant. A celebrity marriage will usually get more coverage than fifty civilians blown to pieces in the Middle East.

Virtually every television channel now spurts out increasing drivel with childlike soap operas, reality TV, and the cynical way in which news is presented to the public at large. More worrying, some news channels in the United States have now simply become extensions of corporate political bias,[3] with specific political agendas dictated to them at their benefactors behest. This trend has also taken root in Britain, through increasing monopoly ownership within the media industry. No-one should be naïve enough to think it just stops there. People are beginning to wake up to the fact that there is not much that we see or hear from the media these days that is not influenced by one source or another. In a wider sense, this partisan vogue is rife within society today, cynically manifesting itself in the behaviour of some of the so-called 'impartial regulatory bodies' and 'independent public inquiries' - whose conclusions in recent times have whitewashed that many contentious political issues their outcomes have, to a large extent, become predictable. It could be said that the lack of, or at times absence of, objectivity and robust scrutiny has facilitated the spread of this insidious phenomenon.

Politicians have had a great time in recent years. They have been shielded from, or in some cases, not been exposed to the proper scrutiny they deserve - which may account for their patronising and supercilious attitude towards the general public. Some politicians now behave as though they are the custodians of realism, believing if they reiterate something enough times as being the truth, people will eventually believe it. The public are constantly bombarded with political assertions backed up by endless statistics which are often arrived at using appropriately obscured statistical formulae. Where is the substance in the world today? A 'good politician' is no longer used as a term to denote someone who uses fair and just reasoning to support decisions they truly believe in. The reality now is that avoiding the question, disguising the real vested interests behind decisions and convincing people of the legitimacy of questionable doctrines has, in many respects, become the hallmark of political competence. It was not so long ago that people in the west used to cringe at the way communist Russia used to shovel its false propaganda down its citizens' throats. Little did people realise then that deceit and even blatant lies would become such an excusable aspect within many western political systems today. In this respect, it is not hard to see why outsiders and, indeed so many other people besides, despair with politicians' duplicity and the political establishment.

Modern society seems hell-bent on casting aside the principles capable of enabling it to properly define itself. People now willingly accept lame excuses to justify others lack of foresight. Some people's increasingly tractable nature is often conveniently redefined as their 'flexibility' or 'adaptability', creating a casino-like atmosphere where they can squander their irresolute values without any qualms of conscience. And yet, when the chips are down, most nowadays just scurry off, with no-one wanting to be seen 'carrying the can' when it might not serve their motives. Loyalty between people, which used to be valued above all things, has now become so dependent upon opportune whims that for many it does not truly exist anymore. It is little wonder outsiders struggle to find any real purpose in the hypocritical and often muddled sphere of everyday life. In today's fickle world, conformity is subtly endorsed as a necessary prerequisite for anyone wishing to better themselves. Following what everyone else does, or deems acceptable, releases people from any presumed responsibility to define the parameters of what they actually think for themselves; bizarrely some people award themselves the liberty of hailing this shortcoming as an achievement in itself, becoming one of society's 'model citizens'.

In many respects, people in general must shoulder some of the responsibility for the state of modern society. It seems inconceivable that so many now choose to indulge and sustain themselves on a diet of apathy and indifference. Their readiness to legitimise baseless ideals to accommodate society's passing fads, has reached endemic proportions. The non-thinking person is already a phenomenon of our time; the most worrying aspect, is that he or she has been created and nurtured by society itself like some perverted science fiction experiment. Technological advancements have catered for this new human fashion, in the way utilitarian inventions are usually orientated towards replacing people's requirement to think or do things for themselves. Instead of being designed to complement the way people interact with their environment, modern technology is often designed to avail people of any requirement to function like intelligent human beings - turning some into little more than gadgetry junkies. The effects of this are already becoming apparent within the younger generation where many appear to exhibit an inadequacy in dealing with simple everyday issues. The never-ending 'advancements' in technology, often designed to replace rather than facilitate human function, is often presented as an example of human progress - the ability to make everything we do increasingly easier or automatically done for us. This ethos, of constantly striving to enhance the efficiency of how things are done, is reflected in the way society is now organised, with people, like tiny parts of one big contraption, being moulded to function (often not to think) in the most efficient way. In this respect, some outsiders find it difficult to foresee a rational basis for accepting many of society's notions of 'progress'.

We now live in an era where contentment is increasingly portrayed as derived from a lifestyle where people are not challenged too much and shielded from the uncomfortable realities around them. The imposition that people must take on a mantle and initiative for having to think, solve awkward dilemmas or, make difficult decisions for themselves, is now increasingly considered as one of society's oversights. Surely society has reached the stage where it does not need to saddle its multitude with the stress or anxiety which might result from people having to deal with predicaments in life for themselves! This ethos has also crept into the workplace where some employees' remit of responsibility has become so abbreviated that what they actually do has lost much of its relevance and, in some cases, can only be described as insubstantial. The outcome of this flawed ideology is the increasing relegation of people's importance and sense of individual empowerment. This in turn, has ominous implications for society's future as more and more people will eventually lose their willingness to initiate things for themselves, in an environment which undermines their resolve to exist as true individuals. It is difficult for outsiders to envisage themselves accepting the authenticity or embracing a worthwhile purpose in a world where originality and diversity of thought are discounted as viable components of society's perceived one-dimensional ideal of functional efficiency. Thus, outsiders are faced with the wearisome prospect of having to overcome the impediments society places in front of anyone who insist on forging their own unique path through life. As Marcuse notes:

> Independence of thought, autonomy, and the right to political opposition are being deprived of their basic critical function in a society which seems increasingly capable of satisfying the needs of the individuals through the way in which it is organised. Such a society may justly demand acceptance of its principles and institutions, and reduce the opposition to the discussion and promotion of alternative policies within the status quo...............Under the conditions of a rising standard of living, non-conformity with the system itself appears to be socially useless, and the more so when it entails tangible economic and political disadvantages and threatens the smooth operation of the whole. [4]

The pressures society exerts on any individual who presumes a right to challenge its format are immense. Some people even consider the outsider's dogged and single-minded attitude as an affront to civilised society, through inadvertently questioning its ability to satisfy their needs by refusing to unconditionally embrace its doctrines. In some people's eyes, outsiders come across as unappreciative when all the apparent overwhelming advantages laid before them to abide by society's standards and, willingly accept its collective legitimacy, are usually spurned. People are often baffled as to why outsiders cannot just unquestioningly accept society's maxims and inevitably some outsiders get branded as bigots, misanthropists or just plain anti-social. Obviously, some people are unable to grasp the concept that an individual may despair with society because they find it hard to sit by watching it squander the means to better itself, often through people's failure to embrace a greater conception of meaning within it.

There have been remarkable advances in technology in recent years. One of the most striking changes is the array of gadgetry available to people now to communicate and pass information in an instant. A large proportion of people now habitually use some form of social media which has made it much easier to gauge people's partialities or opinions at virtually any point in time. Unfortunately, for a good number of people, the fashionable or prevailing view has become the ultimate touchstone from which they now measure how reasonable, well-founded or legitimate their views might be. As a result, public opinion has risen to prominence in recent years, often in conjunction with its increasing manipulation. In the political arena, decisions which appear to endorse the predominant sentiment are usually milked to their fullest, promoting the notion that those making the decisions on people's behalf are receptive to, and take heed of, their opinions. At the same time, it could be argued that people are far more conditioned within society today, which begs the question - what does public opinion really represent in such a society? Can it claim to represent people's free and unfettered opinions? It would be nice if we could believe it. Unfortunately, public opinion has in some cases, become little more than a barometer to society's pressures of influence. It could be argued, it has lost much of its legitimacy through its increasing fluidity and in some cases, people's apathetic attitude towards appraising the merits of others points of view or arguments for themselves. In some respects, the reality is that far from acting as a sanction against unjustified, prejudiced or ill-conceived decision-making, the endorsement of public opinion has simply become a badge which crafty politicians and/or powerful institutions can often acquire at will to push through their particular agendas.

Society has arrived at an unfortunate juncture where people, it seems, are increasingly duped by whatever is thrown their way. And yet, regardless of this, some people still maintain a flawed conception that this amounts to society's amelioration. Over a century ago, John Stuart Mill highlighted the dangers associated with any society where people slavishly followed the will of the majority. In his prophetic *On Liberty* published in 1859, he warned of the misfortunes which he said would befall any society which strove to become too proficient in the way it was organised, at the expense of people's freedom to express themselves as free individuals. He believed that the benefits of attempting to create a society with a singular collective will, by whatever means, should never be pursued by stifling people's individual volition to think and act autonomously. He expounded the theory that the 'only purpose which power can be rightfully exercised over any member of a civilised community, against his or her will is to prevent harm to others.'[5] He added that:

> Protection, therefore, against the tyranny of the magistrate is not enough; there needs protection also against the tyranny of the prevailing opinions and feeling, against the tendency of society to impose, by other means than civil penalties, its own ideas and practices as rules of conduct on those who dissent from them; to further the development and, if possible, prevent the foundation of any individuality not in harmony with its ways, and compel all characters to fashion themselves upon the model of its own. [6]

It could be argued Mill's warnings have not been taken on board as modern society seems to increasingly fashion itself on collective doctrines, so much so that in many respects people's wants and needs are becoming more uniform and even predictable. Society has chosen to define progression through its ability to induce an increasingly heedless generation to think and act in a similar way. Some may argue that this is the way forward to achieving a more harmonious and democratic society, but is this really the case? Can a society, made up of people who are conditioned to act and think in the same way, actually claim to qualify itself as democratic? Put more succinctly, does such a society really represent people's considered opinions or does it merely epitomise the opinions of a conditioned majority? Any society, in which people cheaply surrender their discretion to an unqualified faith in perfecting a collective ideal, becomes a very sad excuse for a democracy. But, it seems that society with every step is moving towards this model - while many people do not appear to have considered the consequences.

The question must be asked, do we really want to live in a world where control, whether it be political, economic, legal, or even down to the way information is relayed to people, is sanctioned by their indifference? Do we want to live in a place where people's apathy or lack of discretion gives those in power an uncapped prerogative to dispense with dissent or deviance from its authority? Have the doctrines of mass production simply been applied to people in the modern world, indoctrinating them to endorse mass-produced ideals, by labelling them as necessary and then advertising them as progress? In many ways, this would appear to be so. The implications for society's future cannot be ignored as it becomes shaped according to the expedient benefits of facilitating increasing degrees of organisational, political, authoritative and these days commercial control - exacted through increasingly cynical means. Indeed the conclusions of J.S. Mill should not be taken lightly:

> .....only through diversity of opinion is there, in the existing state of human intellect, a chance of fair play to all sides of the truth. When there are persons to be found who form an exception to the apparent unanimity of the world on any subject, even if the world is in the right, it is probable that dissentients have something worth hearing to say for themselves, and that truth would lose something by their silence. [7]

Mill's fears are already being realised. Some people's willingness to uphold the truth of what they believe in has already been narrowed, by their willingness to forgo their ability to think or to be influenced by each new whim as it comes along. People's conditioned nature within society removes their function to question the validity of decisions which are accepted en masse. Is it not enough, that the reasoning for the unsanctioned military philandering in Iraq has, like some politician's declarations of the continual progress it was making in terms of improving the lives of the Iraqi people, shown itself at best to be a sham and at worst a complete pack of lies? It is not surprising that so many people, as well as most existentialists, are left confounded by the bizarre ways many of those in power, dress their decisions in auspicious slogans to disguise the inadequacies of their self-serving, overly simplistic and erroneous decision-making. It is the outsider's constant exposure to the sheer absurdity and irrational nature of life, which usually undoes their willingness to accept it seriously, or realistically want to play any role within it.

From an outsider's perspective, there is little doubt the nature of modern life inhibits their desire to become a greater part of it. Instinctively, many develop an appetite for authenticity, a need to create something definitive from life's raw materials, instead of drafting something from society's pre-fabricated design. They often long for some kind of challenge in life which they can equate as being meaningful and yet, most of the time, all they have to look forward to is the prospect of being pitched against the person next to them or, expected to aspire to someone else's notion of success. Each generation of aspiring schoolchildren are brought up to believe people must compete against each other if they want to better themselves; sport probably representing the biggest embodiment of this philosophy. This in turn, establishes society's standards as most people go through life religiously following people's established notions of what they believe success actually amounts to, often learning to do just enough to get ahead of the person next to them. This sets the parameters for many people's success in life, the pursuit of aspirations which have been instilled in them sometimes from an early age, while they themselves lack any real impetus to surpass other people's endeavours in any significant way. Given this circumstance, there is no real expectation placed upon people to really transcend what has already been done before. It cannot be ignored that history's most exceptional achievements have invariably come from individuals who were either not bothered or satisfied with just pitching themselves against their peers. This also explains why outsiders usually abhor the established doctrines within society, instigating rivalry amongst people as a motivational imperative and promoting a contrived vision of what success amounts to, often to preserve its status quo.

Most outsiders' needs in life revolve around finding a purpose which can be authentically reconciled with the way they think, and which is capable of filling their void of meaning. In the modern world, people are instilled with the notion that contentment in life is derived from fulfilling certain needs or aspirations which they have been preconditioned to accept unreservedly. The pursuit of these needs usually shapes their mentality, symbolising the inevitable way their lives often unfold. The presumption that a person must establish a family, work constantly throughout their lives, slavishly aspire to people's prevailing lifestyle or materialistic needs, or continually seek to increase his or her standard of living, are rarely questioned. Many people scurry through life like a dog chasing its tail, as the pursuit eventually becomes the end in itself - with some, in the meantime, suffering increasing levels of mental anxiety in their efforts to realise these perceived needs. Those who, for whatever reason, do not follow this remit or who do not become as successful as their peers, in terms of fulfilling these needs, are often made to feel somehow inadequate. There is a presumption that at certain stages of a person's life, they should have acquired or done certain things such as getting married, getting on the property ladder, or worked their way up in their career. Outsiders on the other hand, are rarely predisposed to such criteria; what most others aspire to tends to mean either very little or nothing to them. People often find it hard to appreciate that most outsiders have different incentives in life which are usually connected in some way to their need for meaning. This often makes them wholly immune from the peer pressures, norms or expectations others presume they should follow or try to impose upon them.

In modern western society, it seems nothing will ever be capable of quenching people's conditioned aspiration for ever greater prosperity. Modern society often caters for this penchant by striving to create everything (often including people's attitudes) as quickly as it is able to cast them aside. Wealth is sometimes created by one generation, spent by the next, leaving the generation after that preoccupied with 'what might have been'. Outsiders generally have little interest in money, or pursuing materialistic ends and are usually too philosophically aware to become embroiled in endlessly striving to increase their affluence or trying to attain some inimitable standard of living. They put the concept of their existence above anything else and exist by who they are, not by their ability to create aesthetically pleasing surroundings, amass wealth, or acquire materialistic ends for their own sake. In terms of the way they think, everyone is born with nothing, leaves the world with nothing and, what is important, is how much meaning they themselves can attach to their existence along the way. Therefore, adopting a purpose in life based on opulence is completely meaningless to the outsider. Joseph Heller aptly reflected this sentiment, when he wrote:

> Men earned millions producing nothing more substantial than changes in ownership. [8]

The outsider cannot be judged according to people's usual wants and needs in life; he or she would never strive to attain anything merely because it occupied some prominence in someone else's imagination. Many people are consumed by the false notion that the acquisition of wealth, or a continually improving standard of living, are the main prerequisites for happiness or contentment in life. This philosophy is continually reinforced and promoted through the commercialisation of people's needs within society. But, once people have satisfied their immediate materialistic aspirations, the net result is often just an adjustment of their expectations - so that in reality all they are doing is striving for a succession of needs, making its eventual realisation unattainable. Even when some people's 'dreams come true' through their lottery win, it is usually a disconcerting experience. They suddenly realise they can now acquire virtually whatever they want in life, but often end up 'all at sea' with nothing substantive to strive for anymore. Most outsiders are content with the most basic of lifestyles; their financial circumstances have little bearing on how content they feel with life or the way they think. As long as they can get by, their material possessions or lack of, are irrelevant to the way they conceive themselves. They are an entity formed through their mind's convictions, and their need to define their existence as something real, surpasses the meagre incentives of some others who aspire to and are prepared to measure themselves against the extent to which their materialistic aspirations are satisfied. In this respect, the true outsider could never equate materialism as an extension of his or her being.

As outsiders start searching for some kind of purpose in their lives, they soon become unstuck. For some the sheer enormity of their undertaking, and the dim prospect of realising a sense of meaning in their lives, generates an inertia which is difficult to dislodge. To overcome this, some believe their best hope lies in gaining a better understanding of the way their mind works. This explains why some existentialists are sometimes drawn to psychology, as a means of understanding why they think the way they do, and which can potentially give them some answers on how they go about generating some sort of purpose. Self-help books are usually out of the question, as many outsiders cannot tolerate their patronising tone or accept their over-simplified precepts with too much seriousness. Notwithstanding this, some outsiders are quite optimistic about the prospect of gaining some control over their thoughts' intensity through acquiring a better understanding of the way they think. The theory appears sound in principle, but the reality is usually quite a different matter. It is now generally accepted, simply knowing how the mind works seldom provides any real answers in itself. In some cases, it can compound a person's disillusionment with life. Outsiders can sometimes find themselves tormented, knowing why they think the way they do, but not being able to escape from the nothingness and despair their minds' generate. Therefore the idea that they will suddenly be able to find a tangible meaning or purpose in their lives through an intricate knowledge of their psychology is usually flawed.

Many outsiders, by their nature, tend to be quite introspective and it is not uncommon for a few to consider academic careers as a means of generating some purpose in their lives. A few believe their character traits are more tailored towards a more studious undertaking, with some even imagining themselves thriving on the detached single-mindedness which academia can sometimes offer. In fact, some see academia as an ideal career from which they can lunge themselves into painstaking study or research, obsessively delving into whatever really interests them. However, even though over the years a few outsiders have found a sense of purpose in their lives through following academic careers, many have still found it difficult to fully realise themselves within the sphere of disciplines academia countenances. Some outsiders actually feel frustrated and dis-illusioned with the relevance and, at times, constrained precepts which underpin many academic pursuits. They find it difficult to accept its legitimacy, when so much of it is built on layers of narrow hypotheses, which to them often detracts from realistically being applied to life in any meaningful way. Therefore, some outsiders do not see any point in continually differentiating the focus of their attentions, in the vain hope of trying to fathom one of academia's many bottomless pits. As Shaw once wrote:

> A fool's brain digests philosophy into folly, science into superstition, and art into pedantry. Hence University education. [9]

It stands to reason that most outsiders would never consider pursuing an academic discipline or gaining knowledge for its own sake. They are not moved by the idea of becoming the next quiz master, or even lining up like lemmings to receive a degree certificate, unless they believed it meant something or had some relevance to them. They often seek opportunities in which they can equate what they do to its impact on their lives or the things around them. With this being the case, many outsiders' focus tend to be drawn towards more humanistic concepts which to them, are considered as more capable of having a profound influence on the nature of their existence. Their instincts make them naturally unsuited to some of the more rigidly defined fields of study which cannot accommodate their freedom of mind. There is no doubt, university graduates and the research they do, are undoubtedly at the forefront of many pioneering breakthroughs and achievements; many of the things people are able to do today would not have been possible without it. However, from some outsiders' perspective, much of academic study appears to exist in a vacuum which, to them, detracts from its application to the real world. Some of the 'test tube' theorems which proliferate out of academic institutions each year have so little relevance to real life that some outsiders find it very difficult to place these in any meaningful context. The ill-conceived philosophy behind many technological advancements has already been discussed, but there are also a few academic endeavours which are conceived on such insular doctrines that their pursuit can only really be described as misguided. For instance, where is the benefit in devising elaborate and monotonous working practices for employees absent of any ethical considerations or people's needs as human beings, in order to formulate a model to enhance productivity or reduce costs? And what is the point in conducting lengthy and painstaking research to prove a highly pedantic theory, which sometimes only serves to reaffirm someone's conception of their own intelligence?

Most outsiders tend to look beyond the immediacy of the everyday world in their search for purpose and its relevance to them. Their perceptions always sway towards the bigger picture. They define themselves by what they think and therefore are more aware of their responsibility for what they do. This is in contrast to a few in the academic world who seem to be quite comfortable discounting or ignoring the broader implications of what they set out to achieve. These academics seem to work in a bubble world where they appear to discard any notion of an ethical or moral dimension in the work they do. One of the most prominent examples of this was a theory which became known commonly as 'the shock doctrine',[10] which emerged from the Chicago School of Economics through the economist Milton Friedman. His economic theory involved initiating the transition of economies into becoming more free-market, offering greater prosperity for all. His theory became a central feature of American economic foreign policy during the Regan era. Friedman's economic theory of transition to free-market economies was applied to numerous economically emerging countries around the world.

Friedman's theory was effectively a system of privatisation which opened up markets for western investment. Within these emerging countries it sought to create a dependency on foreign goods and services, while reaping the benefits of cheap labour and the acquisition of raw materials. It enriched the few at the top, in the countries which it was applied, but also widened the disparity of income in these countries, creating massive upheaval and poverty. On paper, Friedman's theory was meant to make these countries much wealthier and, many economists from all over the world were not only taught Friedman's theory, but actually believed in it and subsequently promoted it. The theory had virtually the opposite effect to what it advertised as being able to create. Yet, even in its early days, with the catastrophic repercussions for the countries who had signed up to it, the theory was still being hailed as a success by many academics. It would appear they simply overlooked the disastrous consequences this policy had on the poorer people within these countries. Maybe today's academic world can best be summed up by some of the new degree courses it now offers, which often grant their own licence for relevance. We already have instances of art being created for art's sake; there is no real reason to think that academics who flex their intellectual muscle for such misconceived undertakings are any different - but the consequences may be.

As early as the 16th century, the French philosopher Michel de Montaigne voiced his reservations about the educational establishment at that time, and the narrow remit of knowledge that was being imparted to students.[11] He made a distinction between purely academic learning and wisdom, which he defined as a much broader and useful knowledge base. He maintained that wisdom had much more application to life, and within his definition, he believed ethics and the ability to solve moral dilemmas were essential to any person's education. He was also an advocate of plain language and did not see any reason why people should express what they meant in any elitist, convoluted, or highbrow way. He believed that real education could not be attained from just studying in a goldfish-bowl. His assertion was that the educational mandate at the time, revolved around regurgitating the quotes and ideas of the academically revered. The educational system, he believed, did not properly encourage people to think for themselves or acquire knowledge which was particularly relevant to their development as individuals with opinions in their own right. It could be argued that in this respect, not much has really changed in terms of education since Montaigne's day. Are our universities churning out ethically aware graduates with a broad knowledge base and an acute ability to appraise and solve difficult dilemmas? It is not hard to see why some outsiders do not consider pursuing an academic career as an avenue for finding purpose in their lives.

It must be acknowledged, that the great social and developmental changes which have occurred throughout history, were never brought about by advancing insular theories to explain how the world works. These changes invariably came about through individuals who used their understanding of people and society, and had the foresight to present a different alternative. The epitome of mankind's progress these days is often narrowly defined through advancements in technology. Yet, in many ways, the new technological gadgetry people now have at their disposal is ill-conceived. It encourages more and more people to languish in an environment in which human endeavour and creativity often amount to little more than entering a configuration of instructions on some device. It is true many technological inventions in recent years have had an incredible impact on the way people now live their lives, especially in the way they communicate and process information. These new technologies have enabled many beneficial breakthroughs in a wide range of fields from medicine to alternative energies. However, in retrospect, the most significant and lasting social changes have nearly always come about through advancing ideas and not simply technological inventions which are capable of transforming people's lifestyles. This explains why many outsiders, would be more inclined to follow an ancient eastern philosophy than to become embroiled in trying to achieve some technological breakthrough, as a worthwhile pursuit.

Outsiders often think much more retrospectively than most others. Furthermore, they often have a stringent and demanding conception of what they classify as being meaningful. This probably explains the fact why so many find it difficult to apply themselves to anything specific for long. Their minds are constantly probing the thin ice which underlies what many others do in life, hoping to find an area dense enough to support them under the cracks of contradiction produced by their penetrating analysis. Their detached perspective, coupled with their strict criteria for meaning, means they are much more partial to advancing a principle or a philosophy than ploughing themselves into a rigidly defined pursuit or gaining an understanding of life like some 'pub quizmaster'. Knowledge on its own is simply a blunt tool to outsiders. They need to feel there is a purpose behind what they learn in life, which is capable of being applied by them, in some meaningful way.

In *The Outsider*, Colin Wilson concluded that the only viable option left for the true existentialist was to become a saint or visionary.[12] The problem with this, is that many outsiders are simply not religiously inclined and their nature inhibits their ability to gain any platform on which to express themselves. Some outsiders even think that entertaining a belief in a religious doctrine obscures their mind's ability to appraise life for what it is. Existential thought challenges individuals to see beyond themselves. Unfortunately, for outsiders, this aptitude is often left dormant by their inability to gain any standing within society's ranks. It is true that throughout history a few existentialists have been hailed as visionaries. These few managed to overcome people's inertia and reticence towards acknowledging their insights often through their uncanny ability to recognise broader trends in life or particular eventualities in people's behaviour. However, society is never ready to accept the blatant truisms of life directly, and therefore, when outsiders do try to generate purpose in their lives through trying to articulate themselves, their discourse is usually received with derision or simply falls on deaf ears. The idea of delivering their insights through falsely claiming some divine authority and using people's religious disposition is not something most outsiders would ever even contemplate. They could not pretend to be anyone but the person they are and would not resort to employing false or underhand means to enhance people's acceptance of views, which they would otherwise have probably dismissed out of hand.

Unfortunately, finding a purpose in life proves as elusive as ever for most outsiders. Many would love to feel they were doing or working towards something they could believe in and want to achieve, but their mind always seems to be ahead of them, undermining their incentive before they can properly apply themselves. There are undoubtedly many people who find a strong sense of purpose in the work they do; unfortunately for outsiders, it is a completely different ball-game. Whatever they commit themselves to, must equate to something capable of matching what they regard as being significant in their lives. In contrast, many people will readily accept that most of what they do in life is simply a means to an end rather than an avenue for finding a real sense of purpose. This ethos is subtly promoted through the materialistic dogma which often determines people's needs. Unfortunately, achieving these needs seldom provides people with any real sense of satisfaction in what they do. To combat this realisation, marketing strategists often continually promote products and services through their ability to enhance or change people's perceptions or lifestyle for the better. The paradoxical idea, that if someone works hard enough, earns enough money, or enhances their status within society - they can somehow escape from or buy their way out of this realisation, is rarely challenged. There is no escape from such subterfuge, even in the work-place. Today's company managers now have no end of strategies up their sleeve, to convince their more gullible or naïve employees of how critically important their work is to their 'personal development'.

There have been significant changes in the last few decades, not only in the nature of the work people do (which in many respects has become more automated), but also in their working environment. Notwithstanding all the equality legislation and changes in working practices in recent years, there is little evidence to suggest that employees are any happier than they were twenty or thirty years ago.[14] Many employees today have had to make themselves increasingly amenable to the bureaucratic, autocratic and, at times, cut-throat cultures which now shamelessly exist in some organisations. In addition to this, employees are now subjected to increasingly patronising language drawn from the cynically contrived managerial tools being applied. What is even more worrying is that more and more employees seem to be duped into believing they are attaining some great personal milestone in their lives, through attaining particular targets or objectives set out by someone in the organisation's hierarchy. Luckily, most outsiders are rarely convinced by any rationale which requires them to measure themselves against other people's expectations or performances as a criteria for success. Indeed, what kind of a person actually buys into the philosophy that reaching particular targets, set out by their organisation, really provides them with an authentic sense of achievement in their lives? Yet, some employees not only embrace, but actually believe in this bogus philosophy and there is a disturbing trend that these types of people are not only becoming more prevalent, but tend to move much more quickly up the ranks in today's organisations.

The simple truth is that outsiders cannot be galvanised into doing something which is drawn from artificial challenges or goals in life. They are like the lone rambler who tackles a difficult assent, in an attempt to push themselves to do or experience something unique or beyond what others may have done. They are not only renowned for not sticking to the beaten track, but will sometimes choose the most difficult way to go about things just to ascend life's monotonous predictability. As employees, outsiders often leave their bosses perplexed. They are often not enthused by the usual motivational incentives most others tend to respond to. Simply going through the motions and bringing home a wage is not enough, even though many find themselves in this exact quagmire. Most outsiders need to feel they are actually doing something which carries some significance in their mind. Their strong sense of conviction makes them wholly unsuited to organisations which are excessively bureaucratic, or which compel them to work to an unreasonably strict or absurd set of guidelines. The reality today is that many employees' responsibilities are increasingly governed by a rigid and narrowly defined plethora of regulations, as the misguided administrative notion of trying to account for every aspect of employee behaviour tends to dominate the workplace culture.

There is now a new and fashionable trend which has enveloped people's attitudes in the workplace, to define progress through continually replacing and updating ways of doing things even if particular systems or working practices are serving people adequately well as they are. It is almost as if changes are necessary for the sake of change and, in order to preserve the notion that progress is continually being made in the way people execute their duties in the workplace. Yet, when a new practice or procedure fails spectacularly with adverse or dire consequences, the causation is often completely misconstrued. The frenzy soon starts to tighten up existing regulations or create new ones whilst making sure everyone strictly adheres to them. Instead of acknowledging the primary or contributory causes which are very often less people using their initiative, common sense, or even becoming so detached from their role they feel little personal responsibility towards what they do, the naïve solution invariably hinges upon constraining people's function with more rules and regulations. This blind philosophy simply engenders more people like the ones whose failings create these types of fiascos in the first place. It is unsurprising some outsiders despair with this state of affairs and have little inclination to become participants in such absurdity.

It is virtually considered as accepted practice in many organisations nowadays to avoid employing anyone with strong convictions or who come across as outspoken in some way. It is almost an unwritten rule in many companies to seek to employ people who are more tractable; willing to abide by whatever system is in place, often regardless of how inept or flawed that system might be. In order for such systems to function effectively, the most servile proponents of company policy are duly elevated to middle management positions, sometimes with little regard to their competence, ability to manage people, or deal with the challenges their role entails. The rationale behind this rests on the notion that these people will be much more partisan to whatever system of taboos is dictated to them by those higher up the administrative chain. Senior managers are well aware these types of people are the ones who can be best trusted to carry out their directives implicitly, sometimes regardless of how unscrupulous or senseless they prove to be. This might explain why some outsiders can often be found in low skilled jobs which bear little relation to their actual abilities. Many often prefer roles where there is no imposition placed upon them to sell themselves short or do something they cannot reconcile with themselves in order to discharge their duties. Some outsiders see this option as the best they can hope for, to preserve who they are by not exposing themselves to the contradiction and unscrupulousness which people often have to swallow to attain success in today's workplace. They will gladly take a boring menial job, rather than compromise themselves and becoming an appendage to the doctrines which underpin the way many of today's organisations function.

It is not surprising then that outsiders are often not the most career-minded, and are usually not in the running for 'employee of the month' award. They cannot be bought by other people's meagre incentives and very often refuse to make any concessions towards anything they do not wholeheartedly believe in. In short, they must equate the relevance of what they do against what it actually means to them. This usually makes them immune from the mechanisms which companies utilise to fine-tune the minds of their employees to enhance their performance in the workplace. In many organisations today, the emphasis is no longer on managing the way human enterprise is utilised, but on treating people like tools who need to be moulded to their particular task, while this is hailed in some managerial circles as a form of human achievement. It seems there is no limit to the contemptuous lengths some employers will go to in the way they treat their employees, if it goes some way to enhance their organisation's competitive edge or serves to endorse their company's status or hierarchical structure. Some of the strategies used by company managers to increase employee commitment or loyalty are often so divisive, that at first glance, it is hard to imagine they were designed for people at all. Many of these devices are often only in place to oblige someone's misconceived faith in striving to attain increasing degrees of efficiency or profitability, with little or no regard towards the means they employ to bring it about. Some of the methods employed are not only an affront to people's dignity, but to anyone with the capacity to see through the faceless and inanimate minions these roles beget.

It seems too much these days to expect some employers to respect and treat people as human beings. We are now witnessing the emergence of a catalogue of cynical phrases such as *to grow with the company* or *to become a key player*, which are meant to convince employees their exertions are prodigiously meaningful. These phrases (and many more like them) are constantly reiterated and reinforced through childish management spiel, until they are firmly implanted in employees' minds like nursery rhymes. There seems to be an implied prerogative that companies are at liberty to override people's entitlement to be treated with a basic level of respect for their intelligence or their regard for them as people in their own right. This often occurs on the back of trying to perfect increasingly efficient means of production or seeking to sustain some untenable hierarchical structure. Many outsiders are not alone when they cringe at the way some employees are treated often as little more than dispensable commodities in today's workplace. In light of this realisation, it is not hard to see why they find it so difficult to find jobs in which they are respected as individuals, are not required to forego what they think, or have some prospect of finding a meaningful incentive behind what they do. It is now (more often than not) presumed that everyone must be prepared to make themselves amenable to perform the increasingly inane roles imposed on them, in order to sustain or advance themselves in their career.

In order for outsiders to derive a sense of self-worth in life, they need to feel they can add form to their existence by being themselves and applying themselves accordingly. Unfortunately, the opportunities which could enable them to achieve this are usually few and far between and for some never really present themselves. This explains why many outsiders often feel disheartened by their inability to influence or change the irrational environment they are in. On occasion, a few develop a type of contrived purpose in their lives by striving for greater prosperity in the hope of being able to make a greater contribution to causes they may believe in. Others sometimes embrace some benevolent cause as a means of furnishing their lives with a sense of purpose. However, no matter how well intentioned their efforts may be, many become increasingly frustrated by their inability to bring about the enduring and dramatic change they can consider as significant. They usually have their eye on the wider picture, being more critical than most of the implications of what they do. They usually cannot accept people's meagre contributions making much of a difference to remedying the root causes of some of the issues which occur in the world today such as social inequality, the perpetual conflicts which occur, or the ever-widening disparity of wealth in the world. Every country in the world has certain taboos and systems of inequality usually enforced by the way their society is structured. There are similar mechanisms at work in the way the countries of the world parley with each other, which more often than not, function in a biased way to maintain the financial status quo of the world's wealthy nations. The issue many outsiders' face is that before they can regard anything they do as being meaningful, they must first equate it as something capable of making a real difference.

The altruistic guise of the International Monetary Fund and World Bank are finally starting to lose their shine, as more and more people are beginning to see through these organisations, as mere instruments of financial imperialism. When people listen to their politicians' banter, especially in relation to foreign policy, some people actually believe their governments want to bring the poorer nations out of poverty to compete on a par with their own. Unfortunately, international trade between the rich and poor nations can be likened to two second-rate teams who turn up for a football match where one team refuses to give the other one of its players, even though the other team is three or four players short. The reality is that the world's wealthy nations have no intention of making a game of it by competing on a fair playing field. It is often left to charitable institutions to pick up the pieces when poverty, conflicts, or natural disasters affect some Third World country. Yet, while charitable contributions may go some way to alleviate the symptoms of in-equality and injustice in the world, they usually do little to alleviate its underlying causes. Most outsiders despair with the reality that whatever individuals and organisations try to do is never really enough, and what really needs to happen is a fundamental change in people's attitudes, and more importantly, the geopolitical landscape. This is provided of course that politicians in general are really serious about helping people or alleviating the causes of poverty in the world, which is questionable considering their track record to date.

In today's world many outsiders are left wondering whether they can induce some sort of purpose in their lives by trying to impose their values on the world, regardless of whether people accept them or not. These outsiders can identify themselves with Schrader's

Travis Bickle in *Taxi Driver* (1976); they struggle to function in normal life while desperately striving to unburden themselves of the despair they feel. They find it hard to derive any purpose from just doing what everyone else does, and become increasingly desperate to make some sort of impression on the nonsensical aspects of life around them. Some become increasingly aware they may never find any meaning through its conventional mediums. A few even give up trying to make any impact on the irrational world they are in, believing no matter what they do, things will simply perpetuate themselves regardless. These outsiders are the ones who have lost any hope of gaining any real sense of purpose in their lives, blaming themselves for being too idealistic; some adopting the feeble convention of calling their submission 'experience'. It is tragic that the incredible passion, energy and insights outsiders potentially have to offer to the rest of society, are usually left dormant by their inability to affect any real change on the world as it is.

In many ways the modern world is a poor source for providing existentialists with the sustenance they demand. Some are made to feel as though they have embarked on life with too many expectations, almost like someone who moves abroad imagining they will be blissfully happy living the life of an ex-pat and ending up with shattered dreams, living an isolated existence and unable to relate socially or culturally to the community around them. Despairingly, the outsider's predicament is compounded by the nature of modern life; its contrived format discourages them from making any serious effort to achieve much within it. Society often chooses to smooth over its distorted edges, always careful not to pierce people's bubble world of equitable misconceptions, making it difficult (if not impossible) for most outsiders to embrace its precepts. It is important to note that whilst many outsiders appear impassive to society's often static motions, they can also excel in extreme circumstances - especially where they feel they can apply themselves unequivocally to a cause they believe in. In some cases this need to do something is only triggered when circumstances determine that any conflicting rationale in their motives are petered out by a clear resolve to act. These extreme situations, for example in times of great social change or adversity, do not often manifest themselves. However, sometimes people's unscrupulousness within society, coupled with the outsider's need to preserve his or her freedom as an individual, is enough to provide an incentive to at least do something.

Inequality or injustice in whatever form usually exacerbate most outsiders, especially in circumstances where people's rights or liberties have been adversely affected in some way. Many outsiders have a natural empathy towards the individual striving to preserve his or her autonomy in the face of others pressures to conform. Assaults or sanctions upon people's individual freedoms strike at the core of their existential instincts and, as such, they often have a strong resolve to respect people's discretion to decide things for themselves. On occasion, some outsiders can react impulsively in situations where they feel they have to do something to censure unjust or biased circumstances - whether blatant or otherwise. For these outsiders the need for action ceases to be a futile proposition; its necessity is generated by their determination to stand up to any system, person or force which discriminates against people's individual volition. Contrastingly, many people today tend to play down or excuse the detrimental effects of society's encroaching impact on their autonomy; they often see it as a necessary expedient in order to somehow protect them, and as a prerequisite for how society functions and sustains itself. There are instances in history which have highlighted how some existentialists have reacted against injustice or oppression. These outsiders undoubtedly discovered a clear rationale for action, where extreme circumstances channelled their thoughts' certainty and resolve towards a particular objective.

One of the most famous examples of an outsider determined to follow his convictions, occurred during Britain's engagement with the Turkish Empire during the First World War. At that time, no-one could have predicted what was going to happen when an intelligence officer working in Cairo was ordered to aid negotiations with potential Arab leaders and pave the way for a possible Arab insurgency. This obscure character later became known to history as Lawrence of Arabia (TE Lawrence). It is clear from historical accounts he had strong existential tendencies reflected in his resolve and the way he set about achieving his aims. Lawrence was initially sent into Arabia by the British High Command to appraise the situation and report back to them, but instead took it upon himself to organise and command small parties of Arab renegades with whom he sabotaged the Turkish supply lines. He surprised many of the Arabs who rode with him by his ability to endure the harsh desert conditions and cover huge distances behind enemy lines to outwit the Turkish occupiers. The energy and zeal with which he applied himself were not merely coincidental - circumstances had provided Lawrence with a deep sense of purpose in what he was doing. He not only saw the Arabs as dispossessed people, but also anticipated their intended role as facilitating Britain's defeat of the Turks - in effect to have one master replaced by another. He was also aware that the Arabs' best chance of independence lay in them making a decisive contribution towards driving the Ottomans out of Arabia.

During his time there, he developed an empathy towards the Arab people. The injustice of the Arab's position and what he witnessed them endure, furnished him with a strong incentive to support their cause. He wanted the Arabs to have basic freedoms such as their prerogative to self-rule and their right to be free in their own land, and strongly believed they were entitled to these basic liberties. His purpose was fuelled by the unjust attitude shown towards them by both the Turkish and British governments' imperialist ambitions in the region. In many respects, Lawrence was governed by his strong altruistic instincts, rather than abiding by any presumed loyalty towards the British crown. His reason could not be set aside. In fact, his existential nature strengthened his motive to seek some sort of redress for the Arab people. But none of this should surprise anyone given the almost pathological determination with which some outsiders can apply themselves, once they find a cause they truly believe in. Lawrence's will to succeed was galvanised by his existential need to apply himself towards a cause which meant something, which would unleash a sense of purpose within him he had always failed to find in the tame country of his birth. Even from Lawrence's younger years, when he travelled alone through Syria documenting archaeological evidence of the crusades, it was evident that he had a need to do more than the average person in both thought and deed.

Sartre and Camus both exhibited this irrepressible need to make a stand for something they believed in. Both were actively involved in the French Resistance in the Second World War. Germany's occupation of France and the treatment of its citizens aroused their sense of injustice and their resolve to uphold their freedom. Here again is another example of the outsider, spurned into action as the existential mind asserts itself in extreme or drastic circumstances. In some respects, extreme circumstances often provide the catalyst enabling a few outsiders to find a clear sense of purpose in their lives. In contrast, the predictable undulating motions of everyday life rarely generate the same incentive or sense of purpose within them. It is hard for some to properly recognise what to attribute their despair to, when so many people appear to acquiesce to the way society is, regardless of how irrational its form or nature may be. It is as if some people derive a type of contentment in their lives through propagating an indifference to its shortcomings. Outsiders are well aware, if they abandon themselves to conventional routines or try to passively acquiesce to everything the way it is, their life in effect becomes a pointless shabby exercise of repressing their instincts and managing their despair. It is frustrating that each time they feel the need to assert themselves they fail to find the crucial purpose they crave for. In some respects, the environment many outsiders find themselves in is often far too torpid to provoke a decisive need to do anything. Having said this there is really no way back for the majority of outsiders. Their nature compels them to keep searching for that meaningful purpose they lack in life; most cannot go through it existing like a lame duck just managing to keep its head above water.

It is evident outsiders demand more from life than going through the motions and following a set of routines which condition their minds to be satisfied living off the scraps of other people's proverbial jargon. They need something which is capable of igniting a desire and their imagination towards wanting to achieve it. They are unwilling to imitate others to acquire the meagre incentives which drive most others down society's narrow conventional corridors. Unfortunately, their attempt to find a purpose they can apply themselves to is made all the more difficult by the inertia generated by their penetrating appraisal of life. This inertia is further reinforced by society's design which draws its impetus from providing people with an illusion of needs - determining the form and nature of their existence. As Herbert Marcuse notes:

> The most effective and enduring form of warfare against liberation is
> the implanting of material and intellectual needs that perpetuate
> obsolete forms of the struggle for existence. [13]

Outsiders often find themselves static in life, with some almost waiting for something to happen, even hoping that some sort of disruption or upheaval will occur which might furnish them with some kind of objective. These outsiders sometimes dream of being placed in extraordinary situations, often the only thing they see as capable of firing their sense of purpose. Unfortunately, the way they perceive life and society's rigid format inhibits their ability to discover that elusive purpose they hanker for; it saps their willingness to aspire to conventional challenges. Nowadays, society is almost fearful of the possible ramifications and chaos which might ensue from providing people in general with a strong incentive to really think outside the box or act on their own initiative. As a result, some outsiders resign themselves to the notion that they will never be truly accommodated within society, its inertia to change and inability to accept their nature seems far too entrenched to be dislodged by them as individuals. Yet, at the same time, they cannot sit idly by either waiting for some sort of circumstance to manifest itself where they might one day find some sort of goal to aim for. The true reality for outsiders is that they cannot measure their expectations with the rest of society, blindly hoping one day to stumble onto something which will satisfy their inherent existential need for meaning. This was Travis Bickle's undoing in *Taxi Driver*, where his aimless life as a New York cabby, mistakenly lead him to believe he could alleviate his despair by forcing himself to be like other people and adopt their accepted behaviour:

> 'All my life needed was a sense of direction, a sense of someplace to
> go. I do not believe one should devote his whole life to morbid self-
> attention, but should become a person like other people.' [14]

One of the most common misconceptions which befall many outsiders is their presumption they can find purpose in their lives like anyone else. This inference leads some to believe they have just been desperately unlucky. Outsiders often set the bar much higher than most, and as such, cannot expect to compare or calibrate their needs with others. They must accept the person they are and acknowledge the underlying force which drives them to think the way they do. Some outsiders defiantly refuse to accept this difference which often prevents them from realising their needs. It is essential they break these chains of comparison, in the same way a traveller can never appreciate another culture unless he or she sees it for what it is, rather than contrasting its difference from their own. Outsiders are in much the same situation - they must take a long hard look at their true needs in life. In essence they must look at what really makes them tick and one of the principal features which distinguishes them from many others within society - their conviction to stand by what they think and believe in - their truth.

# 7

# The Outsider's Truth

What I touch, what resists me – that is what I understand.
And these two certainties - my appetite for the absolute and
for the unity and the impossibility of reducing this world to a
rational and reasonable principle – I also know that I cannot
reconcile them. What other truth can I admit without lying,
without bringing in a hope I lack, which means nothing
within the limits of my condition?

Albert Camus - *Myth of Sisiphus* [1]

Outsiders cannot usually make sense of the world they are in.
It seems completely alien to them in terms of the things they
value in life. Regardless of this contrast, their experience of it often
just reinforces what they think, making much of what is around
them appear artificial. For things to appear real and make sense
they not only need to be enduring, but also hold some substance
behind them by being grounded in reason. In their attempts to
discover some meaningful undercurrent within life, many outsiders
try to apply simple unequivocal principles to its absurd and often
contradictory format. However, the modern world rarely makes
itself amenable to any straightforward exposition and forces them to
turn to themselves for answers. Their minds filter out the transient
and material essence of things, drawing them instinctively to thoughts

and ideas they rationalise with their own perceptions. In their search for certitude, it soon becomes apparent that apart from death and taxes, there are no real certainties in life. They accept they exist, but this is not enough, they need to be able to place their existence in some meaningful context to have any regard for it.

As outsiders strive to add form to their being beyond merely existing in the here and now, they naturally look for constants in the equation, seeking to ally themselves to things in life they can be more certain of. In their efforts to do this, they find themselves invariably drawn to the authenticity of their own thoughts. The unique way they appraise what is around them coupled with their insistence to be who they are, defines them as something much more than someone who just accepts life for what it is. This not only plays a pivotal role in what they do, but also how they conceive themselves. Most accept there is no ultimate truth, everything is relative to how each individual perceives and interprets life. Yet, in an unreal world, the only certainties outsiders can realistically latch onto are the conclusions generated by their own mind. Therefore, in order to consider themselves as anything they must remain true to what they think, and have no reason to portray themselves other than the persons they are. In an irrational world and absent of the substance they demand from it, they must exist as individuals who preserve and uphold their unique nature. The real conflict emerges when their candid disposition and need to be perceptible as defined entities is not reciprocated, understood, or appreciated by the world they are in.

Each outsider's view of life could be described as unparalleled; they have no other cause other than to see it in its plainest format and in terms of what they think it means. Inevitably, their perspective clashes with the way many others tend to perceive it. People in general are sometimes more inclined to brush over their outlook, blurring out its contrasts and anything else they find difficult to reconcile against their conventional portrayal of it. For some these days, the watercolour can always be diluted to suit their own narrative. A few even transform simple choices or decisions into convoluted dilemmas, enabling them to discount any principle or moral doctrine which threatens to impinge on their whimsical behaviour. Some people will resort to using whatever means at their disposal to set aside their intractable instincts. These people actually believe they are being clever in manufacturing ways to obscure the real reasons behind their actions, often making the indefensible justifiable and giving them an implied qualification to practice hypocrisy with impunity. At the other extreme is the outsider, the individual who sees life in black and white; the person whose discordant view not only expounds its paradoxes, but also people's sophistries. The outsider's picture of life cannot be touched up to make it more appealing. It represents their truth, the candid way they see the world and their irreducible need to make sense of it.

Many people cannot appreciate where outsiders' candour stems from. They have no idea of the crucial role truth plays in the way he or she conceives him or herself. Most people tend to work from a different script, and therefore never properly understand what drives the outsider's need for frankness. A good analogy would be to imagine someone who had just lost everything they have ever owned or worked for, including those close to him or her. Once these external things are stripped away, such as a person's material possessions, social bonds, and possible pretence, the only thing that person has left is who he or she actually is. In the same way, the more ephemeral aspects of life such as what most outsiders physically possess or how they are received by others, mean very little to them. They have scant regard for the way others judge them, having no need to appease anyone and, as such, their focus in life revolves around things they can rationalise themselves and rely on their constancy. In effect, it is the outsiders' honesty and ability to abide by what they think, that provides them with the assurance they exist as something distinct and tangible within society. A few would even concede that to be anything but themselves would leave their existence with no real reason behind it.

Outsiders tend to appraise life with a wholly different set of criteria from most others. Their priorities revolve around what they consider as definite and real which makes them scrutinize and interpret things differently; a contrast which often causes a great deal of friction. They are often left perplexed as they watch others go about their daily lives, unable to appreciate how some can consider themselves as having done or achieved anything significant. They look upon society as a whole, forging precariously forward with many people blaming the rigours of contemporary life on their failure to go against the grain when there is something they wholeheartedly disagree with or feel they ought to speak up about. In many respects, truth (as it relates to the individual's ability to maintain it) has become a lost word in the commodity market of modern life, and outsiders feel as though they are the only ones left who place any value upon it. Most outsiders would never even try to conjure up clever rationales or excuses to compensate for their mind's lack of resolve. They have their own standards to uphold, it is they who have to look in the mirror every day and judge their scruples; they have no intention of pretending to be anyone else or hiding behind their own shadow.

When people try to work out the outsider's psyche they are sometimes left baffled as to why they seemingly go out of their way to self-punish themselves by insisting on being so doggedly candid. Many people cannot fathom what (if anything) they gain from this, when all it seems to do is undermine their ability to get along and be accepted like everyone else. They cannot understand why anyone would want to disregard or even go against the format of life most others have acquiesced to. There are times when outsiders can be at cross swords with everyone around them, and all people see are these obstinate individuals who seem intent on upsetting the normal run of things, or who deliberately go out of their way to subvert other people's precepts. And yet, the simple fact is that it is the outsiders' insistence to adhere to their own thoughts in life which casts them into the persons they are. In effect, they are compelled to live by their mind's conclusions; the assurance their existence amounts to something through their insistence to rationalise their thoughts and perceptions for themselves. Truth is a tangible asset to outsiders which can neither be bought nor sold, in a world where most people naively presume that everything has its price.

Within society today people's willingness to abide by what they purportedly think or believe in, is easily excused by an accepted array of justifications. For some, peace of mind is achieved through dismissing what they actually think for themselves or through nurturing a passivity to life's inanity. Most outsiders cannot condone people's lack of resolve to be themselves and, over time, become adept at recognising some people's wavering convictions. They have no reason to lie to themselves, or conduct themselves in the spuriousness of someone else's contrived logic. Unfortunately, society exerts its own leverage to bring them in line with everyone else and to submit to its mandate, while its format usually stifles their attempts to apply themselves instinctively. But outsiders in turn confound most others, usually resisting whatever pressures are brought to bear and not relinquishing the faith in their thoughts' verity. Most people continually underestimate outsiders' determination to remain true to what they think. As a result, they inadvertently become targets for society's inaccurate appraisal; some sort of explanation must be found when an individual defies its presumed legitimacy by following their own values, ideals and reason in life. This view is recanted in Ellison's *Invisible Man*, in which he gives a compelling account of the life of a nameless black man, coming to terms with the racist and contradictory logic of people's attitudes in 1940's America:

> I was never more hated than when I tried to be honest. Or when, even as just now I've tried to articulate exactly what I felt to be the truth. No one was satisfied – not even I. On the other hand I've never been more loved and appreciated than when I tried to 'justify' and affirm someone's mistaken beliefs; or when I've tried to give my friends the incorrect, absurd answers they wished to hear. In my presence they would talk and agree with themselves, the world was nailed down, and they loved it. [2]

This passage also reflects the experiences of many existentialists, as their attempts to apply themselves are often undone by the incompatibility of their ideals with society's conventions, and people's willingness to unconditionally endorse established doctrines and prejudice.

One of the most poignant historical episodes of an individual's unbending will to adhere to what he or she thought and believed in, was documented by Plato in *The Trial and Death of Socrates*. It describes how Socrates' insistence to apply his reason and question the substance of others dogma in Athens' fledgling democracy, led to him being accused by certain Athenians of corrupting young minds and not believing in the Gods of the city. Socrates' only crime seems to have been the fact that he questioned people's apparent indubitable assertions which, in their eyes, threatened the stability of this early Athenian democracy. It is curious that the nation whose civilisation laid the foundations for the modern democracies of today, proved itself unwilling to accept the scrutiny and reason of one particular individual. Plato recounts how Socrates' arguments were able to displace the certitude of the most intelligent men in Athenian society. From all accounts, Socrates' only wrongdoing seems to have been his attempt to reconcile other people's assertions against his own understanding. He believed, his existence meant nothing unless he could live according to what he thought; above all else he had to be true to himself:

> From me you shall hear the whole truth, though not, by Zeus, gentlemen, expressed in embroidered and stylised phrases like theirs, but things spoken at random and expressed in the first words that come to mind, for I put my trust in the justice of what I say, and let none of you expect anything else. [3]

Socrates never wavered in his determination to rationalise the issues of his day. He felt compelled to stand by the way he perceived and interpreted what went on around him, even the possibility of losing his own life was not enough to make him deny any part of what he believed to be true. The Athenians expected Socrates to admit his guilt and renounce his assertions when presented with death as the alternative, but they were naïve in their estimation. A confrontation ensued, one which has repeated itself countless times throughout history - the right of the individual to be free to express his or her thoughts and opinions above the dictates or presumed omniscience of others collective will. Socrates' conviction to exist by his truth prevailed against the Athenians' threat of the ultimate penalty. His resolve proved itself a greater adversary than the measures the Athenians could impose on him to bring him into submission. As far as he was concerned, the idea of any compromise was never in question. He could not relinquish his thoughts to legitimise a society, which had already demonstrated its shortcomings, by feeling threatened enough by his discourse to sentence him to death. However, as the most extreme and final sanction which can be imposed on any individual, death proved itself an utterly useless lever against Socrates, as he confesses:

I would much rather die after this kind of defence than live after making the other kind. Neither I nor any other man should, on trial or in war, contrive to avoid death at any cost. [4]

Socrates' determination to maintain his mind's freedom, regardless of what ensued, reflects the attitude of many outsiders. Like Socrates, they do not see any point and cannot derive any meaning from their lives by denying what they actually think - their truth is not expendable. Unfortunately, there is little room in society's great orchestra these days for the truly independent person who vehemently adheres to what he or she thinks, just an expectation that everyone in one way or another must follow society's score. The notion that people may be selling themselves short by doing so is never entertained by the paragons of contemporary society. People are usually quick to dismiss any alleged suggestion that they may be compromising themselves and, pretexts such as 'good sense', 'practicality' and 'experience' come easy to those willing to blatantly conceal their inability to exist beside their own truth. How many people can honestly say that in their lives, they always conduct themselves according to what they believe in or think is right? For some people, their ability to exercise or project their truth, usually ends up buried under an array of cowardly justifications whose frequent use eventually turns them into their praxis in life.

The outsider is simply not governed by the same partialities as other people, which is usually reflected in how their lives transpire and what they do in life. As previously discussed, there is sometimes a disparate relationship between the job some outsiders do and their actual abilities. Most can hardly be described as career-minded and, for some, whatever they do in terms of getting by is of little real consequence. Much of the time, work is just something they do to keep a roof over their head. For many, it is simply a routine of turning up on time and discharging their particular duties; some cannot conceive anything more substantive beyond this. Their inability to attribute a quantifiable meaning behind much of what they do, especially amongst the more mainstream or conventional career avenues today, means that for some, it becomes almost incidental what they do to get by. There are a few outsiders who forego any hope of reconciling themselves with the world as it is, so much so, they will even make themselves amenable to simply carrying out the roles society demands. These few have ceased to believe their existence can amount to anything substantive or meaningful, and as such, do not think it makes any real difference how they conduct themselves through life. These outsiders will often go with the flow, do what others expect and tell people what they want to hear. They have already given up on who they are and wander aimlessly in life, invariably pursuing any course of action which allows them to defer coming to terms with their wretched existence. Fortunately, there are very few outsiders whose nature allows them to contemplate making such a vain submission.

It is important to note, there are other factors which have a bearing on the types of employment outsiders are drawn to. For some, their despair with life usually makes them more inclined to doing things which are more individually orientated, where they are often left to their own devices. This often allows them to preserve their unique nature, where they are not obliged to expose themselves too much to the irrational or irreconcilable aspects of some work-place environments. Some outsiders are also more inclined to jobs which usually require little responsibility. This is sometimes due to the fact they often cannot take what they do as seriously as everyone else, and also due to their refusal to put themselves in positions where they may be forced to imitate someone else or do things they cannot equate with what they think. Most outsiders will not barter with their truth. It is too precious a commodity to be exposed to the whims of others who rarely understand its dimensions and will often willingly condemn it, unless they see it as something they can use or manipulate to their own ends.

Pragmatism, not principle, seems to have become the buzz word which now typifies any modern 'progressive' society. Whatever fits best at a particular time can be morphed into society's design, often without a ripple of consternation. Many outsiders do not feel obliged to adapt themselves or even accept these ever shifting tides, and are averse to any role in life which makes their ability to maintain their mind's integrity untenable. They have already anticipated the incompatibility of applying their truth against the expectations and constrained perspective they are measured against within society and today's workplace. The real outsider has already decided the outcome of this conflict and this precludes them from committing themselves to any role which ultimately requires them to betray their true instincts. They could never accept the blatant contradiction of doing or saying things they disagreed with or could not honestly reconcile with themselves. Their willingness to uphold their truth is often unyielding and like Socrates, it transcends their hankering for self-preservation, to get on in life, or their desire to be accepted in society like everyone else.

As far as outsiders are concerned, life is not a trade-off; their thoughts are too much a part of them to be relinquished at society's behest. This often contrasts with how others often go about their lives. For some people, something in the back of their mind may be telling them what they should do or how they should stand by what they instinctively think, and yet, they never quite make that transition from pondering the incompatible possibilities to actually doing anything about it. These people's ability to decide things on their terms is often looked upon as some form of idealistic aspiration, reserved for the heroic characters portrayed through history or literature. Regardless of this, the stubborn idealist battling against all the odds, remains an appealing characterisation in many people's eyes. Maybe this is because, for some, it is how they would like to be, whilst realising it would be too impractical or disruptive to their lives to be properly embraced. The psychological impact on people who, in spite of everything, choose to uphold their truth and what they believe in can be immense, and should not be embarked on naively. The equation is different for everyone and normally depends upon how far a person is prepared to go to follow their instinctive thoughts, in light of the impracticality and drawbacks it entails. Who is really prepared to face the consequences of acting on their mind's principles in every instance? Who is prepared to make a stand and disagree with everyone else and express what they truly believe?

In effect, most people are bound by a need to be part of society, and unlike the outsider, their truth is consistently relegated by an unwritten rule to *tow-the-line* or *not to ruffle too many feathers*. Very often, these people have no real appetite for initiating or doing anything which may be considered too out of the ordinary. In many ways, they become little more than expedient components within society; their inhibition to do anything which may *break the mould* firmly wrapped in convention and bound by others expectations. The instant they make that climb-down from the quandaries they encounter, their truth becomes expendable; a tendency so common and accepted nowadays people have almost ceased drawing attention to, or reproaching others for it. Within society today there seems to be increasingly fewer people who show any real desire to remain true to what they actually think - it is easier for most to just go along with things as they are or wipe the slate clean, amalgamating their conscience into the melting pot of what everyone else thinks or does. However, this still does not stop some trying to portray themselves as people of integrity by professing to act on things they are purportedly passionate about; often convincing themselves and others their actions are bound by some principle they claim to uphold. It seems sometimes, people are more content to blatantly delude themselves and those around them than to actually be the persons they claim to be. Truth often means nothing to society's thespians of principle who entertain their audience by creating semantic permutations to obscure the real motives underlying their flippant nature. This is succinctly demonstrated by Roquentin (Sartre's character in *Nausea*):

I admire the way we can lie, putting reason on our side. [5]

Virtually anything is now capable of passing society's pliant scrutiny. Almost any point of view can be justified, as long as someone is prepared to apply a 'clever' rationale to it. Society's blind faith in itself breeds its own ignorance. Outsiders have no desire to use society's trite means to escape its reality; many already regard the modern world as something verging on a virtual reality game. People go about their daily lives like caricatures in a Lowry painting, convinced they are part of a civilisation which is constantly evolving in a positive direction. No-one wants to believe for a moment that western society is not improving itself. No-one wants to entertain the idea that modern society may be languishing in an inflated notion of its own virtue. And yet, there are some signs it is already beginning to fold in on itself. We are now witnessing an increasing reliance on past familiarity as the populist's spring board for inspiration. Society seems to have lost its appetite for raw originality. Less and less people appear to have time to discern whether something has merit in its own right; this provision is often left to the popular critics of their time, or more worryingly, the opinions of some high profile celebrity. Society is now at the stage where, at times, even people's responsiveness has been whittled down to the fine art of manipulating their perceptions to engineer a desired response.

In some ways all outsiders aspire to be part of a more realistic world where people are not placed at a disadvantage by acting on what their instincts bring into question, or expressing what they honestly think. Most outsiders would probably prefer to live in a world which was more uncertain of itself, in which people at least acknowledged society's blind spots. Yet, while they strive for certainty in their lives, they are also paradoxically drawn to uncertain or even chaotic situations. This maybe because they believe they would fare better in circumstances where the pre-judicial forces to change such as indifference or equanimity are less prevalent. A few, from time to time, even crave for some sort of chaos in their lives, even wishing something would happen which would mix things up and even disturb society's calm content equilibrium.

There are some outsiders who tend to identify chaotic circumstances with an increased potential for change and often long for some sort of disruption as a catalyst which might stimulate others receptiveness towards considering things in a different context or light. Some outsiders also feel they have more of an opportunity to apply their instincts in situations where people are less intransigent. Uncertainty usually encourages the creation and consideration of new ways of looking at things. It can sometimes create a fertile environment for the acceptance of different perceptions and opinions, providing individuals with a greater opportunity to apply themselves. Unfortunately, it is often the opposite scenario facing the outsider in modern life. Society has entered an era where there is less obligation and, in some cases, no requirement placed upon people to use their discretion anymore as they allow life's placid milieu to wash over them. It could also be said, that this attitude has been nurtured by society itself, subjecting people to increasingly simplistic and cynical functions, in some instances, specifically designed to comatose their instinct for independent thought.

Outsiders are made to feel like ciphers in the modern world, strengthening their intrinsic need to preserve their truth. They simply cannot envisage themselves becoming just another hopeless component, caught up in what they often regard as society's misguided motion. Their existence must be based on something more than a birth certificate and national insurance number. They need to feel they exist as something tangible in life, unlike (as they see it) some of the more irresolute and fickle characters which now spawn from society's ilk. This resolve to exist as a visible and clearly defined entity was illustrated in Camus' *Outsider* where Meursault, like Socrates, faced a trial in which his life rested upon its outcome. Meursault is questioned by his lawyer, who is concerned with the bearing his nonchalant behaviour at his mother's funeral may have on his trial:-

> Then he asked me if he could say that I'd controlled my natural feelings that day. I said, "No, because it's not true. [6]

During the trial, it is made clear to Meursault that it is in his best interests to play down what he truly thinks. The court gives him every opportunity, and in fact encourages him, to present himself as a character who exhibits the usual human sentiments such as remorse for what has happened, and fear of losing his own life if convicted. His lawyer urges him to show signs of regret so he can mitigate on his behalf, but Meursault does not see any reason to express anything he does not truly feel. He is not unaware that if he displays some remorseful pretence to the court, he will be able to save himself from execution, but his nature compels him to be totally up front about what he thinks. He does not feel threatened by the possibility of being executed as his life has little meaning to it anyway, and the court duly interprets this as evidence that they are dealing with a cold remorseless killer. Meursault does not have any motive to lie about the way he feels, not even to save himself. In his mind there is no point in going back to the actor's workshop, he is prepared to take whatever is thrown at him regardless. Camus explains the characterisation of Meursault in the afterword of the *Outsider*:-

> The answer is simple he refuses to lie. Lying is not only saying what isn't true. It is also, in fact especially, saying more than is true and, in the case of the human heart, saying more than one feels. We all do it, every day, to make life simpler. But, contrary to appearances, Meursault doesn't want to make life simpler. He says what he is, he refuses to hide his feelings and society immediately feels threatened. [7]

In the world of the outsider, self-preservation does not feature very high on their agenda when pitched against their willingness to be themselves. No-one should expect any outsider to do or say things he or she does not mean or believe in, just to make their lives a little easier. This would be like asking them to become a virtual non-entity, turning their existence into little more than a sham. There is usually too much at stake for the outsider to lie or seek to manipulate others perceptions to ameliorate their circumstances; in the long run this is only achieved at the expense of the self. As Colin Wilson explains of Meursault:

> This honesty springs out of indifference to issues of feeling; he does not attach importance to anything; why should he lie? [8]

The despair most outsiders experience in their lives is amplified by the disparity between the way they think and the things which preoccupy most others. They are often frustrated by those around them, who do not seem to have the same attitude or regard for what they actually think and believe to be true. From a young age everyone is taught the moralistic value of truth and the virtues of standing by what they believe in, but would it not be better to teach children the clever ways of bending the truth or twisting reason to their own ends in order to equip them better for later life? At least this way, when they grow up, they would not be under any mis-conceptions about how unscrupulous people can be and how society tends to function some of the time. It has virtually become accepted behaviour these days that if someone can get away with bending the rules or contrives to get something through some unscrupulous means (as long as they do not cross that increasingly blurred moral line), then all the best to them. Unfortunately, this sets the standard for some as any moral or ethical stumbling blocks can be easily by-passed as and when the need arises. Society often champions those who demonstrate a desire and drive to chase after their aspirations in life, sometimes without a qualm for how synthetic or contrived these accomplishments may be. These achievements then get presented as some sort of pinnacle of individual human achievement, engendering an increasingly shallow society.

For some people, it does not really matter anymore how they realise their materialistic or conditioned aspirations. They become respected within society, as long as they follow convention and do not do anything to provoke too much consensual disapproval along the way. This is typified by the revolving doors of Westminster, where disgraced MP's and Peers who flagrantly abuse their position hardly spend any time in the wilderness before being brought back into the fold. In the same vein a football player who wins a foul by going down after a totally innocuous shove, sometimes gets praised by commentators for his or her skill in bringing this about. This attitude permeates through modern society, allowing people to pat each other on the back for their 'cleverness' in being able to work a situation to their selfish advantage. Each endorsement of this crass attitude makes it easier for people to dispense with addressing the issue of whether they need to have any real responsibility towards anyone or anything beyond themselves. Those who embrace this base attitude to life seldom create anything substantive. They go through it plundering what they can at every turn, often slavishly pursuing the attitude to always put themselves first like some primitive being. The self, which should define the individual's probity, all too easily becomes an expedient to society's adulterated form.

There are times, when some outsiders find it hard to conceive any rational basis for the way people in general go about their lives. This is reflected in Sartre's *Nausea* as Rodquentin's gazes upon a great bronze statue and considers what it actually represents in people's minds:-

> At the service of their narrow, firm little ideas he [the statue] has placed his authority and the immense erudition drawn from the folio volumes crushed under his heavy hand. The ladies in black feel relieved, they can attend peacefully to their household tasks, take their dogs out: they no longer have the responsibility of defending the sacred ideas, the worthy concepts which they derive from their grandfathers; a man of bronze has made himself their guardian. [9]

Many people find it very difficult to be blatantly honest in life, their truth is often conditional, trapped within a web of expectation and need for acceptance. The lack of true and honest expression within society only serves to endorse its status quo, as people shy away from their responsibility to scrutinise and judge things for themselves. This makes for a convenient world where virtually any precept, no matter how ill-conceived, can be placed within seemingly acceptable or justifiable contexts. Those who do not consider their lives beyond the here and now do not even require a pretext for the way they think; their ideals handed to them on a plate. Their contentment with life is virtually guaranteed, often manufactured through nurturing increasing levels of indifference to life's adverse realities. This in turn, extinguishes their incentive to question the way their lives pan out, or what they actually amount to as individuals in their own right. These people's lives are like a relentless self-perpetuating life cycle, where each new generation simply pitches up where the other left off. Unfortunately, this mind-set is commonplace today, making the evolutionary miracle of humankind seem as if it has entered some sort of regressive stage. In a world where people seem to be so conditioned by the influences around them, and where unique or independent thought are increasingly seen as out of place, the outsiders' only allies are those who, from time to time, are prepared to remain faithful to who they really are.

This conflict between the individual and the collective formed the backdrop of Ayn Rand's *The Fountainhead* (1943). It describes the tribulations of an architect whose attempts to establish himself through his work's originality are continually thwarted by those who do not want to deviate from the conventional architecture of the time. The protagonist, Howard Roark, is condemned for being too modernistic and original. He refuses to compromise or adapt his architecture to meet people's general consensus of what they believe buildings should look like. His designs cause a wave of public dissent against him and the style of his work. Ayn Rand sets forth the theme of the book, that architecture must come from the individual and that a building must have an integrity of its own, rather than being contrived from any consensus of past architectural forms. As a narrative, *The Fountainhead* is a testament to an individual's enduring faith in the value and originality of his or her work, in the face of seemingly overwhelming pressures to conform. The book concludes with a trial in which Roark's adversaries eventually accept they cannot compel him to renounce his unique architectural talent merely because of people's reluctance to accept his ideas.

In modern life, the unerring legitimacy of society's consensus is constantly drummed into people from all quarters. Nowadays, there is no real responsibility placed upon anyone to formulate their own unique opinions or adhere to them; it is much easier just to pirate attitudes from other people or regurgitate whatever the prevailing opinion may be. It is as if some people will recklessly swallow any pill, if they are led to believe it will make their lives a little happier for a time by nullifying the effects of the real world. This state of mind is comparable to someone who misuses antibiotics, but instead of weakening the immune system to different strains of bacteria, it gradually makes people increasingly vulnerable to the array of simplistic instruments which condition them. Some outsiders would even go as far as to declare that any alternative would be better than a predominantly conditioned society, which explains the ethos behind the creation of Herman Hesse's character (Harry Haller) in *Steppenwolf*:-

> He was capable of loving the political criminal, the revolutionary or intellectual seducer, the outlaw of state and society, as his brother, but as for theft and robbery, murder and rape, he would not have known how to deplore them otherwise than in a thoroughly bourgeois manner. [10]

There is little left to be achieved in a society which measures its progress through its unending technological sophistication and its ability to imbue the masses with an unending succession of contrived needs. The writing is on the wall in terms of the direction society is moving towards. If it carries on in the same vein, people within it will become more conditioned as they immerse themselves in its increasing artificial realism. A situation will eventually transpire where incidental concerns dominate people's attentions as their minds skirt around life's more fundamental issues, trying not to overload itself with too much stark reality. A passivity will eventually emerge amongst the masses, typified by dismissive attitudes such as 'if anything needed to change someone would have thought of it and done something about it already'. Eventually, all that will be left is a vague collection of mediocre people, with no impetus to challenge or influence the way their lives turn out; a society which will one day require the crutch of feeble propaganda for it to do or think anything for itself:

> .....an enemy of free discussion may be supposed to say that there is no necessity for mankind in general to know and understand all that can be said against or for their opinions by philosophers and theologians. That it is not needful for common men to be able to expose all the misstatements or fallacies of an ingenious opponent. That, it is enough if there is always someone capable of answering them, so that nothing likely to misled uninstructed persons remains un-refuted. That simple minds, having been taught the obvious grounds of the truths inculcated in them, may trust to authority for the rest and, being aware that they have neither knowledge or talent to resolve every difficulty which can be raised, may repose in the assurance that all those which have been raised have been or can be answered by those who are especially trained to the task. [11]

Any society which places unconditional faith in the way it is governed, the factuality of the information relayed to it, or the decisions made on its behalf, merely advertises its fragility. No society, in which people within it relinquish their responsibility to think and judge things for themselves, could ever realistically have any auspicious future. Society's strength does not lie in inducing people en masse to subordinate themselves unquestioningly to collective doctrines, or the governance of those it promotes as the ones who supposedly know best. Its strength lies in its ability to encourage and empower people to make reasoned choices and decisions for themselves, from the broadest range of influences and experiences. Society's vibrancy comes from its ability to question and, if necessary, challenge the principles or decisions which are either made by it or on its behalf. Without these challenges any government, body, or individual in an authoritative or influential position would be handed a free rein to pass virtually any law or make any decision without any real sanction; the culmination of which would eventually result in people's almost total subjugation. It is acutely worrying that some believe it is precisely this kind of nonchalance towards the *powers that be*, which has crept across the western world over the last couple of decades. It is now evident that increasing numbers of people are beginning to feel the effects of this encroaching phenomenon as many governments, politicians and authoritative bodies have greatly enhanced their influence on the back of society's failure to scrutinise, challenge or even question the presumed reasoning or legitimacy behind decisions they make.

The current nature of British politics is a prime example of what transpires when an institution is not properly brought to account. Almost all political parties today, seem to be obsessed with trying to ally themselves more closely to the middle ground - a position which makes them better placed to appeal to the more mainstream voter, rather than choosing the more risky option of defining their own unique political stance. In addition, politicians seem to have become self-obsessed with presentation, often used as a means of compensating for their lack of substantive policy, or to conceal the spurious nature of their decision making. This lack of clear discernible political conviction is further compounded by an increasing number of party policies concocted on the undulating whims of public opinion. By seeking the short-term popular vote, many politicians have rendered themselves incapable of forming effective long-term strategies to advance the principles they or their parties purportedly believe in.

Whatever happened to the political party that vehemently stood by its values and carried through its policies, knowing at times they might be unpopular or difficult for people to accept? The only time politicians seem to make a point of declaring they have stood by their principles, is usually in order to excuse themselves when one of their often ill-conceived decisions, in hindsight, turns out to be grossly misjudged. The rhetoric has also changed, with for instance, the increasing use of 'I believe' rather than 'I think', which is obviously used as a means to absolve themselves of some element of moral culpability. It seems that nothing is sacred anymore from the resourceful political opportunists of our time. Politicians now make a habit of adopting a popular stance and then convincing people after the event, often through convoluted and inventive argument, that their position has always been consistent with their political convictions. This also reflects the way modern society functions as many things now follow this back-to-front format, being conceived from some opportune whim and then justified by being introduced on the pretext of a seemingly credible yet feigned rationale.

Most politicians never miss the chance to portray themselves as attentive to current trends and public opinion, especially when it furthers their political ambitions. In the public eye, this is often seen as evidence of greater democracy at work, but how can any party whose principles become expedients to the short-term vacillating trends and inconsistencies of public opinion offer anything worthwhile in the long term. Some politicians nowadays even seek to conceal where their true principles lie, either fearful of them being unpopular, or so as not to curtail their ability to act on some political whim in the future. This apparent lack of resolve gives politicians a flexibility which many now regard as expedient in the modern political arena. It seems all the tricks in the book are deemed permissible, when an attempt is made to influence the increasingly sensitive political landscape from the creativity of initiating immature scaremongering to blatantly cynical showmanship. And yet, the truth is, there is not much real contrasting political opinion amongst most politicians today. Many have simply jumped on the popularity bandwagon with much of their decision-making often formed with two principle variables in mind: the immediate popular political climate and often what they think they can get away with.

It must be borne in mind that although politicians realise that part of their popularity rests upon their ability to calibrate their views more closely with public sentiment, this also becomes less of a prerequisite in any conditioned society. It could be said the goalposts have already been widened as politicians in recent times have devised a proliferation of strategies to dodge the increasingly weak media scrutiny through their ever growing army of spin doctors. In effect, politicians have acquired increasing discretionary powers through their skill in manipulating public opinion to fit their agendas - in some cases through blatant duplicity. The ease with which public opinion can be coaxed along by politicians' banter reveals a fundamental weakness in society. As more and more people are swayed by the feeble instruments of spin and unsubstantiated argument, more unsanctioned power is handed over to those in authoritative positions. This circumstance, which is becoming an increasingly prevalent facet of modern society, only exacerbates outsiders' resolve to uphold what they think. People should recount history before judging or frowning upon the outsider's disposition, which shows that few if any great ideas or changes were ever brought about through creating a society of minions or seeking to appease or manipulate the ephemeral demands of public opinion. The whole concept of public opinion's role in the functioning of any democratic society becomes redundant, when it is reduced to a mere product of the forces which condition it.

For many politicians career success is no longer defined through their ability to stand up and effectively articulate the sentiments or concerns of their constituents. Amongst today's political class it is, for some, all about influence and how useful they can make themselves to the corporate lobbyists stalking the annals of Westminster. It matters little to some of them whether the decisions they influence adversely affect particular sectors of society or even the nation as a whole. Some simply do not see anything wrong with using their political influence to maximise their earning potential, often being reimbursed through pseudo roles, services, or some other means designed to bypass public scrutiny. For many politicians, life has become one big gravy train which usually does not stop when they end their political careers. As long as they have shown loyalty to their party or the vested interests of some corporate third party, they can be assured of a lucrative future role regardless of their ability or competence.

The ethos which now permeates through modern politics is that politicians should keep their heads well under the parapet, allowing them when the need arises, to point their cannon in whatever direction they find most rewarding. Nowadays, political skill is sometimes defined through a politician's ability to formulate opinions which show no trace of being derived from any equivocal political conviction. This not only reduces the prospect of setting a precedent for future decisions, but reduces the chances of politicians being branded as hypocritical. This reliance on damage limitation is indicative of doctors who practice 'safe medicine' due to their fear of litigation. Opinions borne by caesarean section may ensure a safer delivery, but surely it cannot be constructive for any society, to have politicians who constantly seek ways to override the natural scrutiny which their decisions or opinions should be exposed to. This epidemic is increasingly common in the often lacklustre explanations provided by politicians for the decisions they make.

There are even instances today where politicians completely ignore politically direct questions, or distort their meaning to contrive an opportunity to discuss a wholly irrelevant topic. These practices are particularly prevalent within today's political world. In the House of Commons, the habit of asking leading questions to politicians from the same party, thereby inviting them to rant on about what they regard as their party's achievements, is rife. This state of affairs has been allowed to happen. It has been given the green light through too many people's lack of critical awareness and society's general habit of devouring more and more of the tripe thrown its way. It is disturbing to imagine what might happen if society keeps going down the same road, where public opinion might even reach the stage where it ceases to act as any kind of buffer to the excesses of political power. Today's world already seems perilously close to Bernard Shaw's depiction of hell in his play *Man and Superman*:

> [Don Juan]: Here you call appearance beauty, your emotions love, your sentiments heroism, your aspirations virtue, just as you did on earth; but there are no hard facts to contradict you, no ironic contrast of your needs with your pretensions, no human comedy, nothing by a perpetual romance, a universal melodrama. [12]

Within this 'universal melodrama', more and more people seem to be searching for quick fix solutions in life. It could be said that this lottery mentality already has a firm grip on people's attitudes in society today, as far fewer people now are prepared to work diligently towards something, unless it has a good chance of producing an immediate or materially profitable result. There is a presumption everyone is entitled to some form of gratification in their lives, either from trying to buy their way to pleasurable experiences, or being unduly commended for some trite achievement. This is where the real difference emerges between the outsider and most other people. For instance, some outsiders may spend years trying to do or create something which he or she considers as important or meaningful, regardless of whether it is going to be deemed a success in others imagination or in terms of delivering some material reward.

As Camus explains, outsiders have their own criteria to fulfil and define success on their own terms:-

> ......I must sacrifice everything to these certainties and I must see them squarely to be able to maintain them. Above all I must adapt my behaviour to them and pursue them in all their consequences. I am speaking here of decency. But want to know before-hand if thought can live in those deserts. I already know that thought has at least already entered those deserts. There is found its bread. There it realised it had previously been feeding on phantoms. [13]

The crucial question outsiders must ask themselves is whether they are prepared to go through life by being true to themselves and accepting the difficulties this entails. It is clear, the ones who generally 'do well' in life, by society's standards, are those who complement its modus operandi, usually basing their aspirations and needs upon what society classifies as achievement. Those who generally reach the top in society's pecking order, are often fiercely motivated towards fulfilling a set of needs they have been conditioned to identify as defining success. These can range from gaining financial rewards, career success or becoming influential in some way - it would also be unfair to omit those who have a talent for being able to dress themselves in an honourable pretence. Most people are usually so busy aspiring to fulfil these needs, they often go through life without once asking themselves, "What does my life actually amount to, or what do I, as a person, actually represent in the world around me?" For anyone who really starts to think about their lives, they must ask themselves whether or not the impracticalities and disadvantages of following their own truth, outweigh their needs as an individual to define themselves according to what they think. For Socrates this question was answered emphatically:

> ....I have deliberately not lead a quiet life but have neglected what occupies most people: wealth, household affairs, the position of general or public orator or the other offices, the political clubs and factions that exist in the city? I thought myself too honest to survive if I occupied myself with those things. [14]

It is clear Socrates refused to renounce any part of his truth, but for some outsiders the situation is not clear cut. Some can never say their resolve to follow their truth is absolute; circumstances at times may compel some to go against what they would ideally prefer to do. This is quite understandable in the case of a person grappling with difficult circumstances in their lives. Yet, generally speaking, many outsiders' circumstances would have to be extremely desperate before they would consider 'biting the bullet'. In contrast, there are some people who like to portray themselves in this same light, but low and behold, as any mention is made of their pliability, the excuses come thick and fast. The pretexts seldom change from one generation to the next; all that appears to really change is the ease with which some people vindicate themselves - often through their own twisted reason.

Truth has almost become an unwanted commodity in today's world as outsiders find themselves increasingly disenchanted with it. Time and again, those around them prove themselves incapable of comprehending or matching their candid criteria. Hypocrisy has virtually become an acceptable and for some, it could be argued, necessary component of modern life. Many people seem to have bought into a fanciful idea that quality of life is dependent on the ease of a person's existence and that it does not make much difference how he or she conceives him or herself or how they embark on life, just as long as they choose the easiest route through it. This makes people ignorant of their real needs in life and some people always have that bemused look on their face when their lottery win fails to bring them that blissful happiness they had always dreamt of. These days some people have such a trite understanding of the human condition, they go through life completely unaware of the constituents they need to acquire a real sense of fulfilment in their lives. As Professor Herbert Marcuse explains, modern society has numerous means at its disposal to try and fill this ever expanding void:-

> We are again confronted with one of the most vexing aspects of advanced industrial civilisation: the national character of its irrationality. Its productivity and efficiency, its capacity to increase and spread comforts, to turn waste into need, and destruction into construction, to the extent to which this civilisation transforms the object world into an extension of man's mind and body makes the very notion of alienation questionable. [15]

Within modern society it is all too easy for people to become like everyone else and succumb to its whims and yet, outsiders will invariably reject this option. Many have already experienced trying to express their truth at certain stages in their lives, only to find themselves denounced as callow students of life whose ideals are derived from an immature conception of its complexities. People are naturally suspicious of outsiders, they are creatures which cannot be tamed or brought into submission. Even when they do attempt to express themselves frankly, it can be cynically perceived as part of some contrived plan to further some conceited underhand ambition. Those outsiders, who follow their mind's instincts, invariably live an impractical and wearisome life, but to many, the tribulations they face are incidental compared with their need to maintain who they truly are. These outsiders have ceased to weigh up the pros and cons of their situation in deciding how they express themselves; their truth is something real and definite which transcends any motive they may have for self-denial. The real outsider exists by what he or she thinks, and therefore must always maintain what they honestly believe. To do otherwise in the short term, would undoubtedly enhance their ability to be accepted within society. However, in the longer term this would be much more catastrophic, leaving them unable to define themselves as anything and rendering them incapable of attaching a meaning to their lives beyond their mere existence. In order for their lives to mean anything, they need to exist on their terms and as such must always uphold their freedom to do so.

# 8

# Freedom

**In its interference's with personal conduct it(society) is seldom thinking of anything but the enormity of acting or feeling differently from itself; and this standard of judgement, thinly disguised, is held up to mankind as the dictate of religion and philosophy by nine – tenths of all moralists and speculative writers.**

John Stuart Mill - *On Liberty* [1]

The concept of individual freedom is crucial to the way outsiders conceive themselves. In many ways, it shapes the nature of their relationship with the world. They believe freedom must be something tangible and capable of being applied if it is to have any real value. One of the central principles of existentialism is that outsiders ultimately choose who they are and what they become in life. Most do not accept they are limited in any way from thinking or doing whatever they set their mind to. They do not measure their freedom in terms of what society sanctions; it is much more than this. Their freedom encompasses their determination to preserve their uniqueness and independence as individuals who think for themselves without impediment or predisposition. This freedom also brings with it an acknowledgement that they alone are responsible for what they do in life.

Most outsiders are very conscious of their need to maintain their minds' freedom and their unique way of seeing life. As such, they are often averse to anything which might draw them into its conditioned sphere. This explains why they are often so indifferent to the usual demands and expectations placed upon them by others. In order for them to feel anything for themselves, they insist on having a total freedom of mind. They insist on being free to exercise their instincts, often striving towards gaining an authentic meaning in their lives which some will pursue with an unyielding determination. By holding themselves accountable for what they think and do, they refuse to rely on others doctrines, beliefs or prevailing attitudes to excuse themselves from acting contrary to their minds' instincts. Once they decide to do something their resolve to carry it through can be unrelenting, surprising those who try to anticipate to what lengths they might go to bring something about. Their need to maintain and apply their freedom can make them fiercely self-determined. Many will disregard the advice of anyone who tries to counsel them on what they can or cannot do in life, or on what their limitations might be.

In a world which contains so little meaning, outsiders exist within it as a blank canvas, untouched by the motives or partialities of others. All they really insist upon is the freedom to define themselves according to the way they think, and through their natural affinity to probe the substance and meaning of the world they are in. This explains why some are notorious for seeking new experiences in their lives. A few will always seek out the most unconventional challenges, often in areas they may be completely unfamiliar with, just to confirm their assertion that if their will is strong enough, they can do or overcome anything. They alone are responsible for authenticating their realism and this makes them aware of the fact, they often have to do something entirely different or go beyond what others strive for, in order to reach their mind's threshold for meaning. Most outsiders are not prepared to accept the nauseating alternative of watching their lives unfold, simply fulfilling the absurd routine of living an ordinary conventional life.

The extent to which sanctions are placed upon people's liberties within society has little or no bearing on how outsiders conceive their freedom. To many people, the word 'freedom' conjures up images of their neatly preserved rights within society, always there should they ever be bold enough one day to explore their extent. In the west people are often led to associate freedom exclusively with western democracies, as opposed to people living under a dictatorship or other political model - especially in less developed countries. In the western world many people are secure in their belief that their freedoms are extensive, compared with many other countries. Unfortunately, this assertion is rarely questioned by a growing number in western society, whose scope of freedom to do or say anything is rarely explored beyond its conventional remit.

In western democracies most people tend to envisage their freedom as something tangible, upheld and solidly protected by democratic principles and the rule of law (or constitution). In some people's mind, this well publicised assertion is sometimes all that is needed to add credibility to ambiguous political phrases such as 'defending our freedom' or defending 'our way of life'.[2] In recent times people have been fed these ambiguous and self-vindicating pronouncements, some even swallowing the notion that their freedom is somehow imminently under threat. As a result, swathes of the population have virtually been mesmerised into unconditionally endorsing dubious political decisions brought in under the cynical banner of safeguarding their liberties. Each year, more and more aspects of people's behaviour either become criminalised or branded as harmful and written into law. Many people appear to quietly concede to these sanctions on their behaviour, without realising that their culmination is creating an increasingly conditioned and namby-pamby society. These days, people's liberties in the western world are being abbreviated as quickly as the language used on social media. In many of today's advanced democratic societies, the claim that such huge freedoms are afforded to its citizens is often nothing more than a staged spectacle. It is a perception that is becoming easier to convince people of the more they allow themselves to be duped into believing their freedom is something real.

In truth, the greatest threat to people's liberties in the western world today does not come from any particular religion, ideology, nation or group, but from people's vulnerability to the forces which condition them. It seems more important for some people today to maintain the parody they are free, without ever envisaging the prospect of ever putting this hypothesis to the test. In contrast, outsiders are not prepared to regard their freedom as a dormant concept. They consider many others attitude towards their freedom like mariners who set out on voyages in centuries past, believing the world was flat and never daring to travel any distance into unknown waters, perpetually inhibited by the established notions of their contemporaries. Outsiders pride themselves on their will to think outside people's conventional mind-set. Their minds are at home in the vast open spaces where, like a naturally free animal, they can challenge or explore their instincts in life. They cherish their mind's freedom to form its own perceptions and apply its own reason, allowing them to exist as someone authentic. They do not have any grey areas, prioritising the notion of their freedom by resisting any coercive pressures or influence which may threaten their emancipated instincts. Within society today people do not seem to acknowledge that, in many cases, their freedom is effectively conditional upon thinking and acting in accordance with society's general propensities. If they really did try to 'go against the grain' and start testing the extent of their freedom, many would soon find themselves snagged and brought back into line. This can happen in a variety of ways, for instance, either through the inhibitions instilled in them by society, others consensual disapproval, or the application of some existing law.

The outsider's determination to maintain their freedom, and apply their own discretion within society, disturbs some people by its implication. Most outsiders pay little attention to conventional precepts or others usual modes of thinking or doing things and because of this, people often take exception to their dogged attitude. Some people even feel intimidated by the outsider because they feel powerless to influence, control, or sometimes anticipate what he or she might do next. Most outsiders think and act in a way which is separate from and has little or no regard for others partialities - which inevitably unnerves some people. In addition to this, they just do not fit into any of society's rigged out little roles; most would never entertain the prospect of condemning themselves to an existence governed by some extraneous influence. It is unsurprising, given their willingness to uphold their freedom and independence, they are often perceived as a potential threat to the normal and predictable way society functions. They are free individuals, unconstrained by any need to conform to or even recognise the perceived forces which often dictate the extent of others thoughts and behaviour.

In western society, people's concept of freedom is generally measured by their ability to make autonomous choices within the context of society's preferred needs as a whole. Most people are simply content to just mosey along through life, tempering their thoughts and instincts to ensure they remain within its perceived parameters. In exchange, they receive acceptance from the rest of society and reassurance of their unique place within it, while at the same time being closely bridled to its herd instinct. In contrast, outsiders often go to great lengths to maintain their conception of freedom, sometimes testing it in the most unconventional ways to confirm it to themselves. Some people look on the outsider as a dangerous customer and, it could be said, that society as a whole is not overly forthcoming to those who are not bound by a need to stalk its conventions. Modern society seems to be increasingly incapable of accommodating the single-minded individual, who perceives life differently to most others and decides for him or herself what is important, meaningful, or worth striving for.

The outsiders' insistence to preserve their freedom also implies an obligation upon them, to think and act in accordance with their own reason. Their thoughts and perceptions come to symbolise and define their existence and, as such, are stringently adhered to. Their freedom of mind gives them a certain boldness to think or do virtually anything, but this freedom is anchored to how they define what is meaningful. Their actions in life must be rationalised by them as individuals, rather than borrowed from society's self-indulgent banking house, on the proviso of getting away with paying back the lowest possible rate of interest. Everyone wants the best deal in life - unfortunately, some people seem to think the whole point of their existence is to simply get what they can out of it, by begrudgingly giving as little as possible in return. Nowadays, it is easy for some to forego any feeling of responsibility for what they do in life, by amalgamating their conscience with the self-vindicating mind-set of some religious, political or prevailing sentiment. It could be argued that society has much more to fear from itself than outsiders, who simply want to live their lives according to the way they perceive what is important in life and how they interpret meaning.

Some people's reluctance to realise the extent of their mind's potential freedom confounds outsiders. In their eyes, people behave as though they have been traumatised by some past experience, forcing them to live in their own shadow. It seems as if many people do not want to step out of their safe conventional circle, afraid that when their back is turned, the harsh reality of life will seep into their foxhole destroying the assurances of a world they have become used to accepting as real. Is this the elusive meaning of the phrase 'defending our freedom' and, if so, should it not be more accurately expressed as 'protecting our conditioned reality'? Outsiders despair as they see so many people taking their existence for granted, not even showing any compulsion to look beyond the immediacy of their everyday world. People's freedom in life is sometimes not only rendered redundant by their insular outlook, but also by the devices which condition them to follow society's conventions. This leaves the outsider wondering how some people can profess to be free by blindly following what everyone else says and does, whilst at the same time, modifying their thoughts to fit into society's increasingly contrived behavioural and social norms.

There are numerous ways in which the nature of contemporary society curtails people's liberties, many of which are subtle and unsuspecting. When people hear any mention of the terms such as being conditioned or indoctrinated, they immediately think of George Orwell's classic *Nineteen Eighty-Four* (1949). However, in the modern world people are conditioned in a whole host of ways, many of which are not always obvious or discernible. *Nineteen Eight-Four* revolves around the character Winston Smith, and how his naturally inquisitive mind starts to question the basis of a reality he has been conditioned to accept unreservedly. Orwell depicts a society which imposes its authority through excessively monitoring people's behaviour and indoctrinating them with its mandate. Control is exacted though rigorously screening people's thoughts and actions in accordance with a strict behavioural model. This is reinforced by their constant exposure to the highly cynical propaganda of Big Brother - *War is Peace, Freedom is Slavery, and Ignorance is Strength.*[3] In the book, people's constant exposure to this propaganda, compels them to think and behave in accordance with a contrived idealistic model. Unfortunately, even though most might consider these concepts completely alien to the way any free society functions, Orwell's work has ominous parallels with modern society in much more subtle ways.

On the face of it, *Nineteen Eighty-Four* appears to portray life within a totalitarian state; however, the concepts which emanate from it have much more relevance beyond this simple backdrop. Orwell's work highlights some of the key mechanisms used to control people's hearts and minds. In the book, people are constantly shown the image of a man who is declared as the perpetrator of all the evil that goes on in the world and indeed, anything which adversely affects their society. This figure becomes the focus of people's anger and hatred, and special times are even arranged for them to vent their fury towards this individual. Orwell describes the state of Oceania as being constantly at war with one of its two other super-powers. His inclusion of this scenario was intended to demonstrate how the idea of being at war induces fear and uncertainty; it disorientates people, making them more susceptible to embracing the discourse and proclamations of those charged with the task of protecting their supposed freedoms. His inclusion of a singular figure as a scapegoat for every unfortunate or tragic event, reflects how people's minds identify more easily on a singular person or face as a focus of hatred or blame - rather than some other entity, such as a group of people or a particular nation. These concepts may not be too unfamiliar with the world in which we live today and, some believe, such strategies have been applied to military interventions in recent years to manipulate public sentiment. It is true, that western powers (most notably Britain and the United States) have virtually been constantly engaged in some war or other over the last couple of decades. It is also evident, that in nearly every case, a figurehead has emerged to represent the evil wrongdoing. Sometimes these 'faces of evil' have done nothing more than to fall out of favour with the west by, for instance, inadvertently threatening its financial or geopolitical status quo.

In *Nineteen Eighty-Four*, Orwell depicts a society in which people are excessively monitored wherever they go and whatever they do; a concept which is not far from the world we live in today. There is an adage that says, 'you're never six feet away from a rat', which could almost be applied to today's CCTV cameras. These now cover virtually every public place where people conjugate. From their inception, these were brought in under the guise of safeguarding people. They are undoubtedly very effective in capturing a mugger stealing someone's handbag or wallet, but what about the person who looks a bit unkempt and simply wants to spend some time in a certain public place. In some high streets, these people are often approached within five minutes of being there, questioned about their motives and then asked to move on. It is as if anyone who does not appear to be shopping on a High Street has no reason or even right to be there. This has led to situations where the public have naturally become confused with who the police actually serve, for instance, when they remove people from public places simply at the request of the manager of some big chain store.

The ways in which people's individual freedoms are adversely affected within society are often diverse and extensive. The previous example is just one such instance, but it highlights a much wider issue with society today - the converging interests of the public and private sector. In some ways, the responsibilities of public bodies towards serving the people have become increasingly vague. The clear lines which used to define their responsibilities towards serving the public have become blurred. In some instances, a clear conflict of interest has emerged between some public bodies' duties and their support of private companies. With very few exceptions, the now compromised role of public bodies in facilitating the interests of the private sector, adversely affects the whole of society; a phenomenon which is particularly acute in the way public bodies collate and share people's personal information.

There is now an incredible amount of data gathered on people from CCTV cameras, the websites they visit, and ultimately down to what they spend their money on. The information gathered from monitoring people is not simply a means to capture real time events – this information is invariably stored and processed in some way. More worryingly, information is now increasingly compiled on virtually every aspect of people's lives, from their political partialities to their health needs. To some this may seem innocuous enough, and there are undoubtedly beneficial aspects to this too, for instance the ability to match services with people's preferred needs. But what happens when this information is used in a more underhand way, to deny people certain benefits like health insurance or financial services. The difference between Orwell's work and today's world, is that it is not only the state monitoring people and collecting information but also private companies and co-operations often working hand in hand to further their own interests.

One of the most worrying aspects in the collation of people's personal information today by government bodies, is that this information is sometimes readily available to any private company which bids high enough. This has led to the absurd circumstance where people's taxes fund the gathering of information, which is then sold on to the private sector, with the result that certain individuals or sectors of society often become disenfranchised in some way. Most people fully accept the needs of public bodies to gather certain information about people, which enables them to do things like targeting their resources more effectively. The real danger to people's individual liberties lies in: the way this information is compiled, who becomes privy to it, and the purposes for which this information is used or applied. In China, a person's political opinions and those of their friends have already become a component part of measuring someone's credit rating; in effect prejudicially rewarding people for being (in the governments eyes) 'model citizens'.[4] Even if people do turn a blind eye to the fact that the collection of certain information concerning them is often an unwarranted but necessary intrusion into their private lives; the more disconcerting aspect for them is how this information affects their capacity to be treated with equality, fairness and respect for them as free individuals.

There are other factors that pose a risk to people's freedoms which at first glance may not be clearly discernible to many. Today's media bombards the public with constant warnings of impending threats from a whole range of quarters, whether it is from other nations, terrorist organisations, or some other entity. It might not be overtly cynical to suggest that, apart from stating the obvious, the way in which these warnings are sometimes dressed up and relayed to the public at large may be achieving another more clandestine purpose. The frequent fluctuations in the levels of alert for potential terrorist attacks, not only ensures these threats are ever present in the public's psyche, but also keeps many people in a suspended state of fear.

Hardly a week goes by, in which new or existing threats from a whole range of things are not spluttered out by some politician or the media. Nothing seems to escape this constant frenzy to castigate things as potentially harmful or threatening.

If it is not the threat of harm from some terrorist group which grabs the headlines, it is the threat posed by the products we use, the food we eat, and even down to the way we live our lives; all of which is sometimes designated as possibly 'life threatening'. People are often given a focus to worry about something but, in addition to this, the way this information is relayed often generates an exaggerated anxiety amongst many. Even when there are no dispatches to report, the media often resorts to plucking out some obscure set of statistics, presenting them wholly out of context, and then labelling it as 'breaking news'. There is even a growing group of people, predominantly in the United States, who call themselves 'survivalists'. These people have an impending fear that some catastrophic event is going to befall humanity sometime soon, many of whose behaviour and attitude to life becomes focused in anticipation of it. The point is that the creation of a perceived threat from any quarter provides a catalyst for focusing people's attention, often making them much more reliant on the discourse of those responsible for safeguarding them - especially in a perceived crisis. All these things, in one way or another, ultimately narrow the scope and incentive for people to think rationally and act freely within society.

In *Brave New World* (1932), Aldous Huxley presented his vision of a conditioned future society. He described a society which had gone as far as it could in the context of its own utopia and, as a result, could go no further except through devising ways to make itself more efficient. Within this futuristic society, progress is reduced to the decadent concept of perpetually trying to perfect increasingly efficient means of production; a doctrine which some people may not be too unfamiliar with in today's world. Huxley describes a world where science has acquiesced to an insatiable demand for organisational efficiency, by cynically creating groups of genetically identical people who become suited to their particular function within it. It could be said, Huxley was merely portraying a more extreme instance of people being designed and conditioned to fulfil a particular role within society. In his futuristic vision, people have nothing really substantive to strive for anymore and, therefore, their only real satisfaction in life comes from inducing their ignorance of its reality. This is achieved through a readily available drug (ironically called 'soma'), which instantly alleviates people's anxieties and sends them into a blissfully happy subconscious state. The book contrasts this society with the world of a man who becomes known as Mr Savage, born naturally in a village outside this perfect world and who is wholly unfamiliar with this modern utopia. He is brought up freely, unconditioned by this highly advanced society, with his mind nurtured on the works of Shakespeare (considered subversive material in this society of the future). When he is introduced into this conditioned futuristic society, he terms it cynically as 'this Brave New World'.

Initially, Mr Savage is curiously attracted to this 'advanced' society, but his attitude soon turns to scorn. He responds very much like an outsider typically would, maintaining he would rather be free and unhappy with his own thoughts, than live a conditioned life trapped in a manufactured realism. He cannot understand how people within this futuristic utopia can profess to be happy by accepting a senseless life, sustained by a drug-induced form of escapism. He sees the functioning of this advanced society as a direct assault on what is constitutionally human, people's need for unique self-expression and their ability to think and feel things for themselves. Huxley's work shows the misconceived and doomed nature of a society where everyone believes themselves to be free but, as Mr Savage soon realises, are not free at all within its conditioned confines. Huxley's genius lay in his ability to anticipate and portray what might happen in the future if mankind continued to advance towards such a misguided technological utopia. He realised that human endeavour becomes superfluous once people are herded into narrow pens and provided with an illusion of needs which appear to be satisfied. In Huxley's depiction of this future society, progress can only be attained by constantly striving to improve the efficiency of everything it does. In terms of human enterprise, this insular doctrine has little chance of leading to any constructive or satisfying outcome in the long term. This also might explain why some people are so disillusioned with their lives today, especially in their working environment.

Huxley's vision of his 'Brave New World' may be much closer than we think. Some people are already beginning to wonder whether we have reached a dead-end; whether we have expended the ambit of our current capitalist and materialist ideologies. For instance, in most developed nations of the world today, there is little emphasis on sustainability and instead an increasing turnaround from the creation of something to its eventual waste, catering for an ever growing succession of needs and wants. In many ways, society seems to be increasingly chasing its tail, even within some of its more artistic undertakings. Arguably, the world's largest and most influential film industry, Hollywood, which should act as a major hub of creativity and originality, now produces increasing remakes either of previous films or through the reinvention of some bygone cartoon superhero. In many ways, it dare not create anything too new, radical or unique, where there is a risk it may not guarantee the same success without the buffering impact of the familiar. In turn, there seem to be more people now seeking to 'make it' in life, by buying their way into the dead-head market of familiarity or the latest craze.

In this day and age, originality often becomes the first casualty on some people's road to success. Much of what is produced these days is often tainted by its orientation towards generating revenue or enhancing someone or something's status. It appears some have become increasingly averse towards creating anything unique in its own right, capable of incorporating its own meaning. In many respects, capitalism as an ideology has proved itself a poor catalyst for supplying the more essential aspects of human needs. Modern literature is another point in question. Its popularity now increasingly relies on hitting some fashionable genre with light, easy to read page turners, rather than producing something with any depth or significance. The general public's insatiable demand for fast-paced simplistic thrillers, to hyped up celebrity biographies, demonstrates many people's immense appetite for effortless escapism. It seems perfectly normal to people today that much of the adult population should have read at least one Harry Potter book. And yet, some people are already feeling the effects of the immense void they have created in their lives as they allocate more and more of their time to finding ways to flee from its reality. In many ways, their view of life is tainted by the way they allow society to do their thinking for them and colour their perceptions. It could be argued that paradoxically, this comprises some people's conception of freedom in modern society - their ability to exercise their right not to be totally free or judge things for themselves. It could even be said people gain some comfort by being bound to each fad, fashion or role that society conditions or entices them to adopt. However, surely the whole concept of freedom becomes redundant when it is reduced to a mere abstraction.

The media has a significant influence, not only on the way people perceive their freedom, but also on their ability to appraise things objectively. Media protagonists always tend to play down its influential role, arguing that its remit is purely to respond to the demands of its audience for news or entertainment etc. However, over the years, the function of the media has been transformed into much more than just fulfilling this straight-forward role. For instance, in the last decade there has been a gradual shift in the way the media portrays what is going on in the world. News reports have become increasingly partial in the way they prioritise and present news to the public at large. In some instances, people are given an accommodating, insular, or even twisted view of events. This is especially prevalent when these events are linked to politically sensitive issues such as racial tensions within society or the uncomfortable truths which emerge from military interventions. It has become much easier to embed a particular perception in people's minds' today as, for many, their overexposure to a dumbed-down and increasingly biased media has blunted their ability to dissect fact from fiction. Nowadays, all it takes to induce people to believe an authentic connection exists between two things is for someone in authority to assert that this is the case.[5]

The media also has a powerful ability to detract people's attentions from the reality of certain situations often by focusing on bland uneventful themes, giving the impression that there is not much going on to report about in a particular region or part of the world. As the alternative to real news, people are often bombarded with stories of celebrity gossip or encouraged to revere witless sports stars, rather than people who have actually done something significant or meaningful in their lives. The disproportionate publicity afforded to the British Royal Family is a prime example. If their profile were based on what they had actually achieved by their own endeavour, then surely most people would not even be aware of their existence. It is hardly surprising that some people become so confused with what the media's role actually is. Its autonomy and willingness to go after the truth and report it as it is, has been gradually whittled away through increasingly agenda driven news reporting. This has principally come about through a corporate stranglehold on the media industry,[6] the affable nature of reporting to acquire first hand dispatches, and the increasing absence of any discerning or introspective media reporting. When people switch on the news today there is always that daunting prospect they will have to listen to some gormless celebrity telling them their opinions of what they think a piece of news actually means.

It is fortunate that there are individuals who are prepared to question, not only the way information is relayed to people in the west, but the actual truth or omission of truth which is fed to the general public. Two of the most prolific writers in this respect are John Pilger and Noam Chomsky, who have sought to expose this duplicity and consistently brought into question the validity and plausibility of the facts presented to people in the west by its media. The evidence they have uncovered has expounded an array of double standards and, in some cases blatant lies, which have served to cover up the true iniquities going on in the world - especially with regard to western governments foreign interventions both economically and militarily. Many of these interventions have been carried out under cynical blanket terms such as 'promoting democracy', 'protecting people's freedom', 'reconstruction' and even 'humanitarianism'. This flagrantly false propaganda must surely be ranked alongside Orwell's - 'Big Brother'. The deception works because so many of the media's less discerning, or shall we say more willing reporters, lap up this bogus jargon while 'joe public' is starved of the faculty to even imagine how callous or dispassionate the political arena of international relations actually is. People's compliant acceptance of their politicians uncorroborated justifications for decisions they make, destroys the whole function of a free democracy. In fact, democracy cannot claim to have any standing in a society where choice is determined, not by people's opinions, but by the forces which most effectively manipulate the views of an increasingly impressionable public. In *Culture of Terrorism*, Chomsky stated what he believes is the American Government's attitude towards its people:

> It is normal for the state to regard the domestic population as a major enemy, which must be excluded, repressed or controlled to serve elite interests. [7]

The actual extent of people's susceptibility to being influenced by their environment and the roles they adopt within society was brought to light during an experiment carried out at Stamford University in 1971.[8] The experiment was designed to simulate a prison environment, using eighteen students as volunteers to play the roles of guards and prisoners. One of the university's departments was fitted out to replicate a prison layout, with individual cells. The experiment was originally scheduled for two weeks, but after nine days the psychologists in charge were forced to abandon it. The reason given for this was the 'shocking behaviour' displayed by the students participating in the experiment. Over the nine days, each of the student's personalities had gradually, or in some cases dramatically, changed in accordance with their assigned role. During the experiment, those assigned to act as guards gradually increased their dominance and authority over those acting as prisoners by subjecting them to increasingly harsh punishments. Eventually, these punishments became so severe that the guards were in danger of doing real harm to those playing the role of prisoners - psychologists later described the guards' behaviour as 'sadistic'.

The effect the experiment had on those playing the role of prisoners was even more dramatic. Many of them showed signs of serious depression and extreme stress. The real effects of this simple experiment were brought home when it emerged that in a couple of cases, the student's realities' had shifted so much they no longer considered their circumstances as part of any experiment, but real. During this time, many of the volunteers acting as prisoners were completely unaware of the profound effect the experiment had on their personalities, which clearly demonstrates how susceptible people are to the conditioning factors their environment exposes them to. The experiment demonstrated how, in nine days, the characters of these students had been completely transformed through simple role play. The students were given an opportunity to watch the experiment afterwards and many found it difficult to believe the way they had behaved. This brings into question whether anyone is really conscious of how conditioned they are by the roles they adopt in life, or the profound effects this has on the way they behave and how objectively they perceive what is around them.

All outsiders are averse to adopting any role in life for its own sake or because someone else assumes or expects them to. It is not just that they lack any incentive to do so, but it flies in the face of everything they stand for as free individuals. In many organisations and particular job roles, employees are required to adorn themselves in a particular uniform, which in some cases changes their behaviour in accordance with what that uniform represents. This can obviously work in both ways, either having the effect of providing some people with a sense of authoritative empowerment, or enervating others through the bright orange overalls prisoners are made to wear in the United States while performing community service. Throughout history, people have demonstrated how easily they can be conditioned to give unflinching loyalty to a particular person, uniform or flag. This also explains why outsiders cherish their freedom of mind to remain aloof from such subterfuge.

Most outsiders are fiercely individual and are rarely swayed into becoming a part of anything on the back of others displays of unity or camaraderie. They are sometimes frowned upon for not joining in, what they often consider, as merely a charade. Yet, when they truly believe in a cause, they will sometimes go much further than most others to defend it. Most outsiders are not governed by, nor have much time for, the devices which are used to direct people's loyalties towards, for instance, a particular set of doctrines or beliefs. From an early age, people have it drummed into them to revere others ability to loyally carry out their duty or assigned role in life (at times without reservation), which on some occasions can be an honour well placed. Unfortunately, many of the levers used to encourage or compel people to adopt certain behaviours or attitudes are often conveniently portrayed as necessary prerequisites for the effective functioning or betterment of society as a whole. They are seldom revealed as callous devices for setting aside people's scruples, in order to acquire their unreserved obedience to an often inept system of taboos.

Outsiders will always seek to preserve and uphold their freedom, which often extends beyond their own personal circumstances. They find it nauseating having to witness other people being stifled in their ability to be themselves or to think freely. They often see things in a black and white way, and therefore believe everyone has an equal right to be free and treated fairly, regardless of where they come from or what their background might be; their judgement is not usually influenced by others conventions, protocol, or prejudice. Should a homeless person, who seeks to join a local Golf Club, be treated or considered different from anyone else? Virtually all outsiders would consider it absurd to prejudge anyone on the basis of factors such as the way they dress, speak, or whatever their cultural or national identity might be. Most outsiders do not generally believe that deep down there is any real difference between the people of the world and what their fundamental needs are in life, apart from maybe their particular customary habits which have naturally been instilled from a young age. There are many factors within society which exacerbate the notion of people's differentiation, obscuring people's ability to appraise others in an equal light. The biased way society is sometimes structured and the prejudicial attitudes within it usually do not feature in the way most outsiders' form their perceptions.

People's ability to perceive things objectively, is usually undone by their unwillingness to freely weigh up what they think for themselves. For some people, the bigger picture becomes inconsequential to the immediacy of their daily lives. The important aspects for these people are things which have a potential or direct impact on their lives. This is typified by the insular focus of local newspapers, which are often written under a presumption, that the particular area they cover and the events which they report on represent an important microcosm in what is actually going in the country as a whole. Outsiders find it difficult to appreciate some people's naïve self-absorbed attitudes within society. They tend to look to the wider implications of things and firmly believe in judging things equally and impartially, regardless of where they happen to occur or to whom. This is why most outsiders could never be duped into joining any movement or patriotic frenzy which, they often believe, simply exists to distort people's ability to regard others objectively. The most fervent patriots are sometimes people who feel they need others camaraderie or collective accomplishments in their lives, as a way of drawing attention from their own lack of personal achievement. It is very convenient for some people to latch onto patriotism's bandwagon by buying into an inflated sense of pride, based upon the circumstance they happen to come from a particular geographical area, speak a common language, or revere the same flag.

Most outsiders do not concern themselves with people's petty prejudices in life. They do not believe there is, or should ever be, any real distinction between people merely because of who they are or what their circumstances might be. It is curious, that some outsiders also appear to have a natural affinity towards people from other cultural backgrounds, especially those which are generally considered as less sophisticated. It is not particularly surprising they are often attracted by the cultural simplicity of people from less developed regions of the world, as for the outsider, these are untouched by the contradictions and irreconcilable aspects a modern existence usually gives rise to. A few even feel an affinity with cultures where people's lives are not complicated by the demands, expectations and paradoxical nature of contemporary society. Some find themselves naturally drawn to communities in which people live straightforward lives with simple basic needs and clearly defined values; untainted by the inescapable irrationality of the modern world. The endless demand for new things and fast pace of life, which in many ways defines modern western society, sometimes inhibits people's ability to appreciate their substantive needs or to see things for what they really are. Unfortunately, many people are now so conditioned to their 'million mile an hour' lifestyles, they have ceased believing in the possibility their lives could pan out any other way.

In 1754 Jean-Jacques Rousseau wrote *Discourse on the Origin of Inequality*, in which he expounded the idea that simple indigenous tribes in remote islands he visited, were in his view, more content, and living much happier lives, than people striving for cultural and economic sophistication in the west. It is invariably presumed that people in the west are the ones who are further down the developed road. And yet, hardly anyone dares entertain the idea that potentially, western ideologies and the doctrines which underpin it, may not incorporate the best constituents to satisfy people's more essential needs for a happy and fulfilled life. It could even be argued that western concepts such as the need for ever increasing economic growth, the commercialisation of people's needs, and their escalating consumption and waste, may be leading civilisation to some sort of impasse. The promotion of western style democracies throughout the world is often hailed by people in the west as a step towards making the world a better place. In the minds' of the western masses, there is often no better alternative for any nation than to embrace western style political and ethical values. However, in some instances, all that is really being embraced by the countries who sign up to this are elements of western supremacy worded in conveniently vindicating political spiel. Western political proponents have yet to come up with a plausible reason why so many up and coming developing countries, which have embraced western doctrines and thereby received the generous assistance of the World Bank, have become so impoverished as a result. Unfortunately these days, some things are never questioned in their proper context. Furthermore, a growing number of people appear to be drawing their inference from the plethora of childish dogma, either advanced by disingenuous politicians or the celebrities of their day.

Within any society it is only natural for certain stigmas and stereotypes to develop; it is often the way some people make sense of the world around them, grouping people or things into convenient compartments. For some, this need for compartmentalisation can override their appetite for an entirely accurate appraisal - the outsider sometimes being a prime candidate. Some people's need to pigeonhole other individuals or groups, such as outsiders, gives them some assurance through being able to place others in a particular category. However, as far as some existentialists are concerned, this stigmatisation can actually augment their freedom. Their erroneous appraisal by others often makes their links with society all the more tenuous, enhancing their freedom as they in turn feel much less inclined to take heed of or even acknowledge others expectations or protocol. However, outsiders must be aware that any detachment from society can also have potentially adverse effects on their state of mind. In some cases the alienation accompanying it, in terms of their total lack of socialisation, can result in some individuals developing an irrational perspective or even some kind of antipathy towards the people or circumstances around them. People are (to all intents and purposes) social animals and everyone requires at least some interaction with the society they are in.

In many respects, the way outsiders conceive their freedom means they are only really bound by the laws of whatever land they reside in, as Camus explains:

> The only conception of freedom I can have is that of a prisoner or the individual in the midst of the State. The only one I know is freedom of thought and action. [9]

To a few outsiders even laws become incidental when pitched against their need act upon something they truly believe in. Their insistence to maintain and respect theirs and others unfettered freedoms against the instruments which exist in society to curtail people's liberties, inevitably causes friction. It can present a massive dilemma for a few, who may believe in their own mind, they are justified in carrying through something they have resolved to do, while the law and its failure to account for such circumstances or through its expedient origination, places some sanction on their actions or even makes them illegal. And yet, some outsiders will tend to choose their own truth above any impracticality or sanction society or even the law imposes. Therefore, the question of whether society or the law deems an action permissible or not, sometimes has little or no influence on some outsiders whose existence must be based on their own veracity to mean anything.

This single-minded determination which compels some individuals to remain true to themselves was epitomised in Socrates' trial. In his case, the law and the consequences it threatened made absolutely no difference to what he thought or how he chose to conduct himself. His truth came first, above any requirement to make himself amenable to escape, in his instance, the law's sweeping application. In the same vein, outsiders refuse to relinquish their freedom to be who they are, often regardless of the repercussions to themselves or their own personal circumstances. They do not set out with any intention to break or act contrary to any law and accept they alone are responsible for what they do in life. Many of the laws governing people's freedoms often originate from a need to appease the partialities of whatever the majority believes is right or wrong at a certain point in time; with a fair number simply construed to facilitate the law's practical implementation. It is laws such as these which tend to conflict with some outsider's needs to adhere to their instinct to maintain their truth and sense of rectitude. Society should not fear this revelation as the end never justifies the means for the true outsider. Therefore, they are unlikely to carry out any action which conflicts with their notions of individual freedom or which they cannot reconcile in their own mind.

It is easy for some to classify outsiders as being aloof from the rest of society, not caring less what happens around them. But, in actual fact, many outsiders do aspire to have some influence over their lives and the things that happen to them and even to others. The problem is that some outsiders become increasingly frustrated with their impotence to affect any change or control over their lives in a broader sense. Some feel as though they should be doing something to wake society from its deep irrational sleep, but as soon as they take steps towards trying to offset life with their own perceptions, they soon encounter an insurmountable inertia. It does not help sometimes when their frustration and despair boil over, leading some outsiders to choose the most controversial and contentious route in their desperation to make people realise a particular set of circumstances from their perspective. The way many outsiders envisage change and the robust way they believe it needs to be implemented, conflicts with the rather slow subtle and often indirect change that most people, and society as a whole, are usually accustomed to. A few outsiders tend to believe the objectiveness generated by their emotional impartiality gives them some sort of implied right to dispense with the wishes, opinions or even rights of other individuals in choosing a way to remedy society's oversights or other issues concerning people. However, this attitude sets a highly dangerous precedent in society, and is akin to someone in an influential position who makes decisions based on their own self-interests which adversely affect others.

To some outsiders, the idea of trying to change a particular set of circumstances (even sometimes through whatever means) which they may have justified in terms of a wider, or longer term benefit to society as a whole, can appear quite appealing. However, anyone who assumes a right to decide things for other people, or who tries to bring about change through the causation of detriment or harm to others, could never make any truly beneficial contribution to society's future; this not only endorses future change happening in this way, but also sets a precedent for it. Many outsiders refuse to resort to the means which most others accept in order to initiate change, unless they can rationalise and justify these means for themselves. Their objectiveness often renders their reliance on others benchmarks as out of the question. This would not only mar the way they define themselves, but would also promote such actions for anyone who decided they wanted to change something by the same means. A prime example of this contrived logic was the way the Baader-Meinhof Group allied themselves with J P Sartre's works in their attempt to use the principles of existentialism to justify their terrorist activities. The Baader-Meinhof Group originated in Germany in the 1970's.[10] They attempted to link their ideals with existentialism, believing their cause justified a carte blanche approach to use whatever means they deemed necessary to bring about their objectives. This skewed interpretation of existentialism was simply a means by which they could excuse themselves from the deliberate targeting of civilians, in an attempt to justify it in terms of advancing a greater cause. However, whilst there may be some who obscure the underlying principles of existentialism to justify their own ends, most outsiders would never countenance such an interpretation.

The way or means outsiders choose to bring something about is as, if not more important to them, than the end result. In effect, the unbridled freedom through which they define who they are also carries with it a responsibility to apply this freedom according to how they judge what is right or justified. Their need to authenticate their existence and create meaning in their lives implies a wider responsibility, not to use their freedom of mind to assume their unique insight or perspective grants them a licence to do what they want to bring about a desired end. This was the theme of Dostoyevsky's *Crime and Punishment*, which demonstrates how conscience plays an important role in present and past actions, even amongst outsiders. The main character Raskalnikoff, assumed his dire situation gave him an implied right to use whatever measures necessary to change his circumstances. He had justified the old lady's death in his own mind before carrying it out, seeing her as a worthless parasite who fed on other people's misfortune. It was only after committing the murder that Raskalnikoff found he could not entirely 'step over' the ramifications of his actions. He had the ability to plan and act totally without sentiment or feeling for another's life, but the practice of his theory was undone by his tormented conscience. This demonstrates that all existentialists are to some extent bound by the basic laws of human nature.

In terms of the way outsiders think, they could be described as the most liberated within society. Their resolve to be themselves without any inclination to placate anyone else, qualifies their freedom as something real. They are not only fiercely determined to uphold and defend their own freedom, but will often be prepared to make a stand when they encounter other people's freedoms being adversely compromised. From their own experience, many have a natural empathy towards anyone who feels their rights or liberties have been eclipsed by society in some way. They usually often do not accept the arguments put forward which promote society's need to impose its doctrines or ideologies on others to legitimize itself. This often makes them highly sceptical and critical of any authoritative body or the instruments it, or anyone else, employ within society which seek to control, repress or condition people. Any system whose existence is dependent upon a requirement to limit people's freedom or indoctrinate them to any significant degree, merely advertises the spurious foundations underpinning it. Some outsiders even cringe at the methods some individuals and institutions resort to in order to repress people's freedom; usually carried through with the assertion they are purportedly furthering people's overall needs in some way.

There are some prominent existentialists who, over the years, have stood up against oppressive regimes or authority which have sought to deprive people of their freedoms. As mentioned previously, these include people such as: Sartre, Camus and Lawrence. However, in the western world today, the extreme circumstances required to fire outsiders into action and respond in some way against the erosion of people's freedoms has in some respects been nullified. In today's world where more and more people simply acquiesce to the forces which condition them, it could be questioned, who are outsiders really standing up for by taking on the mantle of trying to preserve people's freedoms? With a little scaremongering, public opinion can now be twisted to endorse virtually any law which people are led to believe protects them within society, sometimes with hardly a qualm for the repercussions or liberties they surrender. Outsiders are sometimes left wondering, whether they are the only ones who appreciate the real value and need for people to exercise their freedom in the functioning of a progressive society. It seems some people these days are simply unfazed by the erosion of their liberties within society, and do not really aspire to much beyond a conventional existence where their lives are mapped out before them. It could be said that today's society has become the barometer of subtle conditioning, as we enter a new era ushered in by the 'sheep like' people of our time.

In some ways this new era has already has arrived. Over the last few years there have been significant changes in the methods employed by the commercial sector, the media, and authoritative bodies to influence people's sentiments and opinions. Probably the most notable in this respect, has occurred in the advertising industry and the strategies it now employs to generate mass appeal. These days there is no requirement for advertisements to be creative, original, or even canny. Their form, delivery, and overall impact are, in many ways, achieved through indirectly appealing to people's subconscious. The objectives of media advertising have shifted away from when they once sought to create something artful or distinct, and now rely on increasingly simplistic and familiar concepts (often promoting Brand Identity) which have more chance of circumventing the mind's conscious filter. This technique becomes much easier to effect in any society where people are less inclined to properly appraise what they see and hear. It is also typified by the types of programmes fed to the public by today's media moguls. Viewers' ratings have become the ultimate measure of any programme or channels success. The emphasis no longer seems to be on creating something of quality, but upon a programme's ability to generate mass appeal in which no-one dares risk creating anything too clever or original today, just in case it proves too rich for people's bland appetite. To some extent, originality in film and television have now been reduced to the art of providing people with cheap thrills, the chance to watch the perpetual reinvention of characters or stories of yesteryear, or an opportunity to gore fantastically at the new and inventive ways they can be shocked by the content of what they see and hear.

When people are not being 'entertained' by the graphic scenes or emotional outpouring on TV, or through the telegraphed plots which are so typical of storylines produced today, they are usually being drawn into the brain drain world of the soap opera. Within these dramas, changes in the story become as easy to anticipate as an MP's response to a leading question. Contemporary soap operas seem to be designed to make people switch off completely while they watch the childlike plot unfold. Everything has its place in today's predictable world of familiarity as it strives towards its apparent utopia; a world where aspiring to mediocrity has already become the new religion. Once a society reaches a stage where it becomes a derivative of its media influence (and some would argue this is already the reality in the United States), the need for deceptive conditioning is reduced, the susceptibility of that society to its conditioning forces is enhanced, and the opportunities for any real original thought penetrating the resulting pseudo-reality becoming an ever more distant prospect. Those who work themselves into a frenzy with each media fad as it comes along usually lose all sense of how distorted their realism actually is. This explains why some outsiders close themselves off from what they see as the constant drivel around them and why they choose not to entertain themselves with, or expose themselves to, the content of today's media.

Outsiders are creatures which cherish their freedom of mind and as such can never be domesticated. Their needs in life revolve around their ability to maintain their mind's freedom to define its own existence; beyond this, there is little else that makes much sense. Socrates' case provides a good example of this. He believed that even though he had been wrongly accused and unjustly sentenced, he could not take the advice of his friend Crito and flee his cell before his impending death:

> Socrates: Look at it this way. If, as we were planning to run away from
> here, or whatever one should call it, the laws of the state came and
> confronted us and asked: 'Tell me, Socrates, what are you intending to
> do? Do you not by this action you are attempting intend to destroy us,
> the laws, and indeed the whole city, as far as you are concerned? Or
> do you think it possible for a city not to be destroyed of the verdicts of
> its courts have no force but are nullified and set at naught by private
> individuals?' What shall we answer to this and other such arguments?
> For many things could be said, especially by an orator on behalf of this
> law we are destroying, which orders that the judgements of the courts
> shall be carried out. [11]

Even when Socrates was given the chance to escape he refused,
placing his truth and reason above his concerns for his own life.
Socrates' freedom (like that of the outsider) was in following his
mind's judgement and this is where the real freedom of the outsider
lies. It is not reliant on an apparent perception of freedom, but
represents their assurance to conduct themselves according to their
own truth; transcending the doctrines which constrain most others to
society's persuasive mould. It furnishes them with a unique ability to
think and act according to their instincts and reason, such as in
Socrates' case where, contrary to what anyone else would have done,
he chose to reject the opportunity to save himself. The culmination of
pressures modern society exerts on outsiders compels them to
become individuals with an inherent need to be free to maintain who
they truly are; to be anything but themselves is pointless. They are
not inclined to accept anything unless it has been through their
mind's foundry, which seeks out the substance in everything they see
and touch. These factors make outsiders staunchly independent in all
that they think and do, which in turn enables them to define
themselves as truly free individuals.

# 9

# The Individual

"The worth of a state in the long run, is the worth of the individuals comprising it; and a state which postpones the interest of their mental expansion and elevation to a little more of administrative skill, or of that semblance of it which practice gives in detach of business; a state which dwarfs its men, in order that they may be more docile instruments in its hands even for beneficial purposes – will find that with small men no great thing can really be accomplished; and that the perfection of machinery to which it has sacrificed everything will in the end avail it nothing, for want of the vital power which, in order that the machine might work more smoothly it has preferred to banish."

John Stuart Mill - *On Liberty* [1]

It is clear the unique traits outsiders possess make them stand out from the rest of society. Their compulsion to adhere to their existential instincts makes them wholly unsuited to the format of modern life. It seems inconceivable that the basic human qualities of preserving the mind's freedom, seeking out a more substantive meaning to life, or following through something a person may passionately believe in, have become so incompatible in respect of the way society functions today. In many respects, the outsider's place in the world forces them to exist as distinct entities, individuals who decide things for themselves and independently from society's sphere of influence. Contemporary life is much more tailored to those who obediently stick to society's garden path, usually aspiring to embrace the most opportune or conventional roles they happen to stumble across. The biggest rewards for anyone wishing to make anything of themselves in life(in the way most people are led to quantify success), are generally reserved for those who demonstrate their willingness and flexibility to taper their individual volition to suit some predetermined role. Contrastingly, most outsiders cannot abide the false milieu which transpires when people set aside their scruples and follow others collective whims, or when they simply affirm society's taboos. Like children in nursery school, people nowadays get the greatest plaudit from reproducing and copying the set patterns of their contemporaries; sometimes without a qualm for the type of person they become or the type of society they engender.

It is amazing how easily some people today can just switch themselves off from anything outside their narrowed realism. Some people's lives unfold as if they were writing their autobiography in advance, where they have already decided what to put in or leave out of the next Chapter. As a result, their realism becomes obscured by the way they dodge the realities around them, existing in a contrived world where their perspective is built upon layers of preselected criteria. These people's skewed reality makes them much less inclined to project themselves as individuals in life or act on their own initiative. Some even become convinced it is somehow beyond them to be or do something truly original which has not been conceived previously; an attitude which is all too prevalent in the transient and unoriginal creativity which underpins much of the fabric of society today. There seems to be increasing numbers of people who now shamelessly aspire to the banality of everyday life, as if it were some sort of ideal. The instances where people, especially the younger generation, demonstrate a willingness and determination to choose careers based upon their ideals or things they may be passionate about is fast becoming a thing of the past. There seems to be no place any more for the romantic, idealistic lifeblood of the human spirit. Instead, career paths are nowadays often decided on the vain basis of salary increments, pension plans, job stability and usually a host of other fringe benefits often leading to a facile, conventional but, at the same time, wholly uninspiring existence.

There are now an increasing multitude who appear to pride themselves on becoming archetypal run-of-the-mill people, often indulging themselves on a cocktail of ignorance and indifference to sustain their conditioned notion of a happy life. It is profoundly worrying that some people even consider attaining this state of being as some personal milestone, with even more people apparently unashamed of the fact. Yet, what is even more absurd is that those who adopt this middling philosophy to life, are usually the ones hailed for being the most shrewdest or most discerning within society. While those who often doggedly pursue an enterprise which may bring some meaning into their lives, often get branded as being obtuse or denounced for having their 'head in the clouds'. People often coin the phrase 'Rome was not built in a day' but, if today's society had existed in ancient times, it could be argued whether the thought of actually building Rome would have been conceived in the first place. In fact, it might not be too cynical to suggest that society's design engenders people's spiritless attitude to life, making them less likely to think or do things outside its established mind-set. This often leaves some outsiders wondering how many real individuals there are left in the world. No-one seems to have considered who society will turn to for its creative inspiration when it finally achieves its 'utopia' of producing a perfectly tame tractable population. What, if anything, will people actually achieve when their domestication to conventional precepts becomes so acute, they may one day render themselves incapable of imagining or initiating anything truly unique or original?

Paradoxically, some claim it is outsiders who really lack any gumption in life. They believe it is outsiders who have resigned themselves most to society's scheme of things, through their detached attitude and indifference towards it. However, it may be foolish to infer too much from the outsider's overt passivity, which often belies the fact that they, as individuals, are sometimes the most disaffected with life as it is. It must also be borne in mind that many outsiders often harbour a profound willingness to change society in some way - usually stemming from their need to bring it in line with their own perceptions and what they value or regard as meaningful. Ralph Ellison's *Invisible Man* contains a passage which exemplifies someone who truly resigns himself to society's status quo. The book describes the tribulations of a nameless black man who struggles against the prejudicial racist attitudes of 1940's America. His will to become visible within society is constantly eclipsed by the self-perpetuating and bigoted attitudes around him. His school principal, who is also a black person like himself, tells him:

> 'You're nobody, son. You don't exist – can't you see that? The white folk tell everybody what to think – except men like me. I tell them; that's my life, telling white folk how to think about the things I know about. Shocks you, doesn't it? Well, that's the way it is. It's a nasty deal and I don't always like it myself. But you listen to me: I didn't make it, and I know that I can't change it. But I've made my place in it and I'll have every Negro in the country hanging on tree limbs by morning if it means staying where I am.' [2]

The irony of this passage is that his school principal actually believes he has achieved something in his life, through the esteem and responsibility his role affords him. He believes he can respect himself, even though his role amounts to appeasing white supremacist attitudes instilled in him through incentives to enhance his own meagre niche of authority. His attitude reflects the attitude of a growing number of people today, who manufacture respect for themselves by applying the increasingly contrived logic being banded around. Within society, people are supplied with all kinds of spurious reasoning as a pretext for doing its bidding and consequently, it is hard for the outsider to credit some as being substantive or even to envisage them as real people. Many outsiders are naturally drawn to people who, like themselves, are sincerely driven by a need to equate what they instinctively believe in to the way they think and conduct themselves. Unfortunately, from their perspective, more and more people appear to behave like lemmings constantly flipping from one fruitless fad to another, while acquiescing to virtually every-thing imposed upon them, from adopting each new bureaucratic stipulation to developing an exaggerated fear of saying or doing anything which may offend anyone.

Outsiders usually cannot accept life as authentic. They find it difficult to be optimistic, it often lacks the scope and gravity for them to accept most things seriously. This saps their willingness to bind to or achieve anything within it in the usual way. This explains why many feel as though they are suspended in a state of flux, with only the vain hope that one day they might discover an aspiration they can apply their frustrated energies to. They are fully aware their penetrating scrutiny of life makes them poor candidates for finding a purposeful motive within it like anyone else, through mastering its successive pseudo games. This renders their relationship with society like a climber trying unsuccessfully to ascend a rock-face, whose form keeps breaking away under their mind's grasp. Despite this, outsiders are rarely deterred by this realisation. Their principle needs revolve around their responsibility to be the person they are, to express themselves plainly and simply in accordance with what they think. They place their autonomy as individuals above anything else and at least derive some meaning in life through being themselves, regardless of what ensues or what counsel they receive to the contrary.

In today's world, people's ability to exist as true individuals is often overshadowed by the forces which shape and bind society together. Individuality is often discounted as a viable component in any society which continually seeks to enhance its proficiency in accommodating the majority's needs. This has translated into much less diversity in the way people think and behave. It could be said people are becoming more mainstream and even standardised in their outlook and opinions. Their impetus as individuals to do something different, or seek to change something which may be considered out of the ordinary or radical is often undermined, by the constantly reinforced notion of society's unimpeachable design. It is sad that there are people today who dare not imagine their needs will encompass anything beyond what a conventional existence has to offer. Society's betterment is often promoted through the idea it is continually enhancing its ability to incorporate an increasing plethora of needs and opinions. However, in many instances, the opposite appears to be the case with a greater emphasis these days on 'shooting the messenger',[3] dressing people in the straightjacket of political correctness, or criminalising the expression of an increasing range of opinions.[4] What is left, is a society where people are afraid of saying the wrong thing and usually end up saying nothing at all. This ethos is reinforced by the way society seems to propel itself forward, rearing an increasingly tractable, and in some respects, docile population. It has no answer or remedy for those who find themselves trapped by the realisation of life's increasing existential vacuum, who expect more from it than repeating the heedless patterns of their contemporaries. Is society so short-sighted that it is unaware of the dire consequences which ensue once people's individual volition is dissipated into some collective and anonymous mass will? Do people really want to live in a society where their conditioning to collectivist doctrines, renders them incapable of having any real influence over what it does or what calamities it sleepwalks into along the way?

There seems to be little evidence people in general learn any real lessons from society's mistakes. More alarmingly, some people seem more inclined these days to pick and choose what they consider or even acknowledge as being an oversight. Quick-fix solutions and a failure to recognise the simple realities of situations, is now a prevalent facet of modern life. It appears across the board people are demonstrating a growing lack of foresight and common sense in their ability to address or even appraise things for themselves. It could be said that some people have become so conditioned in their behaviour they have almost lost their ability to reason through certain eventualities or even simple scenarios. To compound this, there is a much more dangerous precedent being set where people selectively choose which views or opinions to acknowledge, often for no other reason than to reinforce their own contrived perceptions. From this 'pick and mix', some simply choose what tastes best at the time or the flavours they are most familiar with, usually leaving contrasting or less acknowledged opinions and anything else hard to swallow on the shelf. Outsiders feel naturally stifled by this state of affairs, which draws its impetus from people's confidence in collective in-fallibility, and the way they are discouraged from appraising things independently and applying any impartial or critical judgement.

Socrates' experiences testify how prejudicial a society can be towards the individual. He was denounced by a group of people who decided that something had to be done about this individual, whose argument and blunt reasoning proved itself too great an adversary for Athenian dogma. Pericles had earlier advanced his vision of a better society, through the notion of the democratic ideal.[5] It was probably inevitable, sooner or later, some people in this early democratic society would feel threatened enough by Socrates' arguments to accuse him of corrupting young minds and failing to worship the God's of the city. An equivalent charge today could probably be brought under the current anti-social behaviour legislation.[6] However, the fact is that Socrates, far from being a seditious radical, was someone whose instincts compelled him to scrutinise life for himself before he felt he could add any credibility to it. Like the outsider, his reason would not allow him to blindly accept other people's assertions. He had to weigh up what people said against his own perceptions. Socrates unwittingly threatened the infallible concept of this early democratic ideal, and it could be said that his fate was sealed by his insistence to rationalise other people's accepted conventions with his own truth.

Pericles' democratic ideal has survived as a model for successive civilisations from Athens to the present day. However, it also sets a dangerous precedent to presume that because a majority within any society believe something to be true or hold a particular point of view, this should override people's individual rights or the rights of certain groups within it. When applied across the board, the presumption of democratic legitimacy can be extremely detrimental to any individual or section of society when implemented without due regard for others basic freedoms. This is not only a facet people should solely identify with less developed countries - there are plenty of examples of arbitrary and draconian legislation being enacted in many advanced democracies of the world today. The sanctimonious attitudes present in some backwater American states and the extreme and fanatical religious doctrines emanating from the Middle East and elsewhere, typifies how people's intolerance adversely affects individuals or groups within society. Without the buffer of vociferous scrutiny and lack of independent opinions, society has little to stop itself from becoming increasingly irrational and bigoted in its attitude.

Any society, which becomes too impressionable to or shaped by its conditioning influences, does not often incorporate much within it to incentivise people to behave as individuals or rationalise things for themselves. As a result, there is usually much less argument, opinion and even imagination generated to temper people's more extreme opinions. In many ways, those who are more conditioned within society are often more prone to becoming intolerant or adopting an irrational point of view based upon the whims of others. Within any conditioned society, people are not only more pliable, but also more likely to follow someone whose views are more extreme as they run out of ideas to address society's predicaments or see the bigger picture. The hopeless inability of the political class to connect with people in recent times has exacerbated this phenomenon. Reams of legislation and endless political policies are sometimes not the answer to dealing with some of the complex issues which exist in modern society today. As political measures often prove themselves short sighted or ineffective, and as more people feel dispossessed of any real voice, they naturally look to other more desperate means for a solution. It is in these circumstances that certain individuals or particular sectors of society can often find themselves marginalised at the mercy of others conceit. Furthermore, the more people become partial to the prevailing attitudes or prejudice within their society, the more difficult and precarious it becomes for any person who stands out as a distinct individual to uphold their rights and freedoms within it.

In any discussion of illiberal attitudes, the effects of political duplicity cannot be ignored. In fact, some of the intolerance within society today has been unwittingly nurtured by politicians themselves. This is not only due to their failure to properly address issues which concern the public at large, but also the way some encourage prejudicial attitudes through headline grabbing policies such as 'anti-social behaviour orders' and other consummate legislation; cynically advertised as measures which empower people, but which inevitably serve as divisive labels within society. Sometimes it does not matter whether someone's behaviour harms or affects anyone else, just as long as enough people or politicians take exception to it. In some states in America people have taken this to its extreme, self-righteously endorsing blatantly bigoted and even draconian laws designed to limit the freedoms of certain sectors or individuals within society. And yet, the most absurd aspect of this is that it is the United States, which brazenly promotes itself as the beacon of freedom throughout the world and the staunch defender of its citizens' *inalienable rights*!

Throughout history, countless episodes have recorded the plight of individuals who sought to express opinions or do something which others, due to their existing attitude, prejudice or superstition, disagreed with. Many of these people found themselves condemned on little more than the majority's partiality. History is littered with accounts of persecution and repression of individuals who entertained or tried to advance views which were not in accord with, or did not endorse, the preferred trends of the day. Much worse than this are the accounts of wholesale murder, either in the case of individuals or certain sectors of society, merely because they were in the minority or because they held conflicting opinions or beliefs. In most advanced democracies, extreme instances of oppression are not usually considered as being the norm and indeed, would probably not be tolerated on any mass scale; however the ethos of control is still prevalent, but pursued by much more refined, unobtrusive and often less obvious means. Within many democracies today, public opinion is usually considered as an instrument of power which needs to be guided, coaxed along and even manipulated, in order to calibrate it with the perceptions those in authority wish to advance. The methods through which this conditioning is exacted, is at times so subtle, it tends to go unnoticed. For instance, there are a whole range of strategies now employed to match public opinion to particular political persuasions, which are often designed to slip under people's radar. The effectiveness of these strategies has been greatly enhanced in recent years by the use of teams of 'spin doctors', often in collusion with our 'independent' media.[7]

It is easy to see why outsiders value their uniqueness as individuals. A few have no qualms about voicing what they truly think of society as a whole or people's conditioned behaviour within it, which sometimes leads some to label them as misanthropists. However, these outsiders' critique of people or society does not stem from any unreasonably nurtured antipathy towards others. Its real source, is derived from the consequences they see for individuals and society, as people become increasingly impressionable to, and conditioned by, the influences around them. Many outsiders despair with society's format, which tends to scupper theirs and other people's will to think and act according to their own reason or grasp of life. It is as if society has adopted the principles of some social mass production model for its future progression. Is society on the verge of an industrial revolution-style standardisation of people, as the interest of facilitating its smooth function, overrides its need to respect people's individual autonomy and their right to self-determination? If we are indeed witnessing this as a product of our age, then surely society is going backwards with the adoption of a model which bears more resemblance to some ant-like subspecies, than an inclusive society of freethinking individuals capable of contributing to society's vibrancy and diversity? Does not the advent of greater control within society eventually engender a more tractable and compliant populous? Should not society, given its presumed advanced status, be encouraging greater self-expression and incorporating more individualism as an extension of humanity? This is surely imperative, if it is to properly and legitimately advance itself from the broadest array of ideas and opinions.

> The human faculties of perception, judgement, discriminative feeling, mental activity, and even moral preference are exercised only in making a choice. He who does anything because it is the custom makes no choice.....The faculties are called into no exercise by doing a think merely because others do it, no more than by believing a thing only because others believe it. If the grounds of an opinion are not conclusive to the person's own reason, his reason cannot be strengthened, but is likely to be weakened, by his adoption to it: and if the inducements to an act are not such as are consentaneous to his own feelings and character (where affection, or the rights of others, are not concerned), it is so much done towards rendering his feelings and character inert and torpid instead of active and energetic.[8]

It would be tragic, if the scope of individual thought and self-expression were marginalised to the extent that they ceased to have any meaningful impact or influence upon society as a whole. Yet, this would appear to be the direction society is moving towards as it strives to facilitate virtually all aspects of human endeavour, often removing people's inclination to think or do things for themselves as free individuals. The right of every person, not only outsiders, to be able to articulate and express themselves is fundamental within any free society. However, this right is increasingly being eroded by people's willingness to delegate their responsibility to decide or appraise things for themselves and acquiesce to whatever the prevailing view may be. Some people's veneration and respect for individual opinion has already been superseded by the apathetic trust they willingly place in the hands of those they believe more qualified to dictate the form, nature and, in the most extreme instance, character of their thoughts.

The erosion of people's sense of individual empowerment is by no means self-inflicted, it has emerged from a culmination of factors such as the way people apply themselves to, and how they interact with, a rapidly changing world. For instance, some people today are assured of society's progress though a circumscribed notion of its ability to create increasingly intricate and clever technology. Indeed, today's technology has made things possible which, in some respects, would not have been imagined ten or twenty years ago. The drawback is that much of the technological gadgetry people now have at their disposal is often specifically designed around speeding up or replacing what they do - in many ways dispensing with their requirement to do things for themselves. Furthermore, much of the new and inventive technology tends to inhibit people's ability to interact with their environment as human beings. In many ways, it creates a disjointed relationship between people and the world they are in, detaching them from the rich experience of real life.

Society has reached an advanced stage, where there is now little or no prerogative placed upon people to develop a good memory, good cognitive skills, or to even possess an intricate knowledge of something. This is, of course, unless it is directly related to the work they do or something which is of specific interest to them. Science teachers are now being taught to introduce any new subject matter to pupils on the back of concepts or stories they are already familiar with. People's receptiveness to learn new things and embrace new ideas has been whittled away through their penchant for solely concerning themselves with things which are directly relevant to them, and the fact they can become an instant 'expert' on anything by Googling it. Advancements in technology have not only had an effect on the way people learn, but also how people think and relate to their environment. More and more people are spending their free time glued to some form of screen, either through watching TV, communicating through social media or simply trawling the internet. Ready meals have, for some, become an indispensable part of everyday life and there is now a separate gadget or machine to do anything people could possibly conceive of doing or making in their kitchen or indeed elsewhere. The upshot of this is today's modern lifestyle, which does little to enhance people's sense of being or self-worth. It foments a disillusionment with life as their senses become increasingly detached from basic yet, in many ways, essential human functions.

It is not only lifestyle which has impacted on people's sense of individual empowerment - their workplace environment often typifies how disenfranchised some now feel. In the last few years there has been an explosion in employee bureaucracy. The elaborate and often inventive job descriptions created for people today obscures the reality, that in many instances, their roles have become circumscribed to a narrow and more specific set of responsibilities. There seems to be a powerful push towards seeking to regulate and account for every aspect of people's behaviour and duties at work. This has, at times, led to an absurd situation where an issue or problem crops up which clearly needs to be addressed, but because no-one's job description or responsibilities specifically refer to dealing with it, the problem is seldom properly addressed in the short term. Is there really a valid argument to endorse the continual redesign of working practices which pigeonhole people's industry into ever more simplistic functions, often confining them to work in increasingly absurd bureaucratic and automated roles? In many respects, people seem to have discounted the adage that a system is only as sound as the skill of the person or persons who devised it. And yet, more and more employees today tend to unreservedly (and sometimes fearfully) abide by each new policy or initiative as it is churned out. Some employees will religiously endorse each and every provincial politically-correct organisational taboo, without even conceiving the possibility that the thinking behind them may be flawed. There seems to be a cannon in some organisations which dictates that to get the best out of people, they need to be increasingly organised and monitored, often streamlining their role through compelling them to perform some robot-like function. This erodes one of the most essential aspects of the human condition; people's need to be able to do or achieve things for themselves. It is naïve for anyone to presume that mankind is more advanced now than at any stage in the past, when for millions human endeavour now consists of mind-numbingly sitting next to a production line or glued to a computer screen all day.

It is not surprising, even outside the workplace, how many people feel plagued by a sensation of hopelessness and anonymity. The cause of such feelings is rarely addressed at source, often being attributed to some extraneous factor in people's lives. Those who do try to express how inconsequential or senseless they feel their lives are, usually get labelled as having some mental indisposition. The treatment prescribed to many, whose only real affliction is their need to acquire a little more meaning in their lives or need to feel that inimitable quality which comes from behaving as an authentic individual, sometimes amounts to a cocktail of 'happy pills'.[9] In many ways, the treatments prescribed mask the blatant reality of modern society's erosion of people's significance as unique individuals. People have an inherent human need to feel, do and often create things in their own way, in order to give themselves a sense of control over their own destiny. By inhibiting this need, one of the essential ingredients required to maintain a person's sense of well-being and contentment with life is removed.

With mental illness continually and alarmingly on the increase almost year on year,[10] maybe people will start to acknowledge the possibility that lifestyle, and the direction society is moving towards, plays a significant role in exacerbating people's mental unease. It may be hard for some to appreciate, that their mental anxieties usually become more acute when their will is eclipsed by society's conditioned format, stripping away their significance as entities in their own right. Few people even seem to want to entertain the idea that mental illness may be the side effect of a society which is achieving its goals by emasculating more and more people through its restrictive design. Are people reaping the dividends of a society which has chosen to discard its essential humanistic aspects, people's ability to exercise their needs as individuals, for a flawed utopian model?

There's no doubt, modern society is a potent catalyst for existential despair; a point which is aptly portrayed through Travis Bickle's characterisation in the screenplay *Taxi Driver*. Throughout the screenplay, Travis finds it hard to contain his despair as the falseness and mundane predictability of his life keep undermining his need to feel his existence is capable of amounting to anything. He keeps fighting against his presumed role as just another guy with a blank meaningless identity. He cannot tolerate the thought of being Travis Bickle, the man who fits neatly into a slot, and in the grand scheme of things becomes of little more significance than just another person to add to the characterless New Yorkers portrayed in the screenplay. Life, for Travis, lacks the substance he craves for: "I cannot continue this hollow, empty fight. I must sleep. What hope is there for me?"[11] Travis' desperation knows no bounds, he is not fazed by anything and even the thought of placing his own life in danger is subordinate to his need to gain some tangible meaning to it. As the screenplay draws to its conclusion, Travis emerges as the hero for rescuing a girl who has fallen into the entrapments of prostitution. However, this is ironic since he could so easily have become the villain had he carried out his initial intention of shooting an unchaste, and in his eyes, deceitful political candidate. The true irony is the lottery of fortunes facing the truly desperate existentialist, and the flawed impression society often generates to make sense of their motives; Travis' motive was the same whether or not he killed the political candidate or saved the young girl.

Virtually all outsiders would like to feel there was some meaningful impetus running through their lives. At times, they can become quite desperate just to do something, even if it is merely to reaffirm their ability to perform an action which is separate and unanticipated from the people around them. This need often symbolises the outsider's position as a person whose hopelessness has reached a defining stage, where in effect they have nothing else to lose. Laws, expectations or even concern for their own welfare, often do not have much bearing on truly desperate outsiders, determined to bring some meaning or purpose into their lives. It is important to understand that this determination is often fuelled by a deep frustration with the way life is, leading some outsiders to take a disparaging view of others or society as a whole. Regardless of this, it is important to bear in mind that they are not some bunch of subversive psychopaths keen to bring about society's demise. Their despair and their attitude towards life in general usually stems from the way they think or perceive society can better itself, especially if people were more receptive to the notion of meaning in their lives and its reality.

Why do the patterns of human nature become so horribly predictable to outsiders? Questions like these add to their frustration and despair, sometimes generating a strong need to change the circumstances they are in. Unfortunately, for many outsiders, their efforts to bring about the profound or far-reaching change they sometimes hope to bring about usually end up as futile gestures. This unrealised need tends to haunt many outsiders who, on the one hand, despair with the irrational world they are in and, on the other, feel helpless through their impotence to change anything. Some outsiders attempt to alleviate their despair by trying to draw a line under the things they despair with. They try to dispel its causes by dismissively thinking - "why shouldn't I leave people to their own devices, why should I despair with other people's antics?", or "why should I feel any responsibility for the way society is?" Indeed, why should outsiders take on the mantle of trying to make society or people more conscious of themselves? They can hardly be described as gallant philanthropists, who selflessly want to make the world a better place. In fact, the real cause of their despair revolves around the issue that, for them, the world makes so little sense and, because of this, many harbour an aspiration to make others see it in the way they do. In addition to this, they also cannot escape from their need, however tenuous, to feel they belong somewhere. Even though some outsiders appear to be completely dispassionate about what goes on around them and the nauseating inevitabilities of day-to-day life, this does not mean they have given up all hope of one day applying themselves instinctively to it in a meaningful way.

It is clear some outsiders already feel they have established some meaning in their lives through their insistence on being themselves. This feature defines them as individuals. It enables them to say to themselves 'I have not shunned my mind's responsibility to itself', however, this on its own is usually not enough. Many outsiders also need to feel they can realise themselves more or somehow make their mark in life, in order for it to mean anything. In effect, they not only need to be themselves, but many also long to find some niche within society where their instinctive expression can at least be acknowledged, reciprocated, or even allowed to flourish. Most outsiders will readily admit that their existential craving for meaning is seldom, if ever, satisfied. A sentiment which is accurately reflected in Thomas More's

*Utopia*. Even though the work is most famous for its depiction of More's vision of a utopian society, which since its publication in 1516 has left an indelible mark on generations of writers and philosophers, it also contains an interesting dialogue from a character named Raphael. In his dialogue, he explains the futility of endeavouring to project his energy and industry to achieve something in the context of other people's realism:

> Raphael  'We'll never get human behaviour in line with Christian ethics,' these gentlemen must have argued, 'so let's adapt Christian ethics to human behaviour. Then at least there'll be some connection between them.'
>
> But I can't see what good they've done. They've merely enabled people to sin with a clear conscience – and that's about all I could do at a Cabinet meeting. For I'd either have to vote against my colleagues, which would be equivalent to not voting at all, or else I'd have to vote with them, in which case, like Micio in Terence, I'd be 'aiding and abetting insanity'.
>
> As for working indirectly, and when things can't be put right, handling them so tactfully that they're as little wrong as possible, I don't see quite what that means. At Court you can't keep your opinions to yourself, or merely connive at other people's crimes. You have to give open support to deplorable policies, and subscribe to utterly monstrous resolutions. If you don't show enough enthusiasm for a bad law, you'll be taken for a spy or even a traitor. Besides, what chance have you got of doing any good, when you're working with colleagues like that? You'll never reform them – they're far more likely to corrupt you, however admirable a character you are. By associating with them you'll either lose your own integrity, or else have it used to conceal their folly and wickedness.' [12]

Many outsiders can easily identify with Raphael's predicament; like him, they just do not feel there is enough scope through life's usual avenues to realise that unequivocal purpose they really hanker after. Like Raphael, they see through it, so much so it often becomes futile trying to exert any serious degree of effort in discharging many of society's unavailing roles. As their need for meaning intensifies, they become more conscious of their impotence to change anything and how insignificant they are within society as a whole. It is this which often accounts for their inertia, and which for some, comes to symbolise their existence.

The ultimate question remains to be resolved - can outsiders find meaning through trying to apply themselves in a world which by its nature thwarts their attempts to bind to it? This question has confronted innumerable individuals throughout history as they have tried, often in vain, to translate their truth or ideals to others. In order for outsiders to have any hope of acquiring any meaning at all, they need to be able to express themselves instinctively. They need to feel they can be true to who they are and define themselves in their own way. They also need to be able to live according to the way they perceive things, what they think, and how they value life. This was the conclusion Victor Frankl arrived as in his most famous work - *Man's Search for Meaning* (1946). Frankl was a psychiatrist by profession, although he spent time as a prisoner during the Second World War in two concentration camps. His book describes the resultant effects upon his state of mind under the extreme pressures of his captivity. However, the most striking feature of Frankl's book is that he declares, regardless of the extreme suffering and hardship he encountered in the camps, he still managed to find meaning in his life which gave him an incentive to survive.

Frankl's approach to the question of meaning involves confronting the issue directly, and unlike some other psychiatric methods of dealing with the issue of meaning, does not try to shroud the individual within any safe psychological framework. Frankl's approach does not dwell on or offer any excuses to the individual for the way their mind works, or the way their lives have turned out; nor does it advocate that anyone needs to go through some kind of grieving process to overcome past experiences before they can find peace of mind. Instead, he shifts the emphasis directly upon the individual by nurturing, what he terms, their 'will to meaning'. Frankl termed his approach *logotherapy*. Its principal focus rests upon galvanising the individual's desire for meaning as something authentic which should not be masked or considered as some psychological flaw, but accepted as part of the human condition. He says, people should not become too preoccupied with trying to pinpoint the particular causes of their despair, but instead should concentrate their efforts more on finding the meaning they demand to properly address its cause. In the same way, Frankl advocates that existentialists should ally themselves to the things they consider meaningful, rather than becoming embroiled in Freudian explanations to account for the way they are. His approach, promotes the idea that people should focus upon pursuing the things which they as individuals believe they need, in order to generate meaning in their lives. As a methodology, Frankl's logotherapy is very relevant to the way outsiders can find meaning. However, the extent of Frankl's panacea from the examples he provides, and its direct application to the outsider's predicament, can sometimes be limited.

In *Man's Search for Meaning*, Frankl believes his theory can be applied to anyone in general who find themselves in what he terms the 'existential vacuum'. This includes those who do not feel their lives contain the degree of meaning they can qualify as leading to a worthwhile existence. It rests upon the presumption that everyone can potentially find a purpose and meaning in their lives by pursuing or doing something more meaningful. Frankl gives examples of a cross-section of people he had counselled over the years, who had gone on to acquire more meaning in their lives. However, many outsiders would probably struggle to equate the examples Frankl cites as qualifying what they define as being meaningful. For a good proportion of outsiders, their predicament cannot suddenly be solved by changing their job or lifestyle; their criterion for meaning is invariably more demanding and profound than the average person. Even though Frankl's theory endorses the idea that anyone who finds themselves caught up in an existential impasse, should pursue the things they believe in - it does not address what outsiders should do when they feel trapped in a world they cannot warrant with any meaning and where everything seems futile. For most outsiders, discovering something in life which they can classify as meaningful, is usually a tall order and often involves acquiring some sort of ability to influence the absurd nature of the world they are in.

In order for outsiders to overcome their predicament, they often have to be much bolder to have any prospect of finding a definitive purpose in their lives. It is not enough to simply explore the conventional avenues; many need to be able to project the person they truly are, which often presents a massive challenge in light of society's lack of provision to accommodate their single-minded nature. Therefore, it is often left to outsiders to look to themselves for ways to overcome their circumstances. For some, this may require embracing a much more flexible approach in terms of exploring different mediums and ways to express themselves. They must move away from contrasting the incompatible differences between them and the rest of society and, instead, focus on the source of their disaffection. In effect they must turn to themselves for inspiration, to truly find the means necessary to bring meaning into their lives. It does not serve any purpose for the outsider to resign him or herself to a dormant existence in which they simply sit there in despair, inhibited by their apparent inability to become anything or even to express who they are. Therefore, the challenge is clear and cannot be embarked upon naively or in any half-heartedly way. The responsibility falls squarely on the outsider to realise him or herself as an individual, to overcome whatever impediments exist within life and find some kind of niche within it, to apply themselves instinctively in a meaningful way.

# 10

# Creating Meaning

**Let us therefore limit ourselves to the purification of our opinions and evaluations and to the creation of our own new tables of values..........We, however, want to be those who we are - human beings who are new, unique, incomparable, who give themselves laws, who create themselves.**

Friedrich Nietzsche - *The Gay Science* [1]

There is no doubt most outsiders live a type of seminomadic existence. They roam amongst society's ranks like natives from a long lost tribe subsisting in a modern metropolis, unable to assimilate its customs or feel any sense of belonging to it. Their thirst for certainty and truth seem unquenchable in the parched environment created by its fickle habitat, where achievement usually revolves around the predictability of fulfilling an established set of needs most strive for without question. The pattern is sustained through successive generations as people embrace these needs, often hailing their fulfilment as something momentous in an attempt to disguise their futility. Their demand is assured through conditioning people to aspire to a perpetual array of wants in life, regardless of how manufactured, false or unavailing they may be.

The outsider wanders aimlessly through this desolate meaningless wasteland, unable to find any fertile ground on which to sow his or her incompatible ideas. In contrast, people's unconditional devotion to society's established behavioural norms ensures that, for many, the format of their lives in a broader sense does not really change from one person to the next; a circumstance outsiders find so nauseating. The great play carries on with most people following their script to the letter, whilst all utterances not included in the screenplay are edited out by the pressures society exerts upon individuals to abide by its conventions and discard their instinctive self. The form and content of the play are undisputed, its legitimacy has already been substantiated through its widespread adoption and the erosion of people's inclination to be themselves or express what they think, against the apathetic demeanour society demands. People are encouraged to regurgitate their simplistic lines, as society in turn reveres those who demonstrate their ability to subdue their intrinsic nature. No one seems to have given outsiders a part in this tragic comedy, which has been so carefully contrived from the most brazen and naïve model of human needs.

The passage of time does nothing to solve the outsider's predicament. To combat this realisation, a few spend their time devising elaborate strategies or rationales to mask their inability to attach meaning to anything - even though fully aware they are only kidding themselves. There is a gaping hole in these people's lives, an unfulfilled need to make sense of things coupled with an assertion their existence must amount to something to have any real value. Their frustrations with life are never far from their thoughts and sometimes add an edge to the way they are, and how they present themselves to others. Their exposure to the 'déjà vu' of the everyday world makes them naturally cynical of people and life generally. Many also find it hard to understand how their lives have panned out, often from childhood innocence and youthful optimism, to the dogged empty impasse they now find themselves in. Unfortunately, there is no one definitive course of action capable of resolving or alleviating every outsider's predicament. Their existential disposition makes them unique and diverse individuals, and any approach must necessarily account for this. They must also look at what their underlying needs are in order to acquire a clearer understanding of what challenges they may have to face trying to realise themselves in life as the person they are.

In 1943 Abraham Maslow proposed his now famous paper on Hierarchy of Needs,[2] in which he listed a succession of needs which he said, once fulfilled, would then lead people to progressively seek to attain more complex needs. He grouped these needs from basic physiological needs, such as eating and sleeping to eventually self-actualisation, which he defined in terms of deriving meaning from life. He proposed that people were bound by this successive format of needs, and he equated the numbers of people seeking to acquire these in a block pyramid structure to reflect the amount of people within each category. For instance, with the largest proportion trying to fulfil basic needs and gradually fewer people seeking to fulfil progressively complex ones. He explained his 'hierarchy of needs' as a continuum, proposing that once people's basic physiological needs were satisfied, they would naturally move on and strive to fulfil more profound needs. These being things like gaining social acceptance or self-esteem, and then eventually for a few self-actualisation (fulfilment of the highest need which incorporates meaning in life).

Unfortunately, whilst Maslow's theory has proved itself an indispensable tool for understanding people's motives and behaviour over the decades, it falls flat on its face when applied as a framework to understand the outsider. This may also explain why existentialists are so misunderstood within society, their priorities are usually completely alien to people's usual wants and needs. They inadvertently confound most people who try to anticipate what their motives or aspirations may be. The simple fact is that outsiders possess an inherent need to affix some meaning to their lives which sometimes even overrides any incentive they may have to fulfil more basic needs, such as having comfortable surroundings or even, for a few, knowing when or where their next meal or paycheque is coming from. The outsider's behaviour often usurps Maslow's theory completely and some people become quite perturbed when they find themselves unable to fathom the outsider in any coherent way. For example, striving for financial security or to be socially accepted is often of little consequence to many outsiders compared with their need to make sense of life or potentially to discover a worthwhile purpose within it.

The crucial question for any outsider should not be what life has to offer them, but in what way they can realise themselves by offering something to the world as it is? Outsiders are aware that whatever they do has to equate to meaning something. They do not believe in half measures and whatever they dedicate themselves to has to either be unique, far-reaching, or capable of transcending the predictable and mundane aspects of life in order for it to be significant. It is this dichotomy which explains why some outsiders are never far from creating some form of friction with others or some kind of discord within society through their attempts to assert, or simply be themselves. Their uncompromising nature, insistence their lives must mean something, and the blunt way they tend to express themselves does not generally endear themselves to others, and often undermines people's willingness to acknowledge their perspective or what their abilities may be. This usually leaves them in no-man's land as their thoughts and potentialities are left on a scrapheap which they are unable to traverse, feeling powerless to gain any foothold in a society which does not provide any real avenue for their instinctive expression.

A few outsiders, whether it is through luck or sheer per-severance, manage to find some sort of leverage to raise themselves up. They find ways around society's incompatible design, often overcoming or changing others attitudes, prejudicial outlook or general inertia. There are even a few who find an outlet for their incompatible nature and expression through more conventional means, enabling them to project their instincts through some mainstream role. However, such conjunctions are rare as most outsiders have unique, specific and stringent criteria to fulfil before they can define an action or aspiration as being worthwhile; they simply do not equate many of the more prosaic roles in life as leading to a meaningful outcome. For many, they not only have (what some would regard as) impossibly high expectations, but also have a tendency to instantly move on to something else once they feel they have achieved what they set out to do. It is as if their mind is always one step ahead, thwarting their ability to feel any long-term contentment with life. In fact, some outsiders' demands for meaning could be better understood as a succession of progressive needs or criteria, which over time are never quite satisfied; a circumstance which inevitably adds to their quandary. However, despite this seeming inability to feel satisfied, the existential will is usually indomitable, with most outsiders rarely discouraged or dissuaded from their search to find something which might enhance their incentive towards life or furnish them with a purpose within it. The issue for outsiders, is in what way they can harness their nature and ability to be themselves in the modern world allowing them to derive something meaningful from it?

For some outsiders the equation is clear, in order to quell their despair and sense of hopelessness with life they must discover or nurture some meaningful application to it. Their success in fulfilling this aspiration is often not a question of how intransigent they are, but sometimes how sagacious they can be. Outsiders have a number of innate qualities which are often left unrealised due to their inability to apply their instincts in a purposeful way. One of these qualities is their penchant for taking a step back and seeing life more for what it is, often from a more detached and broader perspective. Their nauseating experience of it as being unreal makes them more of a witness to it than a participant in it and, as such, their detached outlook is not easily swayed by others sentiment or bias. This ability to see things from the sidelines usually equips them with a strong and often unique sense of impartiality. Their absence of any agenda (apart from finding meaning within life) forces them to be more objective in the way they appraise people and what goes on around them. Their disposition sometimes makes them very reflective and at the same time critical, allowing them to see through the inevitable way things usually unfold. For some, their minds become adept at noticing particular facets like the incessant pattern of people's general behaviour. They become more receptive to things capable of containing or bringing meaning into their lives and, as a result, anything transient or incidental is immediately filtered out allowing them to see life in a unique way.

At times outsiders can be to be wholly disengaged from the world they are in, it is as if they simply exist as a hopeless component of it, lacking any reason or purpose for being there. With this in mind, people rarely appreciate or acknowledge how determined and passionate they can be when they come across something which might propel them to discover a substantive incentive for doing something. Once their imagination is fired up, many outsiders truly believe there are no boundaries to what they can achieve or set their sights on. Faced with resigning themselves to their lot as the alternative, their lack of options usually generates a determination with its own momentum, totally unaffected by others encouragement or admonitions. If they actually believe in what they are doing, factors such as the time it might take them, the drawbacks it entails, or whether anyone else thinks what they are doing is worthwhile, has little bearing on their ability to carry through what they set their sights on. It is this single-minded determination, which does not manifest itself often, that sometimes represents one on the biggest differences between the outsider and many others. The fact that some outsiders never seemingly display much inclination or desire to achieve anything much in contemporary life, should not lead anyone to presume they are any less capable than anyone else. All this really shows is they have not found or do not have the same motives for doing many of the things people usually aspire to. In their case, when they can equate a worthwhile reason for doing something, their efforts can far exceed most others enterprise or perseverance in bringing it about.

Most outsiders' lives are typified by despair in one form or another; for some, it is part and parcel of daily life. Their mind provides them with a mental picture of how things should be, with aspects such as meaning, truth and freedom, featuring heavily in the way they appraise life and conduct themselves within it. In contrast, most people do not have the same inclination to rank these aspects with such importance. For some outsiders, the modern world even seems to be moving further away from where they would like it to be, people seem to draw their sustenance from increasingly absurd concepts and ideals. The fickleness and nonsensical aspects of modern life constantly grate on outsiders, leaving them in a state of quiet despair. For some, this is compounded by their lack of the means to change or influence it in any way. The despair they experience is often unrelenting and some have no respite from the discordant disparity between their world and the irrational one they are in. This contrast cannot be reconciled with accommodating persuasions or by trying to dismiss what they think. In order for them to make sense of what is around them or have any regard for themselves, they must remain true to what they perceive and think. Unfortunately, by doing so, the only prospect they see for themselves is an existence on society's fringes, trying to manage their frustrations and despair in the hope that one day they might just discover something within it, which may come close to reaching their conception of meaning.

Outsiders are unique individuals. They possess a number of traits which sets them apart from people in general. However, these traits in themselves are not wholly unique to outsiders, some being prevalent amongst people who tend to be more unconventional or more creatively inclined. It could be said that the outsiders' character traits naturally lend themselves towards more creative mediums as a means of connecting with the world they are in. At the same time, this seems to run contrary to the forthright and direct way some outsiders tend to convey themselves. And yet, creative expression, in whatever form people choose to portray it, appears to compliment many of the outsider's penchants. For instance, as a way of conveying what they think, artistic undertakings provide individuals the widest possible freedom not only in the way they express themselves, but also through its boundless scope. Whether it be through literature, music, painting, sculpture, poetry or even comedy, the number of avenues is virtually endless, unlocking the means to reach or touch others in a more profound way. It can provide an individual with a sense they are creating something unique, like a jazz musician, authentic to them and brought into existence on their terms. Regardless of its form, creativity has no rules and those within the artistic world often prize the unconventional, people who are willing to go against the grain or who see life in a different context from most others. It rates those who can offer a new or different perspective on things and to others, especially those with an aptitude for capturing the essence of things. Within any creative industry, the people who are usually held in highest regard are those with the ability to step back from life, see it for what it is and effectively translate this through a more imaginative medium; being able to create some sort of impact on the person or persons experiencing it.

The artistic or creative world depends on uncompromising individuals who have an inherent need or fearless determination to present their vision or ideas to others. It facilitates the expression of deeper thoughts and, at times, the uncomfortable truths about life. Artistic expression provides a medium through which the individual can maintain an honesty and integrity in what they create without compromising themselves. Artists and those who choose to apply themselves creatively, are not generally beholden to anyone and, what they have to say is expressed through their own enterprise, in a depth and format which they choose. As a medium, creativity has no boundaries. It provides people with the scope to draw their insights from deep within themselves through their perceptions, experiences, and often frustrations with life. Some artists even use their creativity as a kind of therapy or release for their pent-up emotion and, it is no coincidence that many of those who are more artistically inclined are plagued by despair in one form or another. In essence, the nature and form of what they wish to convey often necessitates its expression through a more imaginative and creative medium. The artist often draws on his or her despair as a catalyst and motivation, to express themselves in a unique way, sometimes to transcend what has been done before. They often have a deep desire to create something which is capable of impacting on people's perceptions; often to produce something original and unparalleled, which for them, is capable of containing its own meaning.

On the face of it, the artist and the outsider appear to be similar creatures. Art, as a means of expression, endorses the outsider's propensity for uniqueness and creativity and can potentially open up avenues through which to express their thoughts or perceptions to others. It can also give the outsider the platform to articulate him or herself in a way which sometimes enhances the sentiments he or she is trying to portray. The single-minded creativity which artistic endeavours often demand complements the outsider's nature, whilst also providing a means by which he or she can overcome the barriers within society which inhibit their instinctive expression. Having said this, many outsiders tend to think in a black and white way and some simply do not believe their nature equips them with the artistic leanings required to generate or convey themselves on a more creative level. Some outsiders simply do not foresee themselves as artistic or creative, and do not envisage expressing themselves other than in a blatantly direct or forthright way. The more artistically inclined are usually highly sensitive individuals, as are some outsiders. Yet, the thing that defines most artists' success is their ability to communicate themselves and their unique insights or sensitivities through their art, on a level capable of resonating with people emotionally or in some profound way. It is not surprising some people are drawn to more artistic mediums through which to express themselves, some of those who are more creative even feel they cannot properly express themselves in any other way than creatively and on some deeper emotional level.

Many individuals, who are more artistically inclined, often have a history of being deeply frustrated by their inability to convey their emotions and feelings effectively in life, especially through more accustomed or conventional modes of communication. Similarly, many outsiders are frustrated by their powerlessness to express their instincts effectively and some even feel a natural proclivity towards more creative means as an avenue through which to translate their thoughts and perceptions. There are some outsiders who even become accomplished or develop a flair for expressing themselves on a more creative level, giving them the scope to translate their perceptions to others – which sometimes cannot be effectively conveyed in other ways. Given the immense scope of creativity as a means of expression, the question still needs to be asked, where does it leave outsiders? Many of whom do not feel they are particularly artistic or capable of immersing or dedicating their emotional energies towards some creative undertaking. Some will just insist on just saying things how they are, rather than interpreting themselves through any deep, subconscious or emotional level. Coupled with this, what they do has to have some meaningful consequence to it, and the impact or influence art may have in a wider context is at times notoriously difficult to define and quantify. Some might even say they are simply not in touch with or do not have the right sentiment to generate anything artistic or creative. However, by dismissing this huge resource as a potential avenue for finding meaning, they are effectively narrowing their potential scope to assert themselves instinctively. In fact, over the years many existentialists have managed to draw meaning into their lives through using creativity as a medium to translate their concepts and ideas to others; especially those which were more profound, far-reaching or insightful.

It is not by chance that many artists and writers have been associated with existentialism over the years. Some of the more prominent painters and sculptors included people like Francis Bacon,

Alberto Giacometti, Jaen Dubuffet and Wols. These were around during the 1940's and 50's. It was also the time that Sartre and Camus were at their most prolific in terms of their writing careers and when existentialism as a movement was at its most prominent. This era represented a time when many artists and writers sought to reflect people's sense of disillusionment with life, capturing their mood in the aftermath of the Second World War. Many key existential concepts such as alienation, existence, meaninglessness, phenomenology and despair were being artistically portrayed, in what has become known today as existential art. The works of Francis Bacon exemplify these powerful existential concepts. His paintings, usually grotesque representations of objects or human figures, often provoke a strong emotional response within people. Many of his works portray the individual's anxiety with the world by detaching the object of focus from its background and carefully obscuring the contrast between representation and abstraction. In his paintings, people's faces are deliberately blurred to emphasise the concept of their loss of identity in the world. He often portrayed figures as being restricted in some way to reflect people's sense of confinement and lack of freedom, which seemed to capture the profound existential mood of his generation. Similarly, Antonio Giacometti expressed the existential ideas of human suffering, anxiety, alienation and loneliness through his sculptures. His thin, elongated figures depict the human inability to reach out and connect with the world. His sculptures show withdrawn and lonely figures reflecting in on themselves in deep contemplation. His works expound the idea of the individual unable to relate to and totally detached from the world as it is.

In the 1950's existential themes were not only being portrayed in art but also in the theatre, through what became known as the 'theatre of the absurd'. Probably two of the notable playwrights whose works typified, and in some ways pioneered these themes, were Samuel Beckett and Eugéne Ionesco. Many of their plays were expressions of the individual's hopeless plight, trying to find a purpose in an indefinable and senseless world. They dispensed with conventional structure and plots in their plays, often disorientating people and throwing their audiences off guard. The plays break down people's preconceived notions of anticipation and certainty. Out of this come powerful existential ideas of alienation, absurdity and despair, often through creating completely nonsensical and unreal scenes. Beckett's most famous play *Waiting for Godot*, features two characters musing under a tree who are passing the time before Godot's arrival. In the play Godot never arrives and the two simply carry on their un-inspiring conversation each day while they wait. The play demonstrates the futility of waiting for something to happen and the meaningless of time.

It could be said that Beckett and Ionesco were simply expounding the themes of their day, but existentialism is not something which just came about at a particular time - it runs much deeper than this. Their plays are still performed today and their themes still resonate with audiences, many of whom can recognise and also empathise with their concepts. Existential themes also form the cornerstone of many contemporary films, whether this is through depicting the individual in a wholly unreal world as in *The Truman Show*, or through the thought-provoking existential questions which emerge from the films such as *The Matrix*, *Blade Runner* or *Groundhog Day*. Existential concepts are also especially prevalent in the works of many current authors, such as Michel Houellebecq, Milan Kundera, Kurt Hamsun and Haruki Murakami. It is often difficult to define an author today as being purely existential, as their works often draw on existential themes in conjunction with an array of other themes. Despite this, the prevalence of existential thoughts and ideas in contemporary literature testifies to existentialism's appeal, often reflecting people's disjointed relationship with the modern world.

Existentialism did not come about in a vacuum in the 1940's and 50's, it has always been there as an intrinsic part of the human condition. In fact, there are many artists, writers and playwrights whose works, although not principally defined as existential, include key existential themes and characterisations. This is true not only in the way some of these individuals perceived life, but ultimately their need to create something meaningful within it - one of the more notable being Vincent van Gogh. His life can be characterised through his constant struggle to fit into the world, trying to find a meaning he could define as authentic. After spending several years working as an art dealer (which he did not find very fulfilling), he decided to turn his attention to religion and the church as a career which he thought would allow him to dedicate himself to something which would give his life some purpose. Van Gogh's initial intention was to study theology, but after failing to secure a place at university, he took a post as a preacher in an impoverished coal mining community. It was not surprising that his altruistic nature led him to develop a strong emotional attachment to the miners and their families. During his time there, he gave away most of his clothes, possessions and food to the poor around him, leaving himself with virtually nothing. Some have tried to interpret his benevolence as an attempt to empathise with the plight of those more impoverished than himself or simply due to his philanthropic nature, but this does not explain his selfless generosity. As an outsider, van Gogh was a man of absolutes; he had to conduct himself by what he believed. He probably thought he could not preach the word of Jesus and, hypocritically, be better off than the people he was preaching to. Unsurprisingly, even though his actions typically reflect what Jesus would have done (as depicted by the Bible's narratives), the church duly dismissed him for setting a poor example through his ascetic lifestyle.

It was only in 1880, at the age of 27, that van Gogh began studying art and the techniques of painting. It was to signify the beginning of a passion highlighted by his unbending will to pursue art, despite at times his desperate adversity. His physical wellbeing and his struggles with poverty were to become almost incidental, when compared to his need to creatively produce works of art which he considered meaningful. It was fortunate, from time to time, that his desperate circumstances were alleviated by his brother Theo's generosity. Van Gogh was very candid in his letters to his brother Theo, which show what he thought and felt at various times in his life. In July 1880 he wrote to Theo explaining the enormous unrealised passion within him and how much he wanted to dedicate himself unreservedly to this powerful urge to create:

> Must I consider myself a dangerous man, incapable of anything? I don't think so. But the problem is to try every means to put those self-same passions to good use. . . . When I was in other surroundings, in the surroundings of pictures and works of art, you know how I had a violent passion for them, reaching the highest pitch of enthusiasm. [3]

Despite his enthusiasm for art, van Gogh still faced the dilemma of, on the one hand, nurturing his need to add meaning to life in his unique way and on the other, maintaining his passion for painting as a career which would sustain him in life (in his case simply earning enough to survive). He realised early on in life that his nature was different to those around him and was under no illusions of the potential difficulties which lay ahead, by allowing his mind to instinctively create paintings which portrayed the meaning he wished to convey:

> For I am afraid that the better my drawings become, the more difficulty and opposition I shall meet. Because I still have to suffer much, especially form those peculiarities which I cannot change. First, my appearance and my way of speaking and my clothes; and then, even later on when I earn more, I shall always move in a different sphere from most painters because my conception of things, the subjects I want to make, inexorably demand it. [4]

Van Gogh's works could hardly have been described as popular in his lifetime, many were considered too abstract at the time for most people to appreciate or even entertain. It could be argued, he could have made his life much more comfortable by adapting himself and his creative talents to suit people's appetite for the fashionable styles painted at that time. Yet, he had no reason to do this. For him, what was at stake was far more critical than any benefit he could possibly gain from adapting his paintings to satisfy people's tastes merely to improve his dire financial circumstances - his need for meaning in life.

> In my opinion, I am often rich as Croesus – not in money, but (though it doesn't happen every day) rich – because I have found in my work something which I can devote myself to heart and soul, and which inspires me and gives a meaning to life. [5]

The depth and energy of van Gogh's work meant it could not be contrived to compliment or reflect the archetypal or existing artistic styles at that time. Van Gogh realised this, and also realised to some extent the torrid times which lay ahead. Like the outsider, he was driven by a need to add meaning and form to his existence in his own way, by creating art which expressed his deep passion for colours and his perceptions of life. He could not relinquish his need to define himself according to his creative impulses which, it could be said, dominated his life. Notwithstanding this, it also provided him with an unsurpassed purpose in his work through his ability to project the realism, despair and the raw emotion of what he thought and felt.

> So I am always between two currents of thought, first the material difficulties, turning round and round to make a living; and second, the study of colour. I am always in hope of making a discovery there, to express the love of two lovers by the wedding of two complimentary colours, their mingling and their opposition, the mysterious vibration of kindred tones. To express the thought of a brow by the radiance of a light tone against a sombre background.
> To express hope by some star, the eagerness of a soul by a sunset radiance. Certainly there is no delusive realism in that, but isn't it something that actually exists? 6

Van Gogh was clearly an exceptional individual. His unrelenting passion for painting and creativity are in many ways a rare phenomenon. The tenacity with which he applied himself predominantly stemmed from his need to generate meaning in his life - it is the same need which drives the outsider. The nature and form this meaning takes is specific to each individual and can range from anything from affirming their freedom, seeking to create something substantive, or simply expressing their thoughts or perceptions in some way.

This need for meaning is ever present amongst virtually all outsiders. It is essentially a creative and individualistic need which can push the outsider to do extraordinary things, or leave him or her in despair with the enormity of the task they have set themselves. It is not only central to how they conceive themselves, but plays a crucial role in the way they approach life and what they do within it. Outsiders are aware their best chance of gaining some contentment from it lies in them being able to derive some meaningful purpose within it; an avenue which is often vigorously pursued regardless of the drawbacks or hurdles which present themselves. This is not to say every outsider should just go out and, recklessly or stubbornly pursue whatever they consider meaningful to its nth degree. At the same time, they cannot derive anything from watering down their expectations or compromising themselves in their pursuit of something they believe in; for the outsider this is self-defeating. A careful balance must be reached, and outsiders must become adept at identifying the necessary means or avenues for them, as individuals, to generate meaning in their lives.

Contemporary western society often likes to portray itself through its flexibility in being able to cater for the needs and tastes of virtually everyone. This premise also infers there is a place in society for anyone who looks hard enough. Yet, for some outsiders this is often notoriously difficult leaving some with little choice than to somehow seek to carve out their own niche, usually through more creative or unconventional means. A few outsiders have even discovered a much greater sense of purpose in their lives by applying themselves in this way, which has not only given their lives some meaning, but has also served to complement their existential nature. For some, finding their niche or forte involves a long hard slog where they have had to keep chipping away or changing how they do things before uncovering the means necessary through which to realise their intrinsic self. Meaning, as each outsider defines it, is something very specific to them as individuals. The way they define or appreciate what is purposeful or worthwhile in life, is usually vastly different from anyone else. It is intertwined with the way they think and how they perceive what is around them. It is conceived differently by each outsider, and often cannot be gained from the usual outlets society advertises as avenues that purportedly lead to fulfilment. Many outsiders are often quite eclectic and require something to be far reaching in order for them to envisage it as being significant. Their demanding criteria sometimes naturally forces them to apply more creative means in their efforts to realise their expectations of meaning.

Most outsiders are fully aware that most people in society are often not receptive to their stark contrasts or to accepting life's blatant truisms, which are so typical of the way they often articulate themselves. As outsiders pursue certainty and truth, the rest of society often seeks some form of concession or climb-down, as more and more nowadays are prepared to barter with their values. As outsiders prioritise more substantive elements in life such as purpose and meaning, others frown, sometimes looking upon them as if they are some-how mentally inadequate. As the outsider discounts the authenticity of society's realism, society dismisses the outsider as some kind of freak. The point is that as people become more conditioned to the prevailing opinions and influences within society, they become much less willing to accept anything which contrasts with or brings into question their established conceptions; the stark perceptions and trenchant opinions of some outsiders being the last thing they would entertain. The more conditioned society becomes, the less receptive it is to anyone or anything outside its diminishing sphere of understanding, and outsiders often bear the brunt of this increasing insular attitude. This in turn inhibits their ability to be themselves or fit in within society. Therefore, the challenge facing them is how to overcome people's inertia and society's intransigent design, to apply themselves to an endeavour they can regard as worthwhile. In this respect, outsiders need to be bold. Sometimes they need to be prepared to take a 'leap of faith' in order to find other avenues or means to apply their faculties in life. For some, it is only through becoming creative in the way they assert themselves that they can have any hope of projecting themselves in a meaningful way.

There are many examples over the years of outsiders who have applied themselves more creatively in a bid to generate some meaning in their lives. This does not mean they have had to compromise on the substance of what they thought or believed in; these outsiders merely adapted the way they sought to do things or portray themselves. Their versatility to channel their instinctive energies through a different medium has often required a complete change in their approach. The impetus to do something meaningful is still there, all that has changed is the way they go about realising it. This need is all the more pressing in this day and age as, some would say, society seems to have veered off course, with many individuals increasingly disenchanted and detached from the absurd and nonsensical aspects of a modern existence. Some people's overreliance on mainstream precepts, their infallible notion of society's design, and dependency on technology is now so acute, it is seriously beginning to narrow the avenues for creative enterprise and people's ability to think and behave as real human beings. In addition, the prevailing dogma which emanates from society today, in many ways, discounts individualistic tendencies or endeavours as beneficial facets to the way it functions. With the direction society is moving towards, it is not difficult to envisage a future where individual input and creativity become increasingly superfluous. The feelings of hopelessness which ensue from people's inability to connect with the world they are in, provides a strong existential catalyst for those marginalised by an increasing sense of futility and detachment.

The rapidly changing environment and pace of modern life leaves many people struggling to keep up. For a few, things seem to change and develop so quickly that the world is becoming increasingly unrecognisable. The misguided presumption that as each change occurs, it inevitably must amount to bettering society in some way or some form of human progress, seems to sit well with a good number of people. Yet, with the advent of today's technology, in which people have the whole world at their fingertips, many tend to feel increasingly inconsequential or even redundant as individuals in their own right. This has triggered a need amongst some people to become tangible again, to seek to express and live their lives in a more unique and authentic way, capable of comprising more than a 'facebook' profile and 'twitter account'. The needs of people as individuals to feel they can have some meaningful relationship with the world around them, is critical within any free society. This is especially true today where many people's ability to conceive themselves as unique individuals has been superseded by the prevailing forces which shape, define and condition society. No-one feels this more than the outsider, where their need to project themselves to exercise some control over the nauseating inevitability and irrational aspects of day-to-day life becomes imperative. The extent to which they are able to turn the tide and apply their instincts often depends on their boldness, creativity and their expectations of themselves. There is no guarantee any outsider will be able to transform their need for meaning into something more tangible. However, given the lack of alternatives and their determination and belief in themselves to ascend whatever challenges life throws at them, anyone would be a fool to bet against them achieving what they set their mind to.

Many outsiders yearn to be able to reach out, to have the ability to engage with or influence the world around them. Unfortunately their disposition does not lend itself to or facilitate this and, therefore, they must often look to more creative mediums to bring this about. Creativity is not simply a process of, for instance, reinterpreting a concept or idea into a form which makes it more likely for people to identify with or take on board. Nor is it a question of forcing a concept into a more imaginative format; anything created specifically to fit solely into a particular model or artistic style is invariably flawed from the outset. The creative process goes much deeper than this, and cannot be turned on and off like a tap as and when a person commands. For any artist, writer, playwright or poet etc., their need to express something or portray their ideas or perceptions through their art, is usually the underlying driving force behind what they create, but they are also vigilant not to allow this need to fully dominate the creative process. Anyone who has ever created anything unique knows it must come from a will to create, coupled with an affinity or love for what they do. Writers who force themselves to write usually find the more they push themselves, the more the content and style of what they write often deteriorates. In a few cases, their work simply becomes a collection of words with no real meaning other than as an example to others of how someone has forced or abused the creative process. Creativity must come from within, it is not something which can be contrived or conjured up as and when a person demands it, like a performance on a TV talent show. An individual's ability to be creative is usually spontaneous; it is a process which does not obey any set pattern or laws in the way it manifests itself. The impetus of the creator, to express him or herself according to what they instinctively think, perceive, or believe in, is essential. However, the ability to create something capable of transcending people's conditioned mind-set and capable of having a meaningful impact, often requires the individual to be astute and savvy in the way they apply themselves and their imagination.

Many argue that creativity is principally a subconscious process and this is essentially true with regard to any artistic undertaking. However, a person's willingness to create must also incorporate their uniqueness and identity as individuals in order to ensure its originality. Being creative, for instance, does not encompass simply improving on or re-inventing something which has been done before. Many people who choose to express themselves through an artistic medium, whether this be through anything from painting, poetry, or even song writing, often seek to transcend the stereotypical or banal themes which underlie conventional enterprise. Some seek to capture elements of the human condition or, for instance, tapping into the essence of how people feel at a point in time. Regardless of the format this creativity takes, it is driven by a strong sense of purpose to bring into being something which is meaningful either in the way it is created and/or through its impact on others.

More often than not the creator's work becomes an intrinsic part of them, an extension of his or her human identity. A good analogy would be to think of the abstract artist. Their impetus is the interpretation of their insights and perceptions through, what they regard as, the most effective medium. The most influential abstract artists have the ability to push certain buttons within people, by communicating with them and appealing to their psyche and emotions on a wholly different level from which they are normally accustomed to. Over the years, abstract art has had this inexplicable ability to somehow touch people's emotions and penetrate their minds' recesses. Some artists find that the deeper they delve, the clearer their work becomes and, for them, the artistic process is simply a method of reducing their perceptions into some form of universal language. It is the ability to reach through to people in a way the usual modes of communication cannot hope to match. Their epitome is often their ability to find that delicate combination of balance, proportion and harmony in which order and chaos seem almost perfectly reconciled. This ability does not come about by chance, but is usually found within people whose emotions have penetrated the thin fabric of life who have found ways to express and explore the different ways to portray their sentiments. The outsider often faces a similar challenge in creatively conveying the value of what they have to offer the wider world.

The sheer scope of creativity for any person as a medium of expression is only limited by their imagination. In effect, all human progress depends on creativity. The outsider's insistence that life must hold some meaning to it can be a potent force and a naturally strong creative catalyst. For some, this need is like a stream which cannot be stopped, continually taking a different route when something obstructs its path. This analogy also aptly reflects the outsider's resilience and how adaptable he or she must become in finding the means necessary to fulfil this need. This may involve completely changing their approach to life, however, for many, it often relies on adopting a more creative and imaginative medium in order to elicit the meaning they demand. Most artists and writers have faced this exact same dilemma, and in common with the outsider, are deeply frustrated by their inability to express their perceptions, emotions, or simply their vision of life. Yet, they have gone on to succeed by bringing some sense and/or meaning into their lives through their creativity. Some have brought this about through creating something which is personally meaningful to them, while others may derive their sense of purpose through the creative process. Some also consider their ability to elucidate ideas or aspects of life to influence or change others perceptions as a meaningful aspiration. The extensive list of writers who have left an indelible mark on people's thoughts and imagination through the ages is a prime example - a few whose works continue to have a profound impact decades or even centuries later.

There is no doubt the spectrum of disciplines creativity offers, provides the individual with the opportunity to express themselves and reach others in innumerably different ways and on different levels. It provides a chance to introduce people to new and imaginative ways of looking at things, enhancing their understanding and ability to identify or empathise with particular circumstances, issues, or points of view. In the first part of the 20th Century, two unconnected playwrights managed to transform the values and attitudes of virtually a whole generation. Henrik Ibsen and George Bernard Shaw were men before their time who had very strong convictions in what they believed. Their plays offered their audiences an entirely new and different perspective on things, daring to question many controversial issues such as social and gender inequality and, which were at that time, considered unquestionable. Shaw, in particular, can be characterised by an unyielding determination not to accept people's conventions and life as it was, and a willingness to challenge every type of taboo which could not stand up to his reason, engendered inequality, or impinged on people's freedom to be themselves. His emergence as a writer and playwright was not plain sailing as one might expect from reading the sheer volume of his works. He suffered numerous setbacks during his initial attempts to establish himself as a writer, writing five novels before the first was even published - even then little interest was shown in his work. It was only when he embarked on writing plays that he found a medium through which he felt he could truly express his egalitarian and altruistic sentiments. People sometimes mistakenly assume that Shaw's emergence as a playwright was straightforward, that all he did was to translate his deep social convictions through his talent in being able to convey paradox, humour, and irony through his works. This ignores the fact that even before he started writing plays, he was at a disadvantage with respect to most other playwrights of his day:

> But to obtain a livelihood by this insane gift, I must have conjured so as to interest not only my own imagination, but that of at least some seventy or a hundred thousand contemporary London playgoers. To fulfil this condition was hopelessly out of my power. I had no taste for what is called popular art, no respect for popular morality, no belief in popular religion, no admiration for popular heroics. [7]

Shaw did not simply go about appeasing current dogma or the fashions of his time, which reduced the prospect of his works being accepted by others. He refused to trade-in his idealistic principles or social conscience, and was well aware of the hurdles ahead in his efforts to induce his audiences to appreciate and connect with his works. Like the outsider, Shaw did not fit into any neat little role, but his perseverance and flair, often in enunciating the paradoxical and humorous aspects of life, created a medium through which to translate his radical social sentiments to a much wider audience.

The most difficult issue in life for any outsider who find themselves unable to draw meaning from its conventional avenues, is finding a channel through which to assert their instincts. Many existential concepts and ideas are so far-reaching and, in some respects, so alien to some people, that the only effective way of translating them to others is through some creative format. Poetry provides a good example of this, and many outsiders have found it as an effective medium through which to convey their existential notions. There have been numerous poets over the years whose works have been identified with existentialism. Some of the more prominent include: John Donne, Johann Wolfgang von Goethe and

Pablo Neruda. Notwithstanding this, there are many more poets and a whole wealth of poetry which conveys existential themes. This of is no real surprise as, for some individuals, poetry is seen as the only avenue to properly express the profound and personal aspects of their feelings or ideas. It could be said, the subtle and yet powerfully imaginative and unconventional use of language woven together in a particular rhythm, is one of the few platforms capable of  relaying some of the deeper existential concepts like phenomenology or despair. Poetry can transport someone from the world they are in, to experience a whole new world or to look on life from a completely different perspective. It can be used to express emotionally charged feelings which the regular use of words cannot hope to rival, and can be written purely as a personal undertaking or disseminated to others to share a unique experience or insight.

The modern world is continually evolving through its fashions, ideas and people's opinions and attitudes within it, which can virtually change on a daily basis. At any given time, people's level of receptiveness often relies upon this constantly shifting tide within society. Anyone who sets out in the hope of making some meaningful impression must bear this in mind. This is especially true for some outsiders who often launch themselves into something only to find the waters too shallow for their vessel or the prevailing winds too much against them. They must be prepared to take stock of life and seek to understand it for what it is. They must realise that people may be more taken with the emergence of something trending on social media, than the unveiling of a truly great artistic work. The lyrics of a mediocre pop song will often reach more people than a carefully crafted and inspiring piece of poetry. A brilliant play will probably be seen by less than will have watched the latest Hollywood 'B' movie. The outsider may despair with these facts, but for those wishing to make the most of their ability to influence or connect with the wider world, they must be aware of what they are up against. In order to be able to realise themseves through their unique endeavour or self-expression, they may need to introduce their sentiments or ideas on the back of some inspired creativity or some other means which galvanises people's consideration or acceptance of their underlying message. The equation is different for every outsider. However, if they are to use a more creative means to project themselves in life, they also must be careful not to compromise their artistic or creative integrity to simply gain an audience. Having said this, it is an easy trap to fall into even amongst the most discerning. Creativity, in whatever form, is not something which simply serves a function. It must come from the individual with an authenticity of its own, from someone who genuinely wants to create or do something which they consider as meaningful; it cannot be contrived from any motive which simply seeks mass appeal.

There has been some incredible art produced through the ages, which has symbolised and even defined people's attitudes and even certain epochs in time. One of the most prodigious artists of modern times is undoubtedly Andy Warhol. His works have manged to sum up the true fickleness of modern consumerist society, from scores of tins of Campbells Soup, or variations of colourful celebrity negatives, whilst also broaching more controversial issues in works such as Race Riot and Electric Chair. Warhol saw what society had become, almost a single entity which devoured and nourished itself on the mass-produced media and celebrity influences of its age. His repeated tinted negatives of Marilyn Monroe and Elvis Presley, mocking their mass-produced appeal by being all things to all people, demonstrated how they are mere tinted variations in people's collective consciousness. Probably one of the most well-known artists of recent times is the graffiti artist Banksy. His depictions of modern day themes, which accentuate many wide ranging issues has left an indelible impression on the perceptions of today's generation. People are drawn to his powerfully profound, yet simple symbolism, which for many captures the essence of the wider issues going on in their lives. His works are often satirical, relating to cultural or political issues to which he adds an ethical and human dimension which resonates with the wider public.

Virtually all outsiders, to varying degrees, need to feel they can have some meaningful application or influence on the world they are in. For the vast majority, who do not find any real meaning within life's conventional remit, they must explore more creative means to gain a sense of fulfilment. Their unique disposition makes them naturally inclined and, it could be said, even better equipped towards more creative pursuits as their source for meaning. They must be prepared to assert who they are, learn new skills or hone existing talents, and if necessary change their approach or way they apply themselves to generate the meaning they crave. They must be resolute and prepared for the possible hurdles and knock-backs along the way. As individuals they refuse to fall in line with society's regimented roles, which very often compels them to create their own unique niche in life. Deriving meaning and purpose from it is not something they can take for granted, it depends as much on the journey and manner in which they seek to realise their needs as on what they ultimately do or create. Outsiders cannot afford to dismiss their ability to explore or apply themselves in a more creative way. To do so may lead to the tragic circumstance, where those who sometimes harbour a profound ability to shape and change life in the most meaningful way, resign themselves to a dormant and unfulfilled existence.

# Notes

## Chapter 1 - Contemplating Life

1    Camus Albert, *Myth of Sisiphus*,(London:Penguin Books.2000), p.12

2    Ibid

3    Søren Kierkegaard argued that each individual has a responsibility for his own life in his book *Either/Or* (1843)

4    Nietzsche Frederick, *The Gay Science*,(New York:Vintage Books.1974), p.181

5    Nietzsche Frederick, *Thus Spake Zarathustra*, (Oxford:Oxford University Press.2008), p.3-5

6    Sartre Jean-Paul, "Existentialism is a Humanism"-Lecture 29th October 1945, (Stanford Encyclopedia of Philosophy)

# Chapter 2 - The Outsider

1    Sartre Jean-Paul, "Existentialism is a Humanism"-Lecture 29th October 1945, (Stanford Encyclopedia of Philosophy)

2    Authors full names: Jean-Paul Sartre, Ernest Hemingway, Franz Kafka, James Joyce, Albert Camus, Joseph Heller, Jerome David Salinger, Fyodor Dostoyevsky, Milan Kundera.

3    Camus Albert, *Myth of Sisiphus*,(London:Penguin Books.2000), p.12

4    Schopenhauer Arthur, *Essays and Aphorisms*,(Harmondsworth: Penguin Books.1976), p,52

5    Camus Albert, *Myth of Sisiphus*,(London:Penguin Books.2000), p.23

6    Hansard: HC Deb 18th March 2003, vol 401, col 767 Tony Blair:The real problem is that, underneath, people dispute that Iraq is a threat, dispute the link between terrorism and weapons of mass destruction, and dispute, in other words, the whole basis of our assertion that the two together constitute a fundamental assault on our way of life.

7    Camus Albert, *Myth of Sisiphus*,(London:Penguin Books.2000), p.24

8    Camus Albert, *The Outsider*,(London:Penguin Books.2000),p.69

9    Ibid p.97

10    Ibid p.99

# Chapter 3 - The Unreal World

1        Nietzsche Frederick, *Twilight of the Idols*,(Amazon Edition.2012), Reason in Philosophy(section 6),p. 17

2        Eduard Husserl first introduced his idea of phenomenology in *Logical Investigations Vol I + II*, (1900/1901)

3        "Nicolas Sarkozy friend claims any 50year old without a Rolex is a 'failure'" (20th February 2009,Telegraph)

4        Sartre called this nebulous sensation nausea in *Nausea*(1938)

5        Camus describes this sensation of seeing life as absurd in *Myth of Sisiphus*(1942)

6        Hess Herman, *Steppenwolf*,(London:Penguin Books.1965),p.39

7        Ibid p.56

8        Nietzsche Frederick, *Beyond Good and Evil*,(Millennium Publications. 2014), p.34

9        Nietzsche Frederick, *The Gay Science*,(New York:Vintage Books. 1974), Book 1[4] p.79

10       I refer here to Charles Darwin's theory of 'natural selection' as explained in *The Origin of Species* (1859)

11       Sartre Jean-Paul, *Nausea*,(London:Penguin Books.2000),p.17

12       Ibid p.225

13       USA Guantanamo: A decade of damage to Human Rights (London: Amnesty International Publications.2011), 16th December, Index 51/103/2011

14       Remarque Erich Maria, *All Quiet on the Western Front*, (London: Vintage.1996),p.88

15       Heller Joseph, *Catch 22*,(London:Black Swan Books.1985),p.61

16       Ibid p.78

# Chapter 4 - Despair

1    Sartre Jean-Paul, *Nausea*,(London:Penguin Books.2000),p.50

2    Camus Albert, *Myth of Sisiphus*,(London:Penguin Books.2000), p.42

3    Hess Herman, *Steppenwolf*,(London:Penguin Books.1965),p.100

4    Sartre Jean-Paul, *Nausea*,(London:Penguin Books.2000),p.224

5    Camus Albert, *Myth of Sisiphus*,(London:Penguin Books.2000), p.20

6    "Full text of Tony Blair's dossier on Iraq", The Guardian (London: Guardian News and Media) 24th September 2002

7    Hess Herman, *Steppenwolf*,(London:Penguin Books.1965),p.35

8    Schrader Paul, *Taxi Driver*,(London:Faber and Faber Ltd.1990), p.55

9    Hess Herman, *Steppenwolf*,(London:Penguin Books.1965),p.82

10   Descartes René, "Discourse on the Method Rightly Conducting One's Reason and of Seeking the Truth in the Sciences" (1637), Part IV

# Chapter 5 - The Existential Dilemma

1    Camus Albert, *Myth of Sisiphus*,(London:Penguin Books.2000), p.27

2    Sartre Jean-Paul, *Nausea*,(London:Penguin Books.2000),p.18

3    Ibid p.19

4    Ibid p.182

5    Ibid p.145

6    Dostoyevsky Fyodor, *Notes from the Underground*,(New York:Dover Publications.1992), p.24

7       The two areas where this is particularly acute is in relation to the Human Rights Act and the Statutory and Common Law relating to people's individual right to Privacy. Examples of which can be found in the following articles: "Good for crooks, bad for human rights" by Daniel Hannan,(16 November 2006,Telegraph), "The injunction is back: Entertainer blocks extramarital affair story" by Owen Bowcott,(22 March 2016, Guardian)

8       I am referring here to the intervention of foreign powers in destabilising and toppling regimes or governments, most notably Afghanistan (2001), Iraq (2003), Libya (2011) and Syria (2011-currently ongoing) and the imposition or attempted imposition of new regimes more partial to western demands and interests which continues to have catastrophic consequences for the civilian populations of these countries.

9       Dostoyevsky Fyodor, *Crime and Punishment*,(London:Penguin Books. 2007),p.156

10      The word 'Superman' (taken from the German word 'übermensch' by Thomas Common's translation in 1896) and the theory behind it was derived from Nietzche's *Thus Spake Zarathustra*(1883)

11      Dostoyevsky Fyodor, *Crime and Punishment*, (London:Penguin Books. 2007),p.52

12      Ibid p.208

13      Schrader Paul, *Taxi Driver*,(London:Faber and Faber Ltd.1990), p.55

14      Schopenhauer Arthur, *Essays and Aphorisms*, (Harmondsworth: Penguin Books.1976), p,69

15      Shaw George Bernard, *Man and Superman*,(New York:Barnes and Noble.2004), p.436

# Chapter 6 - Seeking Purpose

1    Sartre Jean-Paul, *Nausea*,(London:Penguin Books.2000),p.223

2    Wilson Colin, *The Outsider*,(London:Indigo.1997),p.39

3    For further reading:*Communicating Unreality: Modern Media and the Reconstruction of Reality* by Gabriel Weimann (London:Sage Publications. 2000), p.279-322

4    Marcuse Herbert, *One-dimentional Man*,(London:Ark Paperbacks. 1986),p.1

5    Mill John Stuart, *On Liberty*,(London:Penguin Books.1985), p.68

6    Ibid p.63

7    Ibid p.111

8    Heller Joseph, *Closing Time*,(London:Scribner.1999), p.20

9    Shaw George Bernard, *Man and Superman*, (New York:Barnes and Noble.2004), Excerpts ftom The Revolutionist's Handbook and Pocket Companion, p.510

10    The term 'The shock doctrine' was made famous by the book The *Shock Doctrine: The Rise of Disaster Capitalism* (2007) by Naomi Klein

11    Montaigne Michel de,*Essays*,(London:Penguin Books.1993),"On the Education of Children"p.49-85 and "Experience" p.343-406

12    Wilson Colin, *The Outsider*,(London:Indigo.1997),Ch. 8 The Outsider as Visionary p.203-246

13    Marcuse Herbert, *One-dimensional Man*,(London,Ark Paperbacks. 1986),p.4

14    Schrader Paul, *Taxi Driver*,(London:Faber and Faber Ltd.1990), p.13

# Chapter 7 - The Outsider's Truth

1   Camus Albert, *Myth of Sisiphus*,(London:Penguin Books.2000), p.51

2   Ellison Ralph, *Invisible Man*,(London:Penguin Group.2001), p.572

3   Plato, *The Trial and Death of Socrates*,(Indianapolis:Hacket Publishing Company.2000), p.21

4   Ibid p.40

5   Sartre Jean-Paul, *Nausea*,(London:Penguin Books.2000),p.20

6   Camus Albert, *The Outsider*, (London:Penguin Books. 2000),p.65

7   Ibid p.118

8   Wilson Colin, *The Outsider*,(London:Indigo.1997), p.28

9   Sartre Jean-Paul, *Nausea*,(London:Penguin Books.2000),p.46

10  Hess Herman, *Steppenwolf*,(London:Penguin Books.1965),p.63

11   Mill John Stuart, *On Liberty*,(London:Penguin Books.1985),p. 99

12  Shaw George Bernard, *Man and Superman*, (New York:Barnes and Noble.2004), p.435

13  Camus Albert, *Myth of Sisiphus*, (London:Penguin Books.2000), p.26

14  Plato, *The Trial and Death of Socrates*,(Indianapolis:Hacket Publishing Company.2000), p.38

15  Marcuse Herbert, *One-dimensional Man*,(London,Ark Paperbacks. 1986),p.9

# Chapter 8 - Freedom

1        Mill John Stuart, *On Liberty*,(London:Penguin Books.1985),p. 151

2        Hansard HC 22nd February 2016, col 25   Prime Minister (David Cameron): We are a great country, and whatever choice we make we will still be great. But I believe the choice is between being an even greater Britain inside a reformed EU and a great leap into the unknown. The challenges facing the west today are genuinely threatening: Putin's aggression in the east; Islamist extremism to the south. In my view, this is no time to divide the west. When faced with challenges to our way of life, our values and our freedoms, this is a time for strength in numbers.
         Hansard HC 27th January 2016,col 202WH   The Minister for the Armed Forces (Penny Mordaunt): I also thank all hon. Members who have spoken in support of our armed forces today. We send them into harm's way, dressed in body armour, to defend our freedom and national interest.

3        Orwell George, *Nineteen Eighty-Four*,(London:Penguin Group.1989), p.6

4        "China has made obedience to the state a game" by Samuel Osborne (22 December 2015, Independent)

5        I am referring here to George W Bush's assertion prior to the Iraq invasion (2003) that a connection existed between the terrorist incident of 9/11 and Saddam Hussain, even though there was no evidence for this and the assertion was wholly uncorroborated.

6        "The Elephant in the Room: A survey of media ownership and plurality in the United Kingdom (Media Reform Coalition, 24th April 2014)

7        Chomsky Noam, *Culture of Terrorism*,(London:Pluto Press.2015), p.38

8        The Stanford Prison Experiment: A simulation study of the Psychology of Imprisonment by Philip Zimbardo, Craig Harvey, W. Curtis Banks and David Jaffe (Stanford University-California-US, August 1971)

9        Camus Albert, *Myth of Sisiphus*,(London:Penguin Books.2000), p.56

10 Baader-Meinhof - urban terrorist group led by Andreas Baader and Ulrike Meinhof which carried out kidnappings and assassinations in the 1970s.

11 Plato, *The Trial and Death of Socrates*,(Indianapolis:Hacket Publishing Company.2000), p.50

# Chapter 9 - The Individual

1 Mill John Stuart, *On Liberty*,(London:Penguin Books.1985),p. 187

2 Ellison Ralph, *Invisible Man*,(London:Penguin Group.2001), p.143

3 "There were hundreds of us crying out for help:The afterlife of the whistle-blower" by Andrew Smith(22nd November 2014,The Guardian)

4 *The Modern State Subverted: Risk and the Deconstruction of Solidarity*: Toward the Criminalisation of the Other by Giuseppe Di Palma (ECPR Press, Colchester.2014), Chapter 5 - p.55-65

5 Pericles 495-429 BC described as 'the First Citizen of Athens' by Thucydides whose endeavours shaped the democratic ideal.

6 Anti-social Behaviour Act 2003 (section 29)

7 Oborne Peter, *The Triumph of the Political Class*,(New York:Simon and Schuster.2007) p.249

8 Mill John Stuart, *On Liberty*,(London:Penguin Books.1985),p. 122

9 For further reading: *Happy Pills in America: From Miltown to Prozac* (2009) by David Herzberg, also
*Prozac Nation*(1994) by Elisabeth Wurtzel

10 "Rise in mental health detentions shows 'services are struggling'" by Aisha Gani and James Meikle (23rd October 2015, The Guardian)
"Two-fifths of organisations report increase in workplace mental health problems" Source : https://www.cipd.co.uk/pressoffice/pressreleases/mental-health-091015.aspx

11Schrader Paul, *Taxi Driver*,(London:Faber and Faber Ltd.1990), p.76

12More Thomas, *Utopia*,(London:Penguin Books.1965), p.65

# Chapter 10 - Creating Meaning

1Nietzsche Frederick, *The Gay Science*,(New York:Vintage Books.1974), Book 4[335] p.266

2Maslow, Abraham, "A theory of Human Motivation",(Psychological Review.1943)

3van Gogh(Edited by Bruce Bernard), *Vincent by himself*, (London:Time Warner Books UK.1985), Letter from The Borinage July 1880 p.33

4Ibid – Letter from the Hague, March 1882, p.41

5Ibid – Letter from the Hague,May 1883, p.49

6Ibid – Letter from Arles, August-September 1888, p.145

7Shaw George Bernard, *Plays Unpleasant*,(London:Penguin Books. 2000), Preface p.7

# Index

A website has been set up for anyone interested in reading further about existentialism or discussing the concepts contained within this book.


www.insidetheoutsider.com


Furthermore, should anyone wish to send correspondence to the author, they can either do so through a link via this website or by post to:

John Vincent
c/o Freshwater Publishing Ltd
PO Box 340
Prestatyn
LL19 0BP
UK